LEARNING AT THE ENDS OF LIFE

Children, Elders, and Literacies in Intergenerational Curricula

Intergenerational learning programs, such as art, music, and exercise classes for elders and young children, are designed to promote the expansion of communication skills and identity options for participants while forging relationships between generations. These types of programs help to foster different forms of literacy for both generations and promote a sense of community and belonging. *Learning at the Ends of Life* illustrates the unique benefits of such programs through the development and implementation of intergenerational curricula in Canada and the United States.

Based on more than seven years of research, this book details the experiences of educators and participants in a variety of trailblazing programs. Rachel M. Heydon uses a case-study approach that brings to life the possibilities of arts-based, multimodal curricula that draw on participants' existing funds of knowledge and interests. Offering both insightful theoretical analysis and practical suggestions for curriculum planning, Heydon encourages educators to consider the broader application of intergenerational learning and its potential to transform educational processes.

RACHEL M. HEYDON is an associate professor in the Faculty of Education at Western University.

RACHEL M. HEYDON

Learning at the Ends of Life

Children, Elders, and Literacies in
Intergenerational Curricula

UNIVERSITY OF TORONTO PRESS
Toronto Buffalo London

© University of Toronto Press 2013
Toronto Buffalo London
www.utppublishing.com
Printed in Canada

ISBN 978-1-4426-4537-0 (cloth)
ISBN 978-1-4426-1347-8 (paper)

Printed on acid-free, 100% post-consumer recycled paper with
vegetable-based inks.

Library and Archives Canada Cataloguing in Publication

Heydon, Rachel, 1971–
Learning at the ends of life : children, elders and literacies in intergenerational
curricula / Rachel M. Heydon.

Includes bibliographical references and index.
ISBN 978-1-4426-4537-0 (bound).   ISBN 978-1-4426-1347-8 (pbk.)

1. Older people – Education – Curricula.   2. Older people – Education.
3. Education – Curricula.   4. Education.   5. Children and older people.
6. Intergenerational relations.   7. Internet in education.   8. Literacy programs.
I. Title.

LC5457.H49 2012   374.0084'6   C2012-907902-2

This book has been published with the help of a grant from the Canadian Federation
for the Humanities and Social Sciences, through the Aid to Scholarly Publications
Program, using funds provided by the Social Sciences and Humanities Research
Council of Canada.

University of Toronto Press acknowledges the financial assistance to its publishing
program of the Canada Council for the Arts and the Ontario Arts Council.

Canada Council   Conseil des Arts
for the Arts   du Canada

ONTARIO ARTS COUNCIL
CONSEIL DES ARTS DE L'ONTARIO
50 YEARS OF ONTARIO GOVERNMENT SUPPORT OF THE ARTS
50 ANS DE SOUTIEN DU GOUVERNEMENT DE L'ONTARIO AUX ARTS

University of Toronto Press acknowledges the financial support of the Government
of Canada through the Canada Book Fund for its publishing activities.

For my Mother, Papa, Nonna, all the buddies, and our wee Ollie Cavanaugh.

Contents

Preface

A Narrative Beginning

She lifts our slumbering bodies one by one to the car: the lucky ones placed snugly in the bed of the wood-panelled station wagon between boxes of canned goods, suitcases of clothes, and bargain toilet paper expertly packed. It will be hours before sunrise, and these are the best driving hours. Coasting north, wipers beating away the dew, an occasional headlight shining from the opposite direction. We're in pajamas that keep the dark June cool from touching our skin; but she's always hot, always running, so she wears her elastic waist shorts, sleeveless top, and sneakers without socks. Hair short, face scrubbed shining clean, teeth white and proud with their perfection. There is no nonsense in this car: we are single-minded in this mission.

Slowly, the light wakes and we with it. The privacy of the dark switches places with the fullness of the sun in the trees: The race is really on now. Just one stop at the Big Boy in Gaylord, Michigan: mini breakfast, eggs over easy, cup of coffee for her; eggs for us too, although we want hamburgers that won't be offered for a while yet. The last of the chocolate milk slurped through the end of the straw, and we are whisked to the bathroom (don't touch the seat!) en route to the cash register with plans to refuel quickly at the gas bar. While she pays (always leaving a sizable tip – her nod to our mother's profession) we cry for the strawberry pie that whistles so red and bold from the display case. But how shameless to think of pie when the day must be seized and time is slipping.

I spy; geography; word-making from licence plates and road signs; Loretta Lynn; crayons and activity books; magic slates; and belly-aching stories of her training days for nursing complete with renegade enemas and bedpans extraordinaire. This is the way we shrug away the hours while playing the biggest game of all: who will be the first to see the Mackinaw bridge? Her eyes are sharp; never sick a day in her life, so she's probably legitimately number one, but she'll leave it to us to win. Never mind, the tall arch reaching over the pines announcing the gateway to the path to her home is prize enough for us all. The disappointment of never, ever getting to stop to see the world's largest man-eating clam, climb to the top of Castle Rock, or play in the falls is replaced with the glee of knowing we're almost there.

Bridge two linking the two Sault Ste Maries is in eyeshot now, when the second to last pit stop is called to take advantage of cheap gas, milk, and a bottle or two to pay for the dentist. Clackity-clack over the water; smoke from the steel plant; heavy air from the pulp mill; the spot where someone, sometime went high diving and survived. It's hard to remain sober with this much anticipation, but we still have to make it through customs. "Get my face; Get my face!" she implores as we pull up to the wicket. We fight for the chance to rummage through the vinyl purse, digging past Kleenex and Hershey bars to find the identity card that shows her at her most beautiful: the day of immigration. There she was, all lipstick-bow-tie-smile, coal-black hair shiny and smooth, round raven eyes. "Canadian," she asserts, proudly handing the card over to the officer, and nothing to declare other than the legitimate bottle or two and the black and white television in the back that we are reclining on.

We've made it through and need just a detour to Auntie's red and white villa to check in and announce, "Yoohoo!" Kisses and hugs are exchanged with "Thank Gods," road reports, hot soup, and cornetti. Then run back to the car for the final lap from town to country. Visions of the next two months play round and round: early morning freezing swims; witch around the house; hide and go seek; rowboat pirate attacks; inner-tubes pulled from chugging motor boats; tire swings over deep water; sun-burned shoulders she mothers with Ozonol; the "Rosa Express" wagon filled to brimming with fat-cheeked babies; fly swatters, earwig traps, and mosquito coils: her weapons in the never-ending insect wars; soft, sandy beds that sigh and heave with the slightest movement; old bikes squeaking and swaying on bald tires around the square behind the cottages; gallops through the ancient trail with penny candy on the mind; flame-crisped marshmallows balancing on the ends of coat-hanger skewers over raging bonfires; baseball with Our Lady as home plate (the plaster snake around her ankles always giving me the willies); bear-watches; blueberry picking; kid-run concerts and fashion shows and plays; tractor rides to clip acres of grass with her directing traffic from the steering wheel and coordinating the movement of picnic tables; curtains of laundry strung on the line making the whole world feel like a theatre; her games on the porch: Scrabble, Boggle, Chinese Checkers, Uno; pop-and-chip parties; Friday night fish fries; mass on the tennis court in God's open-air basilica with Father storing the host in a Kentucky Fried Chicken container; freighters moaning good night with lights bouncing off the wake like Christmas; afternoon prayers round and round the rosary; Coca-Cola cakes, long-johns, rigatoni, spaghetti, Auntie Izzie's meatballs, deep-fried zucchini flowers, dandelion salad, pasta fazool, eggplant sandwiches, frizini, capelletis, genettis, food glorious food!; duelling guffaws and her in the centre of all the buddies laughing and laughing like there is no tomorrow; "Roll Out the Barrel," "Those Were the Days My Friend," "Seventy-Six Trombones," we're here! log cabin, St Mary's river, summer with Lulu.

In August of 2009, my darling grandmother, Lucille Greco Daly, fell off of the kitchen chair in her suburban Detroit home and broke her hip. She was alone in the house when the accident happened, my grandfather having just the week before been admitted to hospital with a fractured back. I was away from home when I received the news, and sitting on a bus on the opposite side of the continent with the cell phone to my ear, I felt the buckling of the earth that comes only from death or birth. Unfortunately, I knew the former wasn't far away. Indeed, my Nonna died about two months later.

This narrative is one I wrote in preparation for Nonna's memorial mass. She had moved to Detroit from Sault Ste Marie, Ontario as a young woman to pursue a nursing career, married, and stayed in the United States. Every summer, however, Nonna returned without fail to the shores of the St Mary's River where she owned a cottage that was wedged between the cottages of her sisters and their families. Each one of Nonna's children and grandchildren were towed with her to the "Soo" for the yearly pilgrimage home, to live out the summer alongside her and our expansive, one might even say enormous, extended family. In those summers I learned about pleasure, joy, and my responsibility to family and community. Like all the perpetually in motion, barefooted children along the beach, I was cared for by a large cast of elders: fed, hugged, bandaged, offered refuge and solace, played with, and scolded when it was called for. In turn, I cared for the members of my family:

carting babies to and fro, and being Nonna's right hand in the tasks
of daily living. I have, for instance, vivid memories of being called on
to help my great-grandmother dress, girdles and garters and all, even
at the river in the middle of a scorching summer. The ties within the
family were strong, and children did not belong exclusively to their
parents: I lived with my grandparents for a number of years, which was
not at all unusual in our context, and I have cousins who spent great
chunks of their childhoods living with great aunts and uncles, or like
me, grandparents.

The years of childhood have their own sense of time and space and
can feel like a distinct lifetime that make their mark on a person in ways
learning experiences later in life perhaps never can. Growing up within
a family characterized by generational diversity and mutual responsibility and caregiving and where learning happened amongst and
because of different generations was a gift common to my Italian-Cana-
dian heritage, and one that now, in an adulthood far away, feels special
and fragile. I worry that with demographic trends common to many in-
dustrialized societies, intergenerational opportunities, including learning opportunities like my own, are not commonly available. I see that
these opportunities are definitely not as frequent, intense, or sustained
in my son's life. In Nonna's last years, instead of sitting by her side at
the water, I travelled too infrequently with my little boy to spend too
few hours on the footstool next to her La-Z Boy. Instead of the lapping
of the waves and the laughter of women and children, our conversation
was punctuated by the sound of game shows: "The Wheel, Dolly," she
would implore, "watch the Wheel with me." Until the very end, when
every breath was a marathon, Nonna's pleasures were simple, and it
was easy to just be beside her: a presence and witness to her living. On
those visits I would also see my ninety-year-old grandfather with my
son and feel the plain enjoyment they freely offered to each other, and
my heart would break to know that soon it would be time to return
home, my grandparents would be alone once more, and my son bereft
of their company. It was at these times the days of the cottage would
return, and I could feel in my bones the reciprocity of intergenerational
relationships, the responsibilities mutual, and the natural cycle of life
inexorable, poignant, excruciating, and beautiful. It is those days that
Learning at the Ends of Life honours.

Acknowledgments

The following organizations are gratefully acknowledged for providing financial and material support for the research in the book: the Social Sciences and Research Council of Canada (SSHRC Standard Research Grant 410-2006-1160); the Social Sciences and Research Council of Canada (Major Collaborative Research Initiative, Advancing Interdisciplinary Research in Singing, Annabel Cohen, Principal Iinvestigator); Canadian Society for the Study of Education New Scholar Award; Petro Canada Young Innovator Award; Foundation Western; the University of Western Ontario Academic Development Fund; the Faculty of Education, Western University.

The following people are gratefully acknowledged for collaborating or assisting me with aspects of the research: All research participants and the child and elder care centres where the research was conducted; Luigi Iannacci, Trent University; Susan O'Neill, Simon Fraser University; Carol Beynon, Western University; Western University research assistants, especially Magdalena Ciesla, Wendy Crocker, Wambui Gichuru, Fabienne Haller, Megan Merrifield, Joelle Nagle, Francillia Paul, Tara-Lynn Scheffel, Anne VanGilst, and Zheng Zhang; for their collegiality and conversation, and for teaching me about curriculum, my colleagues, especially, Rosamund Stooke, Kathryn Hibbert, and the late, great Geoffrey Milburn; and for sharing with me the beauty of living intergenerationally, my family, with special thanks to my aunt, intergenerational art teacher Bridget Daly.

Parts of the manuscript have appeared in various forms in the following: Heydon, R. (2005), "The De-pathologization of Childhood, Disability and Aging in an Intergeneration Art Class: Implications for Educators," *Journal of Early Childhood Research*, 3(3), 243–68; Heydon,

R. (2007), "Making Meaning Together: Multimodal Literacy Learning Opportunities in an Intergenerational Art Program," *Journal of Curriculum Studies, 39*(1), 35–62; Heydon, R. (2009), "We Are Here for Just a Brief Time: Death, Dying, and Constructions of Children in Intergenerational Learning Programs," in L. Iannacci & P. Whitty (Eds.), *Early Childhood Curricula: Reconceptualist Perpectives* (pp. 217–41) (Toronto: Detselig Press); Heydon, R. (2012a), "Intergenerational Learning from a Curriculum Studies Perspective: New Directions, New Possibilities," in N. Howe & L. Prochner (eds.), *Recent Directions in Early Childhood Education and Care in Canada* (pp. 182–205) (Toronto: University of Toronto Press); Heydon, R. (2012b), "Multimodal Communication and Identity Options in an Intergenerational Art Class," *Journal of Early Childhood Research, 10*(1), 51–69.

LEARNING AT THE ENDS OF LIFE

Chapter One

Introduction to Intergenerational Learning Programs

Early in my studies of intergenerational learning, I made an observation in an intergenerational art class that I enjoy sharing (e.g., Heydon, 2007), as it so clearly illustrates the affordances of well-crafted intergenerational programs for participants' learning, communication, and relationship-building. I have learned that the recounting of this observation can have a productive effect on listeners, opening them up to the potentialities of children and elders or at the very least, inciting them to ask questions and wondering about their own assumptions concerning education. I have, for instance, recently told the story of how I was giving a talk about intergenerational singing programs – programs that bring skipped generations together to create learning and interactional opportunities through singing (Heydon, 2012). The audience was a committed group of early childhood educators who specialized in music. In part of my talk, I shared the observation which I had made at Blessed Mother, a unique shared-site intergenerational program located in a large city in the United States:

> I'm standing with the video camera trying to decide how to capture everything that's going on in this room. Three large tables are populated by children, elders, and younger adults [with disabilities], and all are working hard to solve the problem the [intergenerational] art teacher has set out for them: choose an item from a clear bucket of mystery objects, then use it as a catalyst to create a drawing. As I look about the room I see Susan, the art teacher, move towards a table of four. She is holding large, bright photographs of various forms of art, including some interesting examples of postmodern architecture. Susan gently touches Bonnie (age 82) who is asleep in her wheelchair. Rebecca (age 80), who is across from

them, laughs and says loudly while pointing at Bonnie, "She wakes me up at 4:00 o'clock, so wake her up!" I smile at the casual ribbing of one roommate to another. Bonnie indeed wakes up to view the photographs just as Carl (age 5), who is sitting next to her, looks up from contemplating his strange, wooden object and pronounces, "Let me see!" Katie (age 4) gets in on the viewing, and then everyone begins to discuss his or her object. Rebecca has a neon orange piece of plastic that looks like the letter "E." She holds it up for the others and announces, "I don't know what this is." Katie says it looks like a comb, or if you turn it this way, an "E"! Carl nods, then tries to turn his wooden object into a spinning top. He can't quite get the spin right. Rebecca offers that maybe this isn't a top at all, as the proportions are wrong. Katie suggests that the object looks like a local landmark. Carl makes a face like he supposes so, but then goes on to say it reminds him of a candle. Susan says she likes how Carl uses his imagination to "see" the solid wood as a flame. Rebecca, who has now indicated on the sly to Susan that she's figured out that the object is an archaic juicer, decides to follow the metaphoric route. She therefore interjects with the idea that maybe it's a beach umbrella. While Bonnie sits silently but watches everything and Katie uses the E/comb to trace patterns on a large piece of paper, Rebecca and Carl continue to wrestle with the wooden object, now using drawing to explore its contours. Every single person in this room will continue in this focused, thoughtful manner for an hour and a half until the lunch crew arrives and forces them to disperse. Later, when I'm out of the field and tell this story to my former early-years teacher colleagues, they will gasp in disbelief. No 4- and 5-year-olds, they will claim, can stay on one task this long. And it is then that I am again reminded of the limits so many of us well-meaning educators place on the possibilities for children and their learning.

As with my past experience in sharing this story, one of the music educators, who was pursing graduate studies in the area but had limited teaching experience, seemed somewhat incredulous but also wanted to know more: "How did the teacher get the children to attend for so long?" he asked. He then shared stories of his own "failed attempts" to engage his students in lessons and activities that he thought would be attractive to them. What was the "secret" of the intergenerational art class?

What This Book Hopes to Accomplish

The intergenerational art class and other classes like it are not places of secrets; they are beautiful examples of curriculum and pedagogy that have created opportunities for people to communicate and learn together within the context of relationship. *Learning at the Ends of Life* is an attempt to help address a gap created by the end of days like the ones at the cottage which I describe in the Preface – an illustration and analysis of what can happen when young and old are brought together not through the structures of family, but through formal shared-site intergenerational learning programs where child and elder care share space and programming. My hope is that the book can provide educators, such as the one above and others interested in young children and elders, insights into how the curricula in such programs might expand participants' communication and identity options while helping to foster and support intergenerational relationships. The corollary of this is that the book may also provide a commentary on the learning and communicational opportunities and identity options that are (or are not) provided for young and old in monogenerational settings. Thus, these pages are filled with implications for intergenerational programs and beyond. Perhaps through an understanding of what intergenerational curriculum has meant and can mean to people's lives, readers might come to see generational diversity and the expansion of people's communication and identity options as fundamental to all people's learning, personhood, and well-being. Additionally, through the inclusion of rich descriptions and working hypotheses of intergenerational curricula, literacies, identities, and relationships, the book might aid others in making informed judgments about the transferability and significance of the research to their own teaching and learning situations (Donmoyer, 2001).

A book such as *Learning at the Ends of Life* is novel and needed. There is a lack of literature that deals with intergenerational learning curriculum, particularly curriculum that attempts to expand intergenerational participants' communication and identity options through learning opportunities and that employs a critical theoretical perspective. Moreover, there is a lack of literature that uses the lessons learned from intergenerational learning programs to comment on curricula and participants' identity options in monogenerational sites. *Learning at the Ends of Life* addresses these gaps, in part, through illustrations and analyses that ask readers to consider, What is a child? What is an elder? What is the place of learning in people's lives? What is the meaning that comes from relationship and how does this relate to learning? Finally, while there is a good base of literature concerning children's literacy learning with grandparents and siblings within households and in community settings such as church, (e.g., Gregory & Williams, 2000; Gregory, Long, & Volk, 2004) and some beginning understanding of the literacies of elders (e.g., Robson, Sumara, & Luce-Kapler, in press; Robson, Sumara, Luce-Kapler, Coll, Hogan, Hurst, Innes, Morrissey & Spencer, 2010; Kamler, 2001) this book is among the first that looks specifically at communication from the syncretic theoretical perspective that I define later in the chapter within the context of formal intergenerational learning situations.

Based on over seven years of formal research into the relationship and learning opportunities created by a variety of curricula in shared-site intergenerational programs, especially art programs, with an emphasis on the children and their educators and punctuated by narratives, images, and other demonstrations of intergenerational programming, this book provides opportunities for early childhood educators, literacy researchers, and others interested in intergenerational learning programs or education more generally to understand:

- The benefits and meaning of intergenerational shared-site programming in the lives of participants;
- The experiences of educators in setting up such programs including the strengths on which one can build and the challenges in the process;
- Pedagogies and curricula for supporting learning that promotes broad communication and identity options for participants;
- The relationships, forms of communication, and identity options that such programs afford for the young children, elders, and practitioners who participate in them; and
- The ways in which the examples of intergenerational learning can help educators reconsider what is taken for granted in monogenerational learning sites and to see new possibilities for such sites and the people who inhabit them.

Note that the book contains a great number of narratives from the studies. These are italicized to allow readers to enter into them outside of the regular, academic prose of the rest of the book. The narratives are fashioned from a triangulation of the research data, which includes field documentation in the forms of video, field notes, audio, and the like.

Structure of the Book

Learning at the Ends of Life investigates the coming together for learning, communicating, and relationship-building of young children and older adults, persons who are often socially marginalized. Such inquiries can help to raise questions and clarify issues around learning, literacies, and identity. Thus, this book is interested in the particularities of the people who populate the studies as well as the larger relations in which their practices are nested. To live out this back-and-forth movement from micro- to macro-relations, the book is divided into seven chapters.

This chapter provides an introduction to intergenerational learning programs and their curricula as an important direction in education, especially early years education. It begins with a general contextualizing of intergenerational programs by describing the benefits the literature has identified for participants, the various forms programs can take, the advice the literature gives about how to create learning programs with optimal benefits, and a look at the theoretical proclivities of the intergenerational field.

In Chapter Two, I narrow the lens from a view of the field to the particularities of my own intergenerational research and provide a discussion of the meanings that people have created through their participation in intergenerational learning.

Chapter Three continues in this illustrative vein to give accounts and analyses of how three different locales structured and carried out their programs, with attention paid to one mature and two newer programs.

Chapter Four relates to the subject matter concerns of intergenerational programming and illustrates how art programs in particular can be excellent vehicles for expanding participants' communication and identity options.

Chapter Five provides an account of the implementation of a four-lesson intergenerational learning sequence in an intergenerational art class to provide readers an in-depth look at the possibilities of curricular programming and what participants might do within it.

To address some of the ways in which child and adult participants were positioned in relation to each other and being at the ends of life and some of the implications for their opportunities for learning, communicating, and building relationships and identity options, Chapter Six considers the curricula of death and dying in the intergenerational programs.

Chapter Seven provides a synthesis of the lessons provided by intergenerational learning programs and highlights the implications of intergenerational programs for the education and care of young and old.

The Beliefs That Underpin This Book

Learning at the Ends of Life

Within the very language of the book, I have demarcated people along generational lines. Still, *Learning at the Ends of Life* is undergirded by critical theories and theories of the postmodern age with their respective (and some might say incommensurable goals) of emancipation (Habermas, 1972) and deconstruction (Lather, 1991). Thus, akin to the beliefs espoused in my writing with Iannacci (Heydon & Iannacci, 2008), I subscribe to the view that what constitutes childhood as well as adulthood (including elder, senior, or old age status) is not self-evident. Each of these categories is dependent on sociocultural and historical context (Jenks, 2004; Rogers, 2004) and is mediated by power relationships between and among generations. In general, in the book I employ the term *elder* to describe the persons in my studies who occupied the adult participant role within the intergenerational programming. There is no particular chronological age, however, that signifies an elder. I use this term rather than another (e.g., senior) to connote, I hope, a sense of respect towards these participants and to show that they have experience and knowledge that most others who have lived for a shorter time have not. At the same time, this is not meant to belie the knowledge and full personhood of the child participants; for example, in terms of communication, I agree with the early literacy perspective that sees children's communication practices not merely as lesser versions of adult practices, but as valuable in their own right (e.g., Gillen & Hall, 2003). In response to the simultaneous use of and dislike for hard and fast categories (e.g., children, elders) and in acknowledging the limits of language, I attempt in this book to move between the actualities of the participant's practices within context to larger macro-educational issues. In so doing, like Thew (2000) I hope to highlight the diversity of children as well as elders as a group.

I also attempt within the fabric of my writing, to practice Emmanuel Levinas's ethical linguistic strategy of *unsaying the said*, that is, of refusing to allow my language to suggest absolute knowledge of another. A said, to Levinas, "reduce[s]" the other to a "fixed identity or synchronized presence – it is an ontological closure to the other" (Levinas & Kearney, 1986, p. 29). With Levinas, however, the hope for language is in the saying; "language as saying is an ethical openness to the other (p. 29), it is the way in which I as a researcher can demonstrate the gaps in my knowledge of the other and my refusal to totalize the other and pin her down in my language. In answer to the question "What kind of language is this that accomplishes the nontotalizing relation to the other?" Robbins (2001), referring to Levinas's saying responds, "ethical language is interlocutionary; it never speaks about the other but only to him or her ... The saying is speech before it congeals in the said, which absorbs alterity into thematization; it is a mobile orientation toward the addressee" (p. 4). This, as I discuss later in the chapter, is an ethical disposition towards the other and a promise to respect the alterity of the other by demonstrating through one's language the limits of one's knowledge and separateness as a human being even as one strives to be present for the other.

Theories of Literacy

Understanding how people make meaning through various semiotic resources and the relationship of these practices to their identities within intergenerational contexts is a major focus of the book. As Hicks (2002) noticed in her studies of literacy, I too recognize that no one theory is sufficient for understanding the complexities of literacy, identity, and curriculum, especially within the particularities of intergenerational learning contexts, and thus I draw on a number of interrelated theories in such a way that new theories are realized. Most salient for the studies are multimodal social semiotic theory within education as related to the New Literacy Studies (e.g., Rowsell & Pahl, 2007; Pahl & Rowsell, 2005), and multimodal pedagogy (e.g., Stein, 2008).

First, multimodal social semiotic theory posits that there is a common communicational trajectory that involves three interrelated decisions: what people want to signify, the "relationship" between what people want to signify and what they can use to signify it, and what ways to communicate are "most suitable" given people's assessments of the contexts of their communication (Kress & Jewitt, 2003, p. 11). Kress (1997) identified the notion of people's interests as fundamental to the responses to these decisions. Albers (2007) described interests as coming from people's "knowledge and experiences" (p. 6), and Rowsell & Pahl (2007) expanded the idea of interest by suggesting that it is bound up in people's "identities in practice," which both "create" and "support" interests (p. 392). Identity is "a way of describing a sense of self that is in practice" (Pahl & Rowsell, 2005, p. 155), and the inclusion of identity brings an important social dimension to multimodal literacy. Rowsell & Pahl (2007) argued, for instance, that identities can be made in relation to texts which offer "traces" (p. 391) of the social through several means including that in their text-making people "assemble Discourses ... negotiate them, transform them, and materialize them" (p. 392).

The notion of Discourse comes from Gee (1996) and denotes

> a socially accepted association among ways of using language, other symbolic expressions, and "artifacts," of thinking, feeling, believing, valuing, and acting that can be used to identify oneself as a member of a socially meaningful group or "social network" or to signal (that one is playing) a socially meaningful "role." (p. 131)

In their literacy research Rowsell & Pahl (2007) have offered a variety of examples of how Discourse relates to literacy practice; they have shown, for instance, how one student "assembled Discourses that related to his dispositions, at-hand narratives, and home life" (p. 393) to create text. Looking ahead to the intergenerational studies, one might ask how various Discourses of aging and childhood might manifest within the participants' visual texts,[1] as identities are "generated" and can be "expressed in artefacts, texts, and discourse" (Pahl & Rowsell, 2005, p. 155) and can consequently become "sedimented" (Rowsell & Pahl, 2007) within the very *materiality* (Kress & Jewitt, 2003) or physical nature of a text.

Based on this dual attention to the social and the material, Rowsell & Pahl (2007) developed a heuristic for apprehending the process of textual production and discerning how the social, including its connection to people's identities, can be "instantiated within ... texts" (p. 394). The model begins with Bourdieu's notion of habitus (e.g., 1990) which the authors defined as "ways of being, doing, and acting in the world across generations, time, and space" (p. 391). They claimed, "habitus both drives dispositions and is transformed in the remaking of dispositions ... Dispositions across generations shape and generate identities" (p. 391); it "generates practice" (e.g., the practice of visual text making),

---

1 I use the term visual text instead of artwork to render explicit the literacy theoretical framework that undergirds the study and to suggest that the participants were exposed to learning opportunities that might expand their communication options rather than providing opportunities in the specific knowledge domain or discipline of art (Albers, 2007).

and "these practices generate texts through a slow process of iteration" (p. 394). Foundational is the "contemplation of the moment of production – the context, the producer with his or her set of dispositions, the text and what it points to, and how it reflects the context in which it was made" (p. 394). In sum, within their very fabrics, texts can offer clues regarding their producers' social contexts and identities.

Fundamental to understanding texts and their producers' identities and social contexts is their physical nature. Certain elements of multimodal theory can be helpful in this with two key concepts concerning the terms *mode* and *media*. Modes are a "set of resources people in a given culture can use to communicate" (Bainbridge, Heydon, & Malicky, 2009, p. 4). Kress (1997) uses the term "to indicate that [people] make signs from lots of different 'stuff,' from quite different materials ... and [they] use the physiology of [their] bodies to turn that physical, material stuff into signs: as speech, as music" (p. 7). The term media comes under mode and is used "to focus more on the manner of dissemination: a letter as a medium of communication and writing – the graphic material – as the mode; a traffic sign as the medium of communication" (p. 7). To be fully considered a mode, resources may need to be regularized or organized into what might be taken to be a *grammar*: Grammar is what makes a text "comprehensible to members of the culture in which it is produced and received" (Bearne, 2009, p. 157). Multimodal theory emphasizes that people are generators and not just users of signs (Kress & Jewitt, 2003), and modal grammars can be seen similarly; rather than being a rigid set of rules grammars can also evolve (e.g., in response to the demands of a context; Kress & van Leeuwen, 1996).

What constitutes a literacy practice is also always being generated. Multimodal literacy and the New Literacy Studies hold an ever-expanding definition of literacy that sees literacy as involving more than just the reading and writing of linear print-based texts as they recognize that all communication entails more than one mode at a time. Even an essay contains choices around the stuff it is written on (e.g., good paper or a screen) and the way in which it is produced (e.g., handwritten or through word processor) (Kress, 1997). In her study of multimodal literacy in a nursery setting, Pahl (1999) documented how the children "started working in one particular mode ... then moved across modes as their interest demands" (p. 17). Interests and the desire to express them can propel people to experiment with mode and media in their bid to find the right fit between what they want to communicate and how to communicate it. All signs (i.e., a "combination of meaning and form" [Kress, 1997, p. 6]) are said to be "motivated" (Hodge & Kress, 1993). Thus, people's movement from mode to mode or media to media is not haphazard but driven by interest and the affordances of modes, that is, "what it is possible to express and represent readily, easily, with a mode, given its materiality and given the cultural and social history of that mode" (Kress & Jewitt, 2003, p. 14). Materiality refers to a mode's "physical" features and the social, cultural, and historical side refers to "what has been done in the past with this material, and how the meanings made in the past affect what can be done with a mode" (p. 15). Multimodal theory also allows for a parallel to affordances in relation to media; it calls this the "facilities of media" and refers to "What is readily and easily possible to do with [a] medium" (p. 16). Helping to clarify these notions further is Rowsell & Pahl's (2007) distinction between *materiality* and *multimodality*. Materiality relates "to a micro, fine-grained analysis of specific [textual] artifacts and how their content and design relates to the text maker" (p. 393). To discern the materiality of a text, one is advised to consider both "product" and "process" (p. 393). Multimodality, however, refers to the more macro-oriented organizers of textual production and artifacts as it is "tied to larger discourses and ideologies such as globalization, cultural migration, and technology" (p. 393) and involves the choices in modalities that are available to people.

In terms of what is known about young children and their textual practices and products, of specific import for this book is that a number of researchers have noted that children are meaning makers who "research," discover, and represent the world in myriad ways. Their exploration and communication are "deliberate" and open to possibilities as children have "not yet settled into the fairly narrow range of methods of communication used by the adults around them," language, for example (Fraser & Gestwicki, 2002, p. 249). When compared to adults, children are seen in the literature as freer to move from mode to mode and media to media and able to take advantage of what each mode affords (Kress & Jewitt, 2003). The movement of an idea from one mode or media to another has been referred to as "transformation" (Pahl, 1999) and "transduction" (Kress, 1997), and the connected, cumulative processes and products of communication create a "semiotic chain" (Stein, 2008). Opportunities for the creation of semiotic chains were created frequently in the intergenerational art classes in the studies. These chains can be highly productive as they have been found to create spaces for learning, creativity, and concept development (e.g., Kress, 1997; Pahl, 1999; Stein, 2008).

An important notion related to semiotic chains relates to the notion of *fixing*, which refers to the points in a chain where there is a "textual object" (Stein, 2008, p. 98; Kress, 1997). There is a foundational knowledge of children's fixing, thanks to a few crucial studies. Kress's inquiry into young children's meaning-making provided insight into how drawings, collages, cut-outs, and the like are cogent literacy practices, and Pahl's (1999) study of transformations in a nursery setting uncovered how children can link modes, develop concepts, and "express complex ideas in a material form, without the need for access to written modes of expression" (p. 23). Further, while she did not use Rowsell & Pahl's (2007) specific heuristic in her study of 3D doll/child figures in a South African context, Stein (2003) did operate from a similar understanding of text production and identity sedimentation within a multimodal theoretical framework which enabled her to apprehend and analyse how participants' texts communicated identities forged within and against their specific home, school, and community situations.

Although Fraser & Gestwicki (2002) commented that children have more flexibility in their communication than adults, and Gregory & Williams (2000) have investigated learning to read across generations, currently little is known about the relationship between text, identity, and social context in the literacies of older adults as they compare to those of children. *Learning at the Ends of Life* hopes to add to the current literature by exploring if texts created in intergenerational contexts may produce knowledge about how the young and old of a society see themselves and others and the ways in which they are socially positioned. The goal of a number of studies included in the book was to expand communication and identity options for participants in intergenerational learning programs. Cummins's notion of "identity options" (2000, p. 17) concerns the possibilities learners have for identity formation. Highlighting the dynamic and multi-dimensional nature of identity, Cummins noted that options for learners' identity formations are closely related with the interpersonal space/power relations played out in teacher-learner "micro-interactions" (p. 15). For example, in coercive relations of power, teachers can narrow learners' identity options and potential, whereas in collaborative relations of power, teachers open up identity options by focusing on collaborative critical inquiry where formation of identity is negotiated. Coercive relations of power operate on the assumption that power is a "fixed predetermined quantity" (p. 16) and is exercised over others, whereas in collaborative relationships, power is created with others and shared within a collaborative interpersonal space where forms of communication and identities meet. Groups or individuals defined as inferior or deviant in coercive power relationships have fewer opportunities for learning and identity formation. However, learners who experience collaborative relations of power are more engaged in learning and affirmed in their identities (Cummins, Baker, & Hornberger, 2001).

In the next chapter I relate the ways in which young children and older adults are sometimes socially positioned as inferior or deviant. Now, however, I will provide an example how these relations of power may be played out in the type of literacy that is emphasized in early childhood curricula. Despite the ubiquitous argument that literacy education must include more than print literacy (i.e., linear reading and writing), it continues to be emphasized in most school curricula (Heydon & Iannacci, 2008), and educators may or may not have the ability to help children navigate these curricula in ways that are collaborative. This is ironic and problematic because limiting literacy education to print reduces people's communication options. Ironic, because knowing how to communicate through a variety of modes and media could support one's print literacy (Kress, 1997); and problematic, because learners' "abilities to create and interpret through" a variety of modes and media "expand the potential of what [they] can say and how they can say it" (Albers, 2007, p. 6). Last, there is a reciprocal relationship between identities and text-making, with each informing and enabling the other. Drawing on the work of Kress (1997) and others, Rowsell & Pahl (2007) claimed that "texts can be associated with the expansion of identities in that the making of the text can itself be accompanied by a transformation in the identities of the text maker" (p. 393). Hence, expanded communication options are related to expanded identity options. Importantly, curriculum plays a major role in the availability of these options and the extent to which educators can create collaborative relationships with children (Heydon, 2012a); thus, studies focused on curriculum's role in communication and identity options, such as the ones in this book, might provide the requisite knowledge for creating expansive communication and identity options for learners.

The book was written also in hope of making a contribution in the area of multimodal pedagogy. Thankfully, there are curricula that decry reductionist definitions of literacy and its education. The Preschool and Infant-toddler Centers in Reggio Emilia are a case in point. Their founder has claimed that "school for young children ... should be a giant rodeo where they learn how to ride 100 horses" (Malaguzzi, 1998, p.

88). The reference to 100 horses is metaphorical, referring to the schools' attempts to support the "hundred languages of children" – that is, the varied ways children may express themselves (e.g., Edwards, Gandini, & Forman, 1998). The pedagogies of Reggio Emilia and those inspired by Reggio Emilia would say that the use and further refinement of all of these languages is indeed a child's, a person's, right. Hall and Rudkin (2011), in their discussion of children's perceptions of rights and communication, add that "Children have a right to have their words heard by other people" and "Children have a right to be listened to" (p. 26). Multimodal pedagogies might be enacted also to help realize the following rights: "Children have a right to color with paint or markers and to choose which one" and "Children have a right to sing, and to sing to other people" (p. 26). Significantly, the identification of these rights came from dialogues with child participants themselves, and Hall and Rudkin explained the inclusion of multimodality in the communication rights in this way: "children speak in non-verbal as well as verbal languages" and "children understand that rights, including the right to self-expression, are not contingent on age" (p. 26). We adults could learn much from children, for in the rights discussion, Hall and Rudkin related that "several two- and three-year olds observed that even infants express themselves, conveying their emotions and ideas by shaking and clapping" (p. 26).

An addition to the pedagogies of Reggio Emilia that foster multimodality is Stein's (2008) multimodal pedagogy. Such a pedagogy is another example of an effort to increase people's communicative and identity options within a more explicitly multimodal theoretical vein. Her pedagogies capitalize on semiotic chains as they "work consciously and systematically across semiotic modes in order to unleash creativity, reshape knowledge and develop different forms of learning beyond the linguistic" (p. 123). The specific qualities of these pedagogies and what they can produce is something that literacy researchers have begun to look into.

Literacy Theories That Are Germane to Intergenerational Situations

More specifically in reference to the intergenerational context of the studies, the theories that underlie this book emphasize the situations in which communication happens. Situation matters; unlike a stance that sees individuals as *users* of sign systems that are pre-made and stable, social semiotics sees people who are engaged in meaning-making as *producers* of signs (Kress, 1997; Kress & Jewitt 2003). Kress and Jewitt explain that this production occurs because all signs are metaphors that attempt to find the best fit between signifier and signified (which are never a perfect fit) at a given moment and place. The gap between the signifier and the signified is where the novel is created. New signs can also be created from the reading of signs. This is a process of taking an "outward" sign (e.g., a text) and creating from it, an "internal" sign: "A person receives a sign, in the material form of its signifier, in which it was realized. She or he takes the shape of the signifier as an apt indication of what was signified, and forms from that a hypothesis of what the signified is. But the readers' hypothesis about the likely, plausible, apt, signified is based on *their* interest. It, too, forms a new sign" (p. 13). Signs are, therefore, never "arbitrary" (p. 10), but rather connected to the conditions in which they are created. Individuals do not, however, have unlimited possibilities for generating new signs; possibilities are again tied to the situation in which signs are created (Pahl, 1999). This point raises the importance of how situations might offer individuals expansive or restrictive opportunities for the creation of signs. An additional social dimension enters when one considers Kress and Jewitt's distinction between the making of signs and the communicating of signs: "The first is concerned with the sign maker, and with what he or she wants; the second is concerned with the sign-maker's perception of the audience and what he or she imagines they want" (2003, p. 12). Thus, within the creation of every sign is an implied audience or receiver of the communication rendering all communication *relational*.

Literacy and the Relational

This book uses interconnected theories of literacy that emphasize *the social* to understand literacies as relational practices. First, Hicks's (2002) theoretical approach to literacy seems to extend social semiotician Halliday's (1978) contention that "language is a form of interaction, and it is learnt through interaction" (p. 18). Through detailed portraits of young children's literacies in home and school Hicks's work (e.g., 2002) suggests that one's identity and emotional connections to others need to be highlighted in any discussion of literacy and literacy learning. Perhaps particularly in early childhood, what one learns is reliant on those whom one values and loves: "literacies are cultural and material *practices* shaped by histories, localities, and the persons within them that give form and meaning to children's lives" (p. 16). As such, signs are contingent on persons' past and present experiences and contexts. It follows then that the practice of literacy is relatively high-stakes, in that the moments of communication (both receptive and expressive) are imbued with the weight of relationship.

Further, the work of Bakhtin colours these pages. Often called on by researchers interested in the social nature of literacy (e.g. Kendrick, 2004),it has been argued that Bakhtin's branch of semiotics acknowledges that "the most important thing for making sense of meaning is not the sign, but the whole utterance into whose composition the sign enters" (Ivanov cited in Wertsch, 1991, p. 49). Bakhtin (1986) coined the term *utterance* to signify that: "speech can exist in reality only in the form of concrete utterances of individual speaking people, speech subjects. Speech is always cast in the form of an utterance belonging to a particular speaking subject, and outside this form it cannot exist" (p. 71). The form of the utterance is contingent on the perspective, disposition, and values of the person producing it; this, Bakhtin calls *voice*. Although Bakhtin's language suggests that he is talking about oral language, his theory "applies to written as well as spoken communication, and it is concerned with the broader issues of a speaking subject's perspective, conceptual horizon, intention, and world view' (Wertsch, 1991, p. 51). What is crucial is that the utterance is always addressing another who is present or implicit. As Bakhtin (1986) says, "addressivity, the quality of turning to someone, is a constitutive feature of the utterance; without it the utterance does not and cannot exist (p. 99). This is where Bakhtin's notion of the dialogic enters.

Bakhtin demonstrates the productivity of signs based in "the ways in which one speaker's concrete utterances come into contact with ... the utterances of another" (Wertsch, 1991, p. 54). Thus, the dialogic involves understanding that because reading (or viewing) is productive rather than merely an act of transmission (in keeping with a social semiotic view of reading), one's signs demand an audience, and this audience is present throughout every stage of sign-making. Bakhtin (1981) suggests that the presumption of an audience and the yearning to have one's words be shown back to one's self through another's reading of those signs, leads every sign-maker to include that implied other in meaning-making:

> [The speaker's] orientation toward the listener is an orientation toward a
> specific conceptual horizon, toward the specific world of the listener; it in-

troduces totally new elements into his [*sic*] discourse; it is in this way, after all, that various different points of view, conceptual horizons, systems for providing expressive accents, various social 'languages' come to interact with one another. The speaker strives to get a reading on his own word, and on his own conceptual system that determines this word, within the alien conceptual system of the understanding receiver; he enters into dialogical relationships with certain aspects of this system. (p. 282)

Because of the dialogic, every text is heterogeneous, containing within it aspects of the other. Consequently, the more that sign-production and meaning-making are carried out within a heterogeneous and explicitly social environment in which relationship is valued and promoted, the greater the learning opportunities may be. This raises interesting questions vis-à-vis intergenerational contexts. It forces one to ask, if and how the sign-making opportunities, and by extension, communication options of participants in intergenerational learning may be affected and perhaps augmented because of the intergenerational aspect.

Ethical Relations

The intergenerational literature is replete with attempts to capture, analyse, and organize the *interactions* of children and elders so as to increase these interactions (e.g., Angersbach & Jones-Forster, 1999) and to see how they might inform *relationship* (e.g., see "About Us" in the *Journal of Intergenerational Relationships*). This literature is largely psychological and seems to define interaction as those behaviours that range from an elder observing children playing to elders and children talking and working through their problem solving as they cooperate on a project (e.g., see the Angersbach & Jones-Forster Intergenerational Interaction Scale). Relationships, however, seem to be characterized more as "ongoing interaction" ("About Us," n.d., n.p.) that would presumably be somewhat sustained and meaningful to the individuals involved. The issue of this potential benefit of the intergenerational component on participants' communication is one that is addressed in a number of forthcoming chapters. In contrast, *Learning at the Ends of Life* takes a sociocultural perspective consistent with the literacy theories just described and also engages with the question of how the conditions and structures of intergenerational programs might provide all of its participants (including educators and researchers) with opportunities to form ethical relations with others. The notion of ethical relations is a philosophical one that is largely contingent, as already mentioned, on the work of Levinas.

Levinas's ethical relation centres on his notion of the *face*. In an interview regarding this matter, Levinas explained that the face is "not of the order of the seen ...but it is he [*sic*] whose appearing preserves an exteriority which is also an appeal or an imperative given to [one's] responsibility" (Robbins, 2001, p. 48). The face calls to the person who encounters it and asks for a response. Levinas said, "to encounter a face is straight-away to hear a demand and an order," and this encounter is one in which the face is laid bare; it is "without-defense, the nudity and the misery of the other" (p. 48); the face is "helplessness, perhaps an exposure to death" (p. 145). In the presence of this vulnerability and need, one must respond as "the face offers itself to [one's] compassion and to [one's] obligation" (p. 48). It "makes a demand" on the person who encounters it not "to leave it alone" (p. 127). Evoking the language of religion, Levinas underscored the primacy of the ethical relation and the face's role within it when he attested, "There is a holiness in the face but above all there is holiness or the ethical in relation to oneself in a comportment which encounters the face as face, where the obligation with respect to the other is imposed before all obligation: to respect the other, to take the other into account" (p. 49). And this taking into account is also, for Levinas, a "responding through one's presence to the mortality of the living" (pp. 127–8). In the intergenerational programs in my studies, participants were literally at the ends of life – the start and finish of the human life cycle. I might ask: What special opportunities did this create to develop ethical relations with others? How might the face be that much more salient or recognizable when it and the person to whom it calls are at the ends of life? Further, what conditions, structural, curricular, or pedagogical, might help to create and reinforce ethical relations? In considering these questions, it may be helpful to think also of the importance of a conception of *the other* in Levinas's ethics.

One of the keys of Levinas's ethical relation is that the alterity of the other is maintained, or otherwise put, that the face of the other is recognized and protected as the other's and not one's own. This is not a question of differences in terms of "properties or dispositions in space" (e.g., "your hair is unlike mine or we are different because you occupy another place than me"), but that "before any attribute, you are other than I, other otherwise ... And it is this alterity, different from the one which is linked to attributes, that is [one's] alterity" (p. 49). To be other should not be confused as being "othered" in the sense of being set apart as less than human or deficient based on some kind of minoritized status (e.g., Iannacci, 2005). Rather, in Levinas's terms, acknowledging the other as other is to simultaneously admit the other's uniqueness, to recognize that the other is "irreducible to any other one" (Robbins, 2001, p. 126), to refuse to attempt to totalize that other by presupposing to know her (e.g., Levinas, 1991), and to see that one's "relationship with the other is better as difference than as unity," for "the very value of love is the impossibility of reducing the other to myself, of coinciding into sameness" (Levinas & Kearney, 1986, p. 22). In relation to the project of intergenerational curricula, I might ask if and how the ethical relation might be enhanced through the intergenerational context. Further, I might ask if and how the ethical necessity of alterity might connect to my intent to discover means of expanding communication options in a theoretical frame that recognizes Bakhtin's (1986) suggestion that the difference of the other becomes part of one's utterance and is thereby enriched. These questions dwell in the backbone of *Learning at the Ends of Life*, but, to situate the context in which I am writing for and against, they are pre-empted by the following discussion of more mainstream notions of the benefits of intergenerational programs.

Benefits of Intergenerational Programs

Even without considering the questions I have just posed, the mainstream intergenerational literature points to many reasons that intergenerational programs in general and intergenerational learning programs in the specific are needed and beneficial to participants. Although my personal experience of intergenerational learning was in informal settings, there are many reasons formal programs may be needed today. Current North American demographic and social trends convey the need for innovative ways of engaging children and elders in learning and being together. In Canada, the proportion of elders "is projected to increase by more than 10 percentage points on average over the next four decades" (Spiezia, 2002, p. 109) and in the United States, "the older population is projected to double by 2030 (to 71.5 million) and represent 20 percent of the total U.S. population" (Minnesota Department of Health, 2005, n.p.). Home was once the place where elders resided, cared for by family members, but today there is an ever-escalating call for retirement and nursing homes. Sadly, isolation and depression are too common for elders in such facilities (Kastner, 2004; David, 2010).

Simultaneously, during vital periods in their lives, a rising number of children require out-of home care (Jarrott & Bruno, 2007; McCain & Mustard, 1999). These growing trends are accompanied by social adjustments (e.g., geographical dispersal, urbanization, and divorce in the family) that have weakened and/or changed intergenerational contact (e.g., Kaplan, Henkin, & Kusano, 2002). Intergenerational learning programs attempt to address these issues by building on strengths and resources that might already exist in the community. Elders can be seen as resources, because overall they are becoming more educated (La Porte, 2000), healthier (Thompson & Wilson, 2001), and recognized as having valuable knowledge to pass on (Illinois Intergenerational Initiative, 1997). Thus, while improving their own learning, elders may be enlisted as nurturers of children (Henkin & Kingson, 1999). Children, similarly, have much to offer. In my studies of intergenerational learning programs, children were observed to draw out, motivate, help with idea formation, and give a sense of purpose to the elders with whom they were learning (Heydon, 2005; Heydon, 2007). Intergenerational learning programs are also needed, because interestingly – and contrary to my own situation – some research has demonstrated that positive familial intergenerational relationships do not necessarily translate into generalized positive feelings about a generation (Jarrott, 2007). Furthermore, one study even found that "frequent contact with un-related older adults," that is, older adults who are not family members, is associated "with more positive attitudes about aging in general" (Jarrott, 2007, p. 1).

Formal intergenerational programs (under which intergenerational learning and shared-site programs fall) have been on the continent for decades. The U.S. Foster Grandparent Program of 1963, in which older adults worked with children and youth deemed "at risk" was one of the first systematically planned intergenerational programs in North America (Larkin & Newman, 1997). Since then intergenerational programs have grown considerably (Kuehne & Collins, 1997) but are still not commonplace. That they are not more widespread is surprising, given that intergenerational programs hold many documented benefits for participants. For children, benefits include a sense of continuity in lives where there might otherwise be little intergenerational contact, the understanding that learning is lifelong (Brummel, 1989), the chance to understand older adults better, which can minimize fears children might have of them, a fostering of children's acceptance that aging is a normal and natural part of the life cycle (Penn State College of Agricultural Sciences, 2003), increased appreciation for diversity, (Jarrott & Bruno, 2007), and increased empathy towards older adults (Schwalbach & Kiernan, 2002). For older adults, intergenerational programs can minimize fears they might have of children (Penn State College of Agricultural Sciences, 2003) and create a calming effect in people with dementia (Ward, Kamp, & Newman, 1996). For both generations, programs can create intergenerational understanding, provide opportunities for lifelong learning (Brummel, 1989), help generations locate commonalities across age and culture (Elders Share the Arts, n.d.), and provide opportunities to build intergenerational relationships (Jarrott & Bruno, 2007).

Structure of Intergenerational Learning Programs

Intergenerational learning programs can take many forms under four basic models: older adults providing service to children (e.g., elders rocking HIV-positive infants in hospital settings), young people serving older people (e.g., by reading to people in elder care settings), intergenerational groups performing community service (e.g., environmental projects), and shared-site programs (Marriage & Family Encyclopedia, n.d.). While each model has its benefits and place, shared-site intergenerational programs (also known as co-located programs) where participants come together in formal and informal ways for learning and relationship-building have many strengths:

- More frequent interaction can lead to stronger relationships and better understanding between generations,
- Transportation between the programs is not an issue due to the co-location or close proximity of the programs,
- Informal interactions are possible through routine elements such as shared indoor and outdoor spaces, a common entrance for both generations, and ease of movement between the adult programs and children programs, and
- Scheduling activities is easier since space is shared, staff are [sic] cross-trained, and many sites have an intergenerational coordinator to facilitate activities (Butts & Moore, 2009).

Shared-site programs are not add-ons to existing ones. Rather, their very form and physical structure create opportunities for myriad intergenerational interaction and relationships.

Regardless of whether a site is shared or not, there are other structural concerns that must be addressed for participants to garner benefits from any intergenerational program. These include the need for formal, institutionalized administrative agreements regarding a commitment to intergenerational programming, individual choice over whether to participate, and the provision of *cross-training* for practitioners so they are not focused solely on the populations with whom they typically work (e.g., educators being educated about working with older adults and recreation therapists [RTs] being educated about working with children). Cross-training can also include educating participants before programs begin about the generation they are about to encounter (Jarrott, 2007).

Creating Learning Opportunities

Program models are important to consider, because simply bringing different generations together may not create positive effects (e.g., Aday, McDuffie, & Sims, 1993). Strong prospects for learning and intergenerational interaction come from contexts that support intergenerational *programming* rather than mere intergenerational *activities*. The difference between these approaches is that programming "provide[s] a way for experiences and interactions to take on meaning relevant to one's life," whereas activities "do not allow the level of meaning to exist because they lack depth and long-term significance" (Friedman, 1997, p. 105). Intergenerational activities are usually one-meeting occasions where people are parachuted together (e.g., a panel of visiting elders in a classroom). Activities like this can have some positive outcomes, but more generally, longer-term programming is more meaningful and tends to "reduce ambiguities about ... relationship[s], lessen social distance, and support intergenerational solidarity" (Jarrott, 2007, p. 6). Consideration of some of the structural issues introduced above can help foster intergenerational programs, but the literature has also identified important, more curricular-oriented issues that should be addressed.

Jarrott (2007) found that a particular notion of "equal group status" should be sought in programs where "each participant has something to contribute and something to gain from the contact setting" (p. 5). Equal group status can, at least in part, be accomplished through programs that help participants to cooperate and work towards "common goals" (p. 5). Further, some "essential criteria" (Friedman, 1997) for intergenerational programming, have been identified as: "programs should be beneficial to all [participants]; programs should be on-going, lasting for a significant length of time to establish relationships; programs should serve the community; programs should include a curricular ... component" (p. 105). This last point begs for the inclusion of curriculum studies in any intergenerational learning program conversation.

Theoretical Approaches to Intergenerational Learning in General

Accompanying the birth of intergenerational programs is a growing interdisciplinary intergenerational research tradition. In general, intergenerational research is made up of perspectives and methods from gerontology, psychology, education, and other human development specialties (Larkin & Newman, 1997). Regarding trends in the research, the benefits of intergenerational programs generally and learning programs specifically are thought to be well known. Consequently, more recent research is considering "best practices," such as asking how programs can "build on [the] respective strengths" (Kaplan et al., 2003, p. 7) of participants and create opportunities for them to foster "meaningful relationships" (Griff, Lambert, Fruit, & Dellman-Jenkins, 1996, p. 5). Attention is also paid to the evaluation of programs (e.g., Cox, Croxford, & Edmonds, 2006).

Theoretically, the bulk of intergenerational research draws on developmental theories, especially those of Erik Erikson (VanderVen, 1999) and supports evaluation of programs based on instrumentalist theories (Hayes, 2003; Kuehne & Kaplan, 2001) with the goal of achieving a degree of prediction and control (Habermas, 1972). The focus on a fairly monolithic notion of best practices bespeaks these theoretical orientations. Undoubtedly this type of intergenerational learning research has greatly contributed to the knowledge of intergenerational learning phenomena, which is significant to the development and maintenance of intergenerational learning programs. At the same time, knowledge and understanding of intergenerational learning can only increase through the inclusion of a diversity of methodologies and theories. My own research therefore relies on the foundation laid by the dominant research on intergenerational learning, yet employs theories and methodologies that come from research traditions that make sense to me as both a former teacher and an educational researcher.

My intergenerational studies are located in the field of curriculum studies and, as mentioned, work primarily through a critical theoretical framework with a secondary propensity towards postmodern theory as it relates to social categories. Curriculum studies is an established field within educational studies that queries the various orientations to and conceptions of curriculum and seeks to answer teaching and learning questions that fall into three main "orders" of questions: (1) the "nature of curriculum" (questions relating to issues concerning the "essence" and "properties" of curriculum); (2) the "elements of curriculum" (questions relating to issues concerning the "teacher, students, subject, milieu, aim, activity," and "result"), and (3) the "practice of curriculum" (questions relating to issues concerning action and thought) (Dillon, 2009, pp. 344–8). While curriculum studies researchers might call on methods and frameworks from distinct fields such as sociology, anthropology, psychology, philosophy, and the like to answer these questions, they do so from a unique vantage and approach of curriculum studies. Curriculum studies "may draw on any external discipline for methodological help but does not allow the methodology to determine inquiry" (Egan, 1978, p. 16). This allows researchers to tailor methodologies to suit the specific circumstances under investigation and ground their studies in specific *teaching* and *learning* contexts. Thus, my studies of intergenerational curriculum draw on ethnographic tools from anthropology, but my use of them is "looser" (p. 16) than in a classically anthropological sense. This is the consequence of curriculum researchers' need to tailor methodologies to suit the specific circumstance under investigation. Given that intergenerational programs and research are in a nascent stage, this flexibility is particularly welcomed and necessary.

When coupled with the aforementioned theoretical orientations, curriculum studies decries the ability of any practice (or curriculum) to be best, for this perspective sees curriculum as multiple and dynamic and not as something that can be predicted and controlled. Although "the curriculum" is sometimes reduced to what is "intended" to be taught (Eisner, 2005) and equated with a "document" (e.g., a paper copy of a provincial curriculum guide), educators like Routman (2000) counsel that curriculum is a "dialogue" (p. xxxviii). Schwab's (1973) curricular "commonplaces" – teachers, learners, subject matter, and social milieu – clarify what might be included in this dialogue. Together, the commonplaces create the "operational curriculum" (i.e., how the curriculum is actually "played out"; Eisner, 2005, p. 147). The "null" curriculum (Eisner, 2002) can also be considered; that is where the very absence of teaching something has an effect, and of import may be the "hidden" curriculum (e.g., Apple, 1971), which accounts for the unstated goals of curriculum. There are also many types of curricular orientations that affect the degree to which the commonplaces, especially teachers and learners, are provided opportunities to be "curricular informants" (Harste, 2003). These orientations run from rigid, "prescriptive" forms to more flexible "emergent forms" (Heydon & Wang, 2006).

The specific critical component of my studies comes through the goal of emancipation, which refers to the desire to "free human-kind of what presents itself as 'natural' or given by making apparent the points of view from which such a version of 'reality' are constructed" (Habermas, 1972, p. 311). Considering phenomena critically means asking questions such as: What is taken for granted? What are other ways of seeing this? What sociopolitical issues are at play? What actions might forward the goal of social justice? (e.g., Lewison, Flint, & VanSluys, 2002). For instance, one might question the notion of a universal best in early childhood education and care (ECEC) or elder care, asking best for whom? What are the different iterations of best? How do they relate to a person's social positioning? Whom does this notion of best serve? The taste of postmodernism here allows me to see social categories as fluid and power as relational rather than something that is owned.

A Curriculum Researcher Discovers Intergenerational Programs

I began studying intergenerational learning programs after visiting an intergenerational art class at Blessed Mother (the facility in the vignette that opens this chapter).[2] Created by the Catholic Church, at the time of the visit Blessed Mother was a long-term care facility that included retirement apartments and ran what it called the Generations Together Learning Center (hereafter referred to as the Center), a child care program for children aged 6 weeks to 6 years that was part of a shared-site program. The mission of the Center was to create opportunities for intergenerational learning and interaction, thus many measures were taken to ensure shared facilities and programming. Foremost was that the entire building was licensed for child care, making the facility a space that literally and symbolically invited children to be present. Next, the architecture of Blessed Mother supported its intergenerational mandate. The Center was prominently housed in a main part of Blessed Mother and had large windows to the hallway, so that adults and children could see each other and adults would be more apt to stop

---

2 All names have been changed.

in and visit. An outside play area was located close to the adults' living areas, and an observation area was included allowing more chances for intergenerational interaction. Moreover, there was a satellite Center area for toddlers located in the heart of two *neighbourhoods* (i.e., where the adults had their bedrooms, lounge, and eating areas). This room was a shared space for elders and children and maximized intergenerational contact. Apart from the architecture, Blessed Mother also offered many formal intergenerational programs (e.g., art classes, music, and exercise). Thus, it was a prime example of a mature intergenerational organization that met many of the essential criteria the literature lists for intergenerational programs.

Trajectory of the Intergenerational Studies

My first inquiry into intergenerational shared-site learning was a naturalistic study of the intergenerational art class as part of the intergenerational shared-site program at Blessed Mother. The research questions were: What are the constituents of learning opportunity-rich intergenerational learning programs, and how are they organized? What (if any) literacy-related learning opportunities are created by the intergenerational art class? What forms of collaboration occur among participants? How does this collaboration build individual and communal capacities? I recorded through video and fieldnotes what was occurring in two intergenerational art classes and one adult art class (which I used as a counterpoint to the intergenerational classes). I interviewed participants, faculty, staff, administrators, and Susan, the art teacher who functioned as a key informant. In my analysis of the class, I found many learning opportunities created by an "asset oriented" (Heydon & Iannacci, 2008) form of curriculum: a curriculum that focused on participants' strengths and knowledge and recognized their need to communicate in a wide variety of ways. Thanks to the theoretical approach to literacy introduced earlier in the chapter (most importantly multimodal literacy), I was able to identify that many of the learning opportunities were literacy-related. Participants were provided opportunities, for example, to learn how to work through fundamental communication decisions: to consider their interests that drive what they want to communicate, learn a number of different ways of communicating their message, and decide, given the context, the most apt way to structure their message (Kress & Jewitt, 2003). These learning opportunities were created through the class structure, which was organized around five components, all of which are expanded on in Chapter Two: (1) strategies to (re)acquaint participants with each other and foster community and a sense of safety (e.g., games to remind each other of participants' names); (2) a catalyst for that day's project that could induce conversation and activate schema related to the subject matter and/or media to be used; (3) explicit instruction, modelling, and support to use the media in the project (e.g., print making); (4) sustained opportunities to work on the project and to draw on fellow participants for support; (5) opportunities to share the work with an audience (e.g., in class, displays in the hallways, at a yearly public art show).

Following the initial studies at Blessed Mother, I wondered how other intergenerational shared-site learning programs might provide similarly rich learning opportunities (in particular as they related to communication) and create productive forms of collaboration and relationship-building. Thus, I visited a number of intergenerational shared sites in southwestern Ontario and undertook a similar study to the one at Blessed Mother at a site called Watersberg. I chose Watersberg, because it seemed representative of the other intergenerational sites in the southwestern Ontario area that I had visited. It was run by the same child and elder care organizations and employed the same type of intergenerational structure, elder care philosophy, and curricular orientation in the child care portion of the program (i.e., an emergent curriculum). Located in a suburban/rural area, Watersberg was a secular, privately run, for-profit assisted living facility for elders that rented space to a private, non-denominational Christian, non-profit child care organization. The shared site was less than five years old at the time of the research, and the building was planned and built to house a child care facility on its main floor. A Watersberg administrator told me that although elder care was more profitable per square foot than child care, they chose to include child care because their guiding philosophy was to provide their residents with opportunities to engage with nature, animals, and children.

Adults and children at Watersberg participated in pre-planned intergenerational learning activities, and there were some opportunities for adults to visit the child care centre unannounced. In general, although I identified some opportunities for interaction and learning at Watersberg, they did not seem as rich as at Blessed Mother. This observation was substantiated by the practitioners who, although they all said how much the intergenerational component brought to the program, admitted they had difficulty "coming up" with what to do with the participants, or when they did decide on an activity it sometimes "wasn't so great." Watersberg struggled to turn activities into programs and to have a true curricular component; thus, there were few or unidentifiable learning opportunities. For instance, a number of practitioners pointed to a teddy bear social as a ubiquitous yet "failed" activity. One educator explained, "We sat in a circle and each person sat there with their bear on their lap." Other frequent activities that were slightly more successful but still did not challenge or create much meaning for participants were "beauty parlor," where participants did each other's hair and nails; "ice cream social," where participants watched as practitioners made and served sundaes; and "free play," where bins of children's toys were placed on tables for intergenerational participants.

The educators expressed ease in programming for young children and the recreation therapists were comfortable programming for older adults, but neither group had much experience or training in working with intergenerational groups. Thus, wanting to support practitioners such as the ones at Watersberg, I wondered if I could create a resource from a curriculum studies perspective to allow practitioners to offer intergenerational programming that created rich learning and interactional opportunities, in particular in the area of communication. Over a three-year period, I built and field tested an intergenerational curriculum support guide that had the goal of capitalizing on the creating and viewing of visual texts as a way of expanding participants' communication options and as a medium for relationship-building. I adapted many of the projects from Blessed Mother's art program and authored others to be used by non-artists. Practitioners took these projects and with support implemented them at a site called Picasso.

Picasso was a secular, for-profit retirement home in urban southwestern Ontario. At the time of the research it was approximately twenty years old and rented space to Picasso Child, an independent, secular, not-for-profit child care centre. Prior to the research there was no shared programming, and there was a stark delineation between children's and adults' spaces. Picasso consented to have my research team work with them to create an intergenerational art program and in turn develop the curriculum resource guide. The team worked with Picasso's own resources and existing structures to build an intergenerational art program as an entrée into intergenerational programming. The practitioners used the guide as a starting point for teaching in the program and provided feedback so we could revise the guide. We documented this process and collected data that related to the participants' responses

Table 1.1 Programs Studied

Participants	Blessed Mother (United States, large, urban centre; established program)	Watersberg (Southwestern Ontario, Canada, rural; <five year old program)	Picasso (Southwestern Ontario, Canada, medium-sized urban centre; program established by research project)
Children (ages 3–5 years)	25	37	24
Elders	16 + 10 adults only class	32	40
Early Childhood Educators	2	7	2
Recreation Therapists	4	5	3
Administrators	2	2	2
Other	1 intergenerational art teacher 2 volunteers		1 family member of adult participant

to the projects and the program as a whole. Table 1.0 shows the break-down of participants in the three sites over the life of the studies.

For data analysis I used a modified version of the constant comparison method (Handsfield, 2006). Data were coded according to predictive themes and pattern matched. To retain their complexity, data that fit between themes did not automatically discredit themes but were included and the discontinuities presented. Some of the findings from the research have been published elsewhere (e.g., Heydon, 2005; Heydon, 2007; Heydon & Daly, 2008; Heydon, 2008; Heydon, 2009). What *Learning at the Ends of Life* does is bring these findings and others together in one place for the first time.

Conclusion

Learning at the Ends of Life is a sustained narrative about what I have learned about intergenerational curricula within the context of shared-site intergenerational programs. It is the first book I know of that looks at intergenerational programs from a curriculum studies perspective through a critical theoretical lens. Through its content and structure *Learning at the Ends of Life* seeks to understand critically how forms of curricula, as value-laden entities, are constructed and implemented in intergenerational programs and address their relationship to participants' learning opportunities and identities, and the structure of the social categories they occupy (e.g., childhood and old age). In general, my findings substantiate and illustrate the literature review I introduced in this chapter, while the critical theoretical framework adds a further dimension. In deciding which findings to include in the book I let the spirit of the question of the educator at the beginning of this chapter be a primary guide: What are some of the curricular, pedagogical, and structural features of intergenerational programs that can help to create rich communicational learning opportunities for participants? In addition, the inclusions and exclusions in the literature on intergenerational programs, literacy, and young children also bespoke the need to include other elements, most specifically those related to gaps in the body of knowledge in areas such as understanding elders and children's text making when they do it together, curricula and pedagogy to support expanded communication learning opportunities and identity options, and issues many educators choose to ignore, such as death and dying.

Chapter Two

Who Can Say What Is in My Heart? Illustrations of What Intergenerational Learning Programs Have Meant to Their Participants

As discussed in Chapter One, mainstream research has focused heavily on the outcomes of intergenerational learning programs with an eye to identifying their benefits. The notion of benefits, however, is a rather instrumental one, and suggestive of attempts to predict and control outcomes. My concern is that in all of the measurement and evaluation, the view of participants in intergenerational learning as living social actors, as people with feelings, desires, and intentionality may be lost. I worry that intergenerational learning programs thus become something that is done *to* people rather than *with* people. I would argue that the search for and focus on quantifiable benefits is premised on a problematic *needs discourse*. Related to developmental psychology, the needs discourse advocates the fulfilment of what it perceives to be a social group's needs (e.g., those of children), based on its own social and cultural understandings of what is valuable. Such a discourse runs the risk of not being culturally sensitive or respectful of people's personhood and intentionality. In relation to children specifically, for example, the needs discourse advocates: "doing things for children simply because they are 'good for them' ... For example, if we accept that children cannot thrive and flourish unless they have warm and caring relationships – this is not all that intimate relationships mean to a child. Adults don't regard being loved and cared about as just about having their 'needs' met. Neither do children. For a child, being loved is profoundly meaningful and valuable in itself" (Rogers, 2004, p. 134). Such a discourse raises a question. If the right benefits of intergenerational learning programs were not identified would the powers that be still help to bring different generations together? This question begets others, such as: What opportunities might the bringing together of different generations for learning offer to participants? What is the meaning of intergenerational learning programs and the relationships that stem from them to the people who *live* them? Based on my intergenerational research and in dialogue with the mainstream intergenerational literature, this chapter begins a response to these questions and focuses on each of the applicable curricular commonplaces (learners, teachers, subject matter, milieu; Schwab, 1973) to do so. It should be noted, however, that in some instances, divisions between commonplaces are somewhat arbitrary because they do, of course, overlap.

The Opportunities of Intergenerational Learning Programs: A Repositioning of Generational Categories and the Meaning of Education in People's Lives

In many ways intergenerational leaning programs are an example of radical curricula that have much to teach about the young and old of a society and how they are positioned. The intergenerational literature claims that intergenerational programs should seek to foster "equal group status" (Jarrott, 2007) whereby programs and participant relationships are planned for and viewed as reciprocal and meaningful to all generations. Taking this further, a critical reading of intergenerational curricula requires a focus on sociopolitical issues. Therefore, early in my intergenerational studies this required me to identify and analyse the positioning of the social categories of the participants in the programs: childhood and old age. One of my findings was the ubiquity of human capital theory in early childhood education and care policy and curriculum. This theory emphasizes the "development of skills as an important factor in production activities" (Olaniyan & Okemakinde, 2008, p. 157) and only (or primarily) because of this is education taken to be important. The significance, then, of education is never in the present and does not belong to the learners themselves but is rather always delayed to the future and belongs primarily to the economy.

As I describe in detail elsewhere (e.g., Heydon, 2005; 2008) human capital theory has been adopted in early childhood education and care policy and curriculum as a response to the rapid social changes of the new millennium. There have been far-reaching technological (Kress, 2003) and economic changes that have caused concern and anxiety on the part of governments and their citizenry. In turn, discourses that set out an "efficient" (Stein, 2001) plan for early childhood education and care that focuses on raising young children into able workers have become very popular. Even before the global economic crisis of 2009, David and her colleagues observed that the "adult manipulation of the childhood experience has come to the fore with a severity not seen since children's direct involvement in industry in the eighteenth century" (David et al., 2000, p. 21). Human capital theory and its ensuing educational practices and policies can deny children's full personhood and belie the many reasons engaging in learning can be significant, meaningful, and pleasurable for people in the here and now. Related to this, the social category of old age holds much in common with that of childhood. Most notably, the similarities between the categories exist in that members are judged against the "normate" (Thomson, 1997): "the constructed identity of those who, by way of the bodily configurations and cultural capital they assume, can step into a position of authority and wield the power it grants them" (p. 8). Here, the normate is the able "adult" who contributes directly to the economy. In a society that defines itself primarily in post-capitalist economic terms, young children and older adults are not generally considered to be contributing members of the citizenry. Thus, they are seen as in need of control with the dominant means for control being segregation and scientific technology (e.g., Thomson, 1997). One can see these controls in operation in the way that older adults and young children are generally segregated by age. For young children, curriculum tends to be scientific and instrumental (e.g., Bobbitt, 1971; Tyler, 1949) in that it constructs knowledge as a product that can be predicted and controlled (Heydon & Wang, 2006). The kindergarten program in Ontario (e.g., Ontario Ministry of Education, 2006), for instance, has been built around academic expectations that are prescribed and relatively easily measured outcomes for children's knowledge and behaviour (e.g., "As children progress through the Kindergarten years they ... use, read, and represent whole numbers to 10 in a variety of meaningful contexts"; pp. 44–5). This is in direct contrast to early years curricula in countries like Sweden, where the child's quality of life (e.g., enjoyment and pleasure) is foremost and educators focus on evaluating the opportunities the environment creates for children rather than evaluating children against a standardized set of expectations. As one Swedish educator put it when comparing her system to the instrumental system in England, "A very big difference between the English and Swedish system is that it is in our curriculum it says it is not the child we should evaluate. It is processes in the school, how we do things, we should evaluate, but not the child, which is a very big difference" (Teachers.tv, n.d., n.p.). Similarly, a scientific approach is also used in "curricula" for elders. Most elder programming in residential institutions or day programs follows a medical model that is evident even in the titles of the workers in such places. For instance, in all of the study locales, even at Blessed Mother, which followed a resident-directed format which fights the medical model, the workers who planned and carried out recreation-related activities were called "recreation therapists." Thus, therapist-run curricula can be seen as following a scientific instrumentalism that is designed to cure some perceived ill in the elders rather than be undertaken because the elders find it inherently meaningful.

When intergenerational participants are understood in critical terms such as the ones above, then bringing the generations together to engage in learning and interactions that defy instrumental ends can be seen as radical. The intergenerational benefits literature is often couched in terms that are commensurate with human capital theory (e.g., Jarrott's 2007 speech to the United Nations was at a conference whose title concerned strengthening "economic" ties), but the value of intergenerational programs need not be defined through outcomes. Instead, a critical approach calls for an appraisal of what one recognizes as benefits, why, and on whose terms. This entails an attempt to respect participants' personhood by allowing their perspectives on what is valuable to at the very least take priority in the discussion.

The Opportunity for the Building of Meaningful Relationships within Ethical Relations

In addition to the opportunities for the forging of ethical relations that I theorized in the last chapter and provide an illustration of in the next, in my intergenerational studies participants expressed, both explicitly and implicitly through their behaviour, that being with people of another generation and forming relationships with them was important to them. This substantiates the literature's identification of the creation of intergenerational relationships as a major feature of intergenerational programs (e.g., Jarrott & Bruno, 2007). I have documented hundreds of interactions between participants that suggest that such relationships were established and important in their own right. I saw children asking for older adults and being disappointed when an adult was absent from class, physical displays of affection (hugging and kissing) and smiling between participants, and participants saving seats for each other in class (Heydon, 2009). I also recorded adults saying things such as, "These children are so inspiring" (Rebecca, age 90); "Oh yes, I like it when the children come!" (Pete, age 83); "[The children] are getting a good education. They're not afraid of old people or wheelchairs ... They add life to the building" (Ida, age 77); "This is my day! I love these children" (Frieda, age 96; Heydon, 2008). Consider too the juxtaposition of the following images: Figure 2.1 shows the hands of two participants collaborating on a project entitled *Intergenerational Hands* (see Appendix I for lesson plan details). The project was adapted by a lesson inspired by Picasso's *Fleurs et mains* (1958) and in the case of the photo, implemented in an intergenerational art and singing program. The image on the cover of this book is a finished text from this project which became the invitation for an intergenerational art show.

What these images begin to show is how the participants were present to each other: the physical coming together, the problem-solving around all the communicational decisions outlined in Chapter One (e.g., what to represent and how), and the meeting of two people within the larger context of art class, the shared site, and the goal of the art show to create a shared visual text. Also, I saw long-term relationships established. The case of Keith, an adult participant at Picasso, the intergenerational shared-site art program that my research team helped to establish, is just such an example.

Keith and Roger

The relationships that were forged between child and adult participants at Picasso definitely affected what participants represented in their visual texts and also the form of their representation. One group of children and adults had spent two years together and evidently bonded. Keith had been ill and missed a number of classes. On a cold February day we held a class focusing on Heartmaps (visual renderings that asked participants to represent what they felt was figuratively in their hearts; Bainbridge, Heydon, & Malicky, 2009; see Appendix II for lesson plan details). Happily, Keith returned to class. He entered the room and took his seat before the children arrived. All that the other adults could talk about was how much the children had missed Keith: "Lisa asked for you, Robbie asked for you ..." Keith replied, "I seem to have adopted another six or seven grandchildren. I'm not sure that I needed them, but I have them!". Keith's joke referred back to the previous spring's art show we held to showcase the intergenerational class's work. At the show, Keith proudly introduced his biological grandchildren to his "adopted" grandchildren, hugging each and ensuring everyone shook hands. Shortly after this joke the children came in

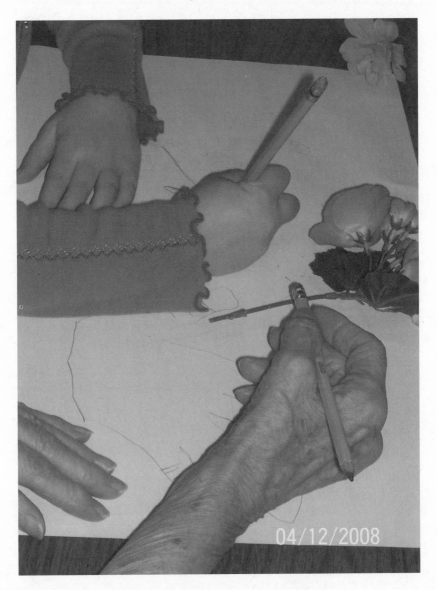

Figure 2.1 Intergenerational Hands Project Participants

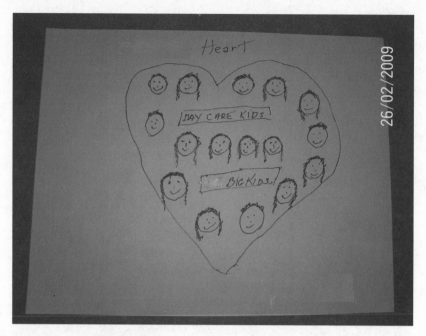

Figure 2.2 Keith's Heartmap

the room and lit up on seeing Keith. Roger, a kindergarten-aged child partici-
pant, ran to sit beside him, and the buddies caught up with each other (e.g.,
Keith answered many curious queries about his new oxygen tank). Then the
instructional component of class began. Wendy Crocker, veteran early years
teacher, doctoral student, and study research assistant, led participants in an
exploration of maps of all kinds and then shared Sara Fanelli's (1995), My
Map Book. *This book highlights a series of maps that Fanelli has made of key*
components of her life including her dog and her heart. The participants en-
gaged in a discussion about what might be in people's hearts, and Wendy made
a heart, talking aloud through the process and paying special attention to how
participants could use words and image in their design. Participants were then
invited to make their own heartmaps.

In discussing with Nora, another adult participant, what he might put in his
map Keith laughed, "I have four daughters and twelve grandchildren so that
pretty much fills (my heart) up. All girls." Nora widened her eyes, "All girls
then, no grandson." Keith looked down at Roger drawing beside him and an-
swered, "Just Roger." When the maps were finished, Keith's contained sixteen

Figure 2.3 Roger's Heartmap

smiling faces within a heart shape (see Figure 2.2). The faces were explained by the captions "Day Care Kids" and "Picasso Big Kids." In response, Roger smiled at Keith and decided it was his turn to show his map. Roger displayed it to Keith and pointing to it said, "I've got you on my map." Indeed, within a cluster of faces just beneath a representation of his "dad," which is in its own section and offset by a box, is a drawing of Keith (see Figure 2.3). "You like me," beamed the honorary grandfather.

As the story of Keith and Roger and other examples of intergenerational relationships throughout the book suggest, participants were provided the opportunity to construct and maintain positive relationships that could last over time, and because half the participants in such programs were in the last "days" of their lives, the adults taught by example that learning is not about preparation for the future but about what it can add to today. Finally, I am intrigued by the possibility that the occasions when participants encountered difference, or better perhaps, recognized the alterity of the other, were important pedagogical moments that have implications for the creation of ethical relations while begging for Deborah Britzman's (1998) notion of *queer pedagogy*.

In her pedagogy, Britzman questions what might be thought of as conventional education's "repetitious offer of tidy stories of happiness, resolution, and certainty as if life were something to be overcome and mastered with as little disturbance as possible" (pp. 79–80). Queer pedagogy "proposes to think identities in terms that place as problematic the production of normalcy and that confound the intelligibility of the apparatuses that produce identity as repetition" (p. 81). This is a type of pedagogy where what is taken to be normal is questioned, with implications for people's sense of identity and where identity can be multiple, contradictory, and in tension. This is also where people can learn to read others or a text in ways that search out alterity as difference that not only makes the other the other but is also "the precondition for the self" (p. 92). In relation to queer pedagogy I ask if and how a context like an intergenerational art class that explicitly teaches the reading and writing of texts of all kinds, where the other in these texts is central, and, it is hoped, where the other's alterity is recognized, the participants' own identity options might in turn become expansive.

Opportunities for the Overcoming of Fear

Many conditions and factors created the relationships and relational opportunities just discussed. The mainstream intergenerational literature speaks of one of the benefits of intergenerational programming being the lessening of fear that children may have of elders (Penn State College of Agricultural Sciences, 2003) which is arguably a prerequisite for relationship-building. Certainly relationships such as the one between Roger and Keith cannot not be possible if participants are fearful of each other. While it is outside the scope of this discussion to account for the precise reasons that some children might be fearful of elders or be thought to be fearful of elders, what is pertinent here are illustrations of the opportunities the program sites created for children to feel sufficiently comfortable with elders that they could work with them and even enter into relationships with them. The following narrative shows how orientation time in intergenerational art class, the use of physical proximity, teachers' modelling of comfort with elders, support for children to know how to communicate with elders, and elective participation all coalesced to provide participants with learning and relationship-building opportunities.

At Blessed Mother, every class began with Susan, the intergenerational art teacher, leading a formal period of welcome where participants reminded each other of their names and became (re)acquainted. If there is such a thing as a typical beginning to class, the following example of introductions that took place in the art room might be it. This episode reveals the layers of emotion and the types of interactions germane to the class. Evident are the playfulness of the routine, the slight apprehension on the part of the children, and the excitement of the adults. Characteristic too is the way in which Susan and Gary, a Generations Together Learning Center teacher, worked together to facilitate interaction and connection-making between participants.

Orientation

Susan models for the participants in a big, clear voice, "Hi, I'm Susan, and I'm the art teacher. Who's here today?" Participants say their names, with Susan and Gary coaching them to look at each other. It is then child participant Carl's turn.

"My name's shy boy." Carl squeaks out these words as he pulls the neck of his T-shirt over the bottom of his face.

Gary doesn't push Carl; instead he looks to Carl's friend, Arthur (another child). "Arthur's been very excited about today. He's been greeting all of his friends at the door telling them who's going to art studio." As Gary says this, he moves behind Arthur and places his hand reassuringly on his shoulder. Arthur smiles, and I notice Carl peeking out.

Frieda (age 96) calls Gary over. She extends her arm to him and smiles widely. Gary takes her hand. "I like your overalls," Frieda beams.

"You like my overalls?" Gary puts his thumb under his suspenders and does a little twirl, showing off his outfit. The children giggle.

"Yah!" Frieda reinforces.

Susan allows this enthusiasm to be a way to bring Carl back into the introductions. She says to Frieda, "The boy next to you says he's shy boy. Do you think so? Do you think he's shy?" Carl covers his eyes, but I can see him smiling between his fingers. Frieda smiles and points at Carl. Susan eases the interaction further. She moves over to Carl and touches his arm. "He says he's shy. Do you think he's shy?"

"Are you shy?" Frieda asks as she reaches for Carl.

Gary, too, eases the interaction. He speaks in a booming voice, makes eye

contact with most of the participants, and uses inclusive language so that eve-
ryone in the room is in on the conversation. "He's not shy when he visits
Frieda on our Grasshopper days.[1] Then he has his hand out for M&Ms! Carl,
you like M&Ms?"

"His real name is Carl," Susan clarifies for Frieda. She repeats his name
clearly and bends down so that she's right at Frieda's ear. Then she spells Carl's
name aloud: C-A-R-L.

"His real name is Carl!" Another child in the room repeats.

Frieda looks at Carl and coaxes, "I can be shy too, but I'm not going to hide
my eyes." Frieda is matter o -fact.

"Shy boy!" Carl asserts after hearing his "real" name said aloud.

"Hey, shy boy," Susan allows Carl to name himself, "Do you know who this
is? Do you know who's sitting next to you?" Susan gestures towards Frieda.

"Yes."

"Who is it?"

"Frieda!"

"See," Susan says, "he knows without even looking."

Watersberg routinely used opening songs to make connections and
share names around the room, something that was also experimented
with at Picasso. Introductions like these framed the text-making that
was to come by highlighting the social aspect of the practice. Participants, by engaging in the routine of sharing names, were reminded
that their work was not independent but rather grounded in community. These types of "round robin" sharing of names, however, were
not always necessary at Picasso where classes were smaller, the people
who participated more stable from class to class, elders were generally
healthier and thus had an easier time remembering names, and where
over time, the same groups of people worked together over years.
Thus, at Picasso, a slightly more ad hoc strategy was used, where artefacts related to that day's project were set out (e.g., travel brochures for
a collage project) and with the support of an educator, participants explored and discussed them. For instance, in a class where participants
made multimedia *Passports* (see Appendix XIII), participants eagerly
looked through brochures with Wendy Crocker asking, "Are you curi-

---

1 In the Generations Together Learning Center the children were grouped according to
  insect names. On Grasshopper days, the children from this particular group went to
  the neighbourhoods to visit residents and sometimes participated in pre-planned
  activities.

ous about what all of these pictures might be for?" "Yes!" exclaimed the children, while many of the adults giggled and smiled. "Well," began Wendy, "last week we travelled inside ourselves to think about maps of our heart. This week we're going to be travelling in our imagination anywhere you would like to go [in the world]. So I would like you, right now, to turn and look at the big [and little] partner you'll be working with today. Who is it?" This kind of questioning prompted responses like "I'm with Gertrude!" and when participants could not recall each other's names Wendy prompted them: "Crystal [age 5], who are you going to be with today?" Crystal pointed to adult participant Monica. "What's her name?" asked Wendy giving a hint: "Starts with an M." "Monica!" interjected Roger. "Perfect!" Wendy said, turning to the duo and helping to add a connection, "You're going to make a good pair because you both like to draw and are very imaginative."

Still, even at Blessed Mother, which was a considerably larger facility than Picasso and had a much less stable elder participant population, the shared-site structure often allowed the orientation at the beginning of classes to be a time of reconnection rather than new connection-making. At Blessed Mother many if not all the participants would have encountered each other in other parts of their day and other spaces of the building. Thus, classes did not stand alone. Added to this was that Blessed Mother accepted children at six weeks of age (the short duration of maternity leave in the United States rendered the placement of such young children in programming necessary); thus many of children in the intergenerational art class had been at Blessed Mother since infancy. Also, aspects of the facility enhanced natural (i.e., unscheduled) interaction through, for instance, the architecture of the building and the proximity of children's physical space to adult space. There were also scheduled interactions outside of art class, such as sing-alongs and strolls through residents' neighbourhoods. Embedded within a shared site, the art class could draw on participants' prior experiences with each other. Most had already met or at least seen each other. These connections were chances for stronger connection-making within the art class. For instance, in one class, adult participant Mina engaged child participant Chloe in conversation by telling her that she could see her playing from her bedroom window: "I wave to you, but evidently you can't see me." Mina explained, "It's way above where you play in those houses. If you look straight up, you'll see my window. There's all kinds of windows in my room and there are flowers. There are lots of flowers and green. I love flowers." The playground with the "houses" of which

Mina spoke was part of the strategic intergenerational architecture at Blessed Mother. Whether or not Mina had actually seen Chloe from her window is debatable, but Mina had seen children playing in that location and Chloe would have played there. The conditions for connection were therefore met and extended through Mina's orchestration of the conversation.

At Blessed Mother and Picasso orientation went hand in hand with the class seating arrangements. Susan insisted insofar as possible that participants sit in a pattern of adult, child, child, adult. Gary (educator), Marianne (volunteer), and the two recreation therapists from Blessed Mother who were interviewed all commented on the effectiveness of this seating plan. It allowed children and adults to be accessible to each other, but did not isolate children from each other. At Picasso, we originally employed this seating plan but then gradually adapted it in response to the children and specific projects. For instance, we noticed that over time, once participants began to form intergenerational relationships, the children in particular would ask to sit with specific adults and were usually not concerned with sitting with other children. This was especially the case with Roger and Keith. There was also a situation where Gregory, a child participant at Picasso, did not want to sit with anyone. Gregory was three years old when he began art class. He called the educators and adults names and cried and said he did not want to sit with anyone. Gregory was interested, however, in making visual texts. Thus, we offered him the option of sitting on his own but where he could see people. Gradually he moved closer and closer to the other participants. Eventually Gregory became one of the most enthusiastic participants in class. Some elders also had seating preferences, wanting, for instance, to be close to the door so they could have access to the washroom; others had hearing or vision requirements that made some parts of the room easier for them to work in than others. It is also important to note that at Blessed Mother, art classes were offered in an art room as well as in elders' neighbourhoods. When classes were held in the neighbourhoods a central table housed the art project with participants in an adult, child, child, adult pattern, and other adults who wanted to participate through observation could sit in a circle around this. Regardless of the specific seating configuration, the goal in all cases was to ensure a sense of comfort and safety for participants (e.g., to ensure that children could reach the table top and adults had arms on their chairs to prevent falls) and provide opportunities for optimum interaction between participants and participants and materials.

In sum, orientation and the classroom set-up allowed a sense of safety by providing the opportunity for participants to locate themselves in relation to each other. For example, in the Orientation narrative, Frieda and Carl, despite Carl's apparent shyness, did connect. In fact, Carl's shyness, when taken in context, may have been a catalyst for the connection-making. Notice that Carl played at his shyness and ironically placed it in the foreground as a means of being at the centre of conversation. In the end, one could see that he knew Frieda all along, and his peeking and smiles tempered his supposed apprehension. This is reminiscent of a young child playing peek-a-boo with a caregiver. Carl created a character of "shy boy," and he brought him back out in subsequent classes. Some of the other boys participated in the play, and they eventually began to introduce themselves as "shy boy number two," "shy boy number three," and so on. Orientation, therefore, became a light-hearted time when participants could play with each other.

Physical Proximity

Physical proximity including touch also played a role in helping participants become acquainted and gain a sense of safety. I observed this as being particularly important for children who were new to Blessed Mother. As Gary told me,

> Well, when they get in here too, it's interesting to see the kids who aren't used to being with residents. They will, when we go and visit, they'll hide behind my legs. They will just peek around. I had one kid tell me he doesn't want to shake the woman's hand because she's going to eat him, 'cause for a lot of kids, the elders, the wrinkles, and the discolouring, it's very intimidating to them. And after a month or two, at first by example, I have them see me touching the residents, hugging them, touching their hands, speaking softly with them, and eventually we get to… what I really like to do is do the lotion with the hands, with the residents. Take them and put lotions on their hands, and of course at first some of them won't. A lot of them instantly will, and they're loving it. It's fun to see the transition from the beginning of the year where those students who had nothing to do with it, now are the first ones that want to run up and have their favourite residents. And, when I put the lotion out, they're proud to bring their little toys and whatever it is they have. They want to come show the residents. So the circle of life ... is just great here because we have babies to our residents who are on their last days. It's a little, little community in the centre here.

Lotion and structured opportunities for touch were additionally used for fun and connection-making at Watersberg in a beauty parlour activity they regularly offered. This activity created opportunities for children and elders to style each other's hair, give each other manicures, and primp each other with accessories such as scarves, beads, hats, ties, and the like. While the learning opportunities here were obvious quite different than in the art classes, beauty parlour did allow participants to practise the life skill of grooming, be close to each other, care for each other, and to communicate verbally and non-verbally. Although female adults outnumbered males, all genders participated and seemed to find the activity pleasurable and engaging. My fieldnotes and the videos of beauty parlour, for instance, are characterized by recordings of the sights and sounds of laughter, smiles, and a great deal of physical and verbal intergenerational interaction.

Touch, was also, as can be seen in Gary's interview, a way of soothing adult participants. I saw this again in all three intergenerational sites through regular practices such as handshakes and the placement of shawls on adult participants' shoulders. Frequently, I observed staff bringing participants together by touch. For example, when Susan wanted two participants to interact, she would squat down between them and stretch her arms around the participants' shoulders, thus making a physical link between them. Touch was also used as an opportunity to alleviate fear of illness in both children and adults. For instance, Frieda had been absent from class at Blessed Mother for a few weeks because of illness. When she returned, she was frailer than before, and she had an oxygen tank. During a portion of class when Frieda was working with child participants, she began to cough aggressively. Volunteer Marianne provided an opportunity to calm Frieda and to let the children know that she wasn't frightened. She did this by using a gentle tone of voice, rubbing Frieda's back and engaging Frieda and the children in conversation about the visual text they were creating. These last two examples are explored in more detail later in the book.

The adult participants also instigated the use of touch as a form of connection between diverse participants. During the orientation portion of one art class, adult participant Alma was very interested in child participant Clara. As Alma's voice was not strong enough to catch Clara's attention, she reached over and touched Clara's arm. At first Clara recoiled and looked frightened. Her eyes were wide and she stared at Alma. Marianne, however, noticed this and intervened to facilitate positive intergenerational interaction. She put herself between

Alma and Clara, squatted down to be at both of their heights and said to Clara, "It's okay. Say hello to Alma." Marianne then modelled this for Clara: She allowed Alma to touch her; she touched Alma on the arm in return and said, "Hi Alma." Clara then released the tension from her body; her shoulders relaxed and her eyes shrank and she moved towards Alma and started to talk with her about the impending project.

As the example above suggests, connection-making through touch was something that needed to be fostered. Gary related that some children were hesitant to interact with adults whom they didn't know – particularly when those adults looked different from those they were used to. Consequently, modelling of behaviour that was conducive to connection-making and safety was necessary. Susan echoed this need to model how to feel safe with disability and aging in addition to the importance of the overall intergenerational structure of Blessed Mother. When I asked her about the possibility of the children being afraid and the changes that occurred in children's attitudes over time she said,

> I can address this partly as a parent of a child in [the Generations Together Learning Center], and that was one of the reasons I want[ed] my kids to be there, because we don't have elderly relatives nearby that they would be exposed to regularly, and have interactions with. Just by eating in the cafeteria with them you get used to seeing people in wheelchairs, and, say, being around. If somebody is trying to push the wheelchair through a doorway, and some other adult will come and just help them with it ... it doesn't become something weird. I mean, it becomes part of their regular life, and they start to see the people that are in the wheelchairs and not the wheelchairs, not the walkers. They also, I think, start to see ... that when you are around somebody that's that age, you don't run, so they get to be a little more empathetic. But just even in the course of one class, sometimes frequently, I can see, they come in, they don't want to sit next to a certain resident, maybe that resident has never been there before, or they might be mumbling to themselves, or they might be asleep. And those things are, the kids would think might be odd. But once the class gets going, they might have me or [Gary] or [another] teacher. They see that person being comfortable with this resident, and talking to them, and maybe even encouraging them to talk to the resident. It gets easier and they get more comfortable, and by the end they'll go up to them and maybe shake their hand, or let [Frieda] kiss them.

Susan used the term comfort, but this comfort may have been a form of safety. Safety requires that all participants learn how to live and work together. As Susan said, the art class provided children the opportunities to learn how to comport themselves around the adult participants. She used the example of children learning that when they ran around in art class, it felt less safe for the adult participants.

Children were also provided the opportunity to learn how to communicate with elders, which is essential for relationship-building. For instance, many adult participants had difficulty hearing. Children were therefore taught that if they wanted to be understood, they needed to speak loudly and clearly. At Picasso where some adult participants were visually impaired, children were also alerted to how to assist such adults in the making of visual texts.

Finally, children were provided with the occasion to learn how to resolve conflict and to talk about their fears. In an interview, Marianne highlighted such an instance:

> These kids, a lot of them have been with the Generations Together Learning Center since they were real tiny. ... And [the educators in the Center] take the kids out onto the [neighbourhoods] on a regular basis. They're very comfortable with the adults. They're comfortable with them being in a wheelchair. They're comfortable with their drooling or the fact that they fall asleep ... Sometimes an adult... We saw it a couple of weeks ago, somebody got angry about a little boy 'cause he kicked her chair... And he was good about it. I mean she was rude and it was not a good thing ... I think it upset him. He didn't start [to] have a temper tantrum ... Johnny [the child] was up on the [neighbourhood]. There was no room to really separate the two. And I talked to him about it, and I explained that she may not have understood what she was saying ... And I praised him because I thought he was really ... good about it. I think he understood. He was a little uncomfortable with it, a little scared about it, but he held it all together and he was able to talk about it.

At Watersberg, and when art classes were held in the neighbourhoods at Blessed Mother, some adult participants had illnesses that affected their behaviour (e.g., Alzheimer's disease). Sometimes these adults had difficulty with impulse control, memory, and the like. Living and working with people who had such illnesses provided opportunities for children to learn about normate behaviour as well as how to resolve conflict and to understand one's fears. A number of times I observed the children responding in positive ways to adult participant behaviour that was incommensurate with the norm. At Blessed Mother, for example, Frieda would forget that she had just introduced herself to the class, and so she would repeat, "Hello, I'm Frieda!" Without missing a beat, the children's response would simply be to return the good humour with an equally gleeful, "Hello, Frieda!" At Picasso, adult participant Flora gradually began to tell longer and longer stories that seemed not to fit pragmatically with what was going on in the conversation. Everyone was very patient with these stories and would listen then sometimes simply pick up and continue their own text-making.

Despite such occasional unconventional behaviour, in no programs were any participants ever put in danger. While some adult and even child behaviour was unpredictable, when participants were in a class, it was because they had chosen to stay and participate. Moreover, participants could leave at any time, as Marianne made clear:

> We have to make sure that the adults we bring down want to be there because the kids are there. You have to have adults who are interested in children. And a lot of adults, you know, they find the kids too loud or too noisy, or sometimes the kids will kick them by mistake and they get very upset at that. And sometimes they just don't really want to be around children. So we have to make sure that the adults know that this is [a class] with the kids, and do they want to come down and visit and watch and work. And even if they don't want to do anything, I'll ask them to come down anyway: "you know, if you don't want to stay, I'll take you right back," so they don't feel that there's any pressure to go down and do artwork.

Children also had the choice of where and when to participate and for how long. In my observations, however, it was usually adults who left class early (for such things as checking insulin levels and toileting). The children did not ask to leave early, and on several occasions, the children asked to stay longer. Community in this sense meant that all participants in the class were viewed as full persons with decision-making capacity[2] and the right to exercise it. In sum, despite moments of fear, overall the children demonstrated behaviour consistent with

---

2 Legally, not all adult participants had decision-making capacity, yet this did not interfere with their right to make choices within the art class.

feeling safe in the classes. From this I extrapolate that they also felt safe in the face of disability. An instance of this was when Mark (age 31), one of the younger persons living in Blessed Mother, was invited to an art class. Mark had never before participated, and his physical disabilities were very pronounced. Like many of the adults at Blessed Mother, Mark used a wheelchair, but his wheelchair was much larger than most, because it needed to support his upper torso and head. Further setting him apart, Mark's body did not look like most others'. His arms were smaller than average and were twisted up by his head. His fingers were splayed, and he seemed to have little control over his limbs. When Mark approached the table, child participant Kevin stared with wide eyes. His staring, however, was not due to Mark's disability. Instead, Kevin exclaimed, "Whoa, he's got a Hooter's shirt!" His interest in Mark was in his shirt, from the chain of restaurants famous for its scantily clad female servers. I remarked in my field notes that evidently stereotypical gender practices can surmount the gulf between generations and abilities!

Educators

Finally, it bears noting that participating adults and children may not be the only beneficiaries of intergenerational programs: they can be powerful professional development tools for practitioners. As my opening narrative in Chapter One shows, intergenerational learning programs taught me to readdress taken-for-granted ideas about young children and their attention spans, and practitioners at all the research sites told me that mixing the populations they typically worked with helped them see children, older adults, themselves, and their work in new ways. Stunningly, I have documented how Generations Together Learning Center educator Greg reoriented his world view when he began working in an intergenerational context (e.g., Heydon, 2005): It forced him to come to terms with his fears of aging and death and made him determined to help the children in his care avoid similar fears. This is particularly significant for the children, because as Hicks (2002) teaches, children learn best from those whom they value and love. In all sites the child participants were seemingly greatly bonded to their teachers; for this reason educators themselves needed to model feeling safe for the children to feel safe with people who were different from them. As formal preparation to become an educator in an intergenerational setting is rare, most had to learn on the job.

Feeling safe with people whom he saw as old and/or disabled was not automatic for Gary; it was a gradual process that required him to face his own mortality. In our first interview, Gary confessed his fears just after starting at Blessed Mother. He spoke about not having prior experience with older adults or with people with disabilities. He explained that his first performance appraisal at the Center suggested that he improve his interaction with the adult participants in art class. Gary said that suggestion "was really good for me 'cause it really brought out more of what you see now." I asked him if he meant the various forms of interaction with the adult participants that he modelled for the children. He answered,

> Yeah, that's a big thing at first I wasn't doing enough of. I was interacting with my kids, trying to make them do the art, and I would a little bit talk to the elders, but I didn't know the residents that good. I was still a little bit uncomfortable. I didn't want to offend people. I was trying to be, you know, too politically correct.

Gary signalled that rather than interacting with adult participants as peers, individuals, or fellow human beings, he perceived them as a homogenous group that was other. This distancing of himself from the group hampered Gary's interaction and communication with the participants.

A couple of months after our first interview Gary talked about his recent bout with cancer and the effect it had had on his relationship with the adult participants. He then said,

> To tell you the truth, when I first started interacting with residents, at first I wasn't comfortable with the touching and everything. My fears of being old and at the same time going through cancer. Now, when cancer came I felt more on par with the residents all of a sudden, you know, because I was walking around with radiation in my body, going slow, so I got this whole new love for the residents too, realizing I'm closer there than I am with ... In my head, my mind, my heart, it's closer to the kids, 'cause I feel like I'm a big, goofy kid. But the body, I have to remember, is closer to this side.

Gary attributed his increased sense of safety, interaction, and effectiveness as an educator, particularly within the art class, to his illness, and to the realization that the other is in fact "us." He recognized that his fears were getting in the way of his development as a teacher. Gary stated,

> In America we joke, you know, when you're 18, you're American, you think you own the world type attitude. That's where a lot of Americans are anyway. When you're 18 you think you have the right to totally own the world. So I think any time we are faced with those things, we realize [our] mortality. [It's like the album by] Sting, *Nothing Like the Sun* ... and he had a song there called "Fragile," how fragile we are, and that song just stuck with me 'cause it's so true. We walk around with an invincible attitude. But there's a fine line between an attitude and the vulnerability we all face every day. A lot of us just don't admit it because part of that is the ego that keeps you going.

In the former interview clip, Gary still distanced himself from the other adult participants in the class. This was communicated in the distinction he made between his mind that he aligned with youth and his body that he aligned with old age. Yet Gary's talk and actions in the classroom demonstrated that he had been consciously working on feeling safe with himself in relation to the adult participants. Moreover, through his descriptions of how to foster a sense of safety in the children, Gary noted that this sense was fundamental to the children's own relationship-building with the adult participants. Finally, Gary's story reflects a movement towards respecting the alterity of the elders but not othering them as he could recognize their common humanity.

Conclusion

Instead of talking about the benefits of intergenerational learning programs, in this chapter I advocate thinking about the meaning that such programs can take in participants' lives and the opportunities that they can provide. Specifically, such programs can create opportunities for educators

- to reappraise the place of education in people's lives and the social positioning of childhood and old age,
- to support participants in the building and maintenance of meaningful relationships,
- to support participants to grow intergenerational understanding and reduce or eradicate fears, and

• to help participants' lives to be enhanced through connection and relationship-building.

Not covered in this chapter, however, are the learning opportunities inherent in intergenerational programs, especially as they pertain to a broad understanding of literacy. The documentation and analysis of these opportunities is of central concern to *Learning at the Ends of Life* and they are dealt with in Chapter Four. Before getting to this, however, I would like to offer readers a larger sense of the context in which the learning takes place; thus, the next chapter concerns the larger structural issues associated with intergenerational programs as understood through the case studies.

Chapter Three

Cases of the Building and Maintaining of Intergenerational Shared-Site Programs

Narrative Beginning: Yearning for a Different Way

I arrived at what was known in the geographic area and seniors' websites as one of the premiere rehabilitation centres in the area. *Greenhills* was located on the grounds of the local Jewish Community Centre, surrounded by carpet-like lawns, and mature, perfectly groomed trees. The asphalt drive was the deepest black, and seemingly the only place anyone every used to get from one place to another, as there were no sidewalks and undoubtedly no one ever stood on the grass. The low, sprawling building spoke of a newer facility, well kept, but definitely nobody's home. I opened the front door to the sticky-sweet, acrid smell of sickness, cleaners, and potpourri, signed myself in and received directions to my grandfather's room. My grandmother, too, had been transferred lickity-split to Greenhills from the hospital following surgery to repair her broken hip, but I thought it best to start with my grandfather, who was in another wing. He was recovering well from his broken back and would be able, I thought, to cushion the shock of it all.

Through winding, convoluted hallways from which I could see directly into people's beds and onto which I thought I would need to drop breadcrumbs to find my way back, I twisted and turned, finally reaching the room with my Papa's name on the door. I knocked in deference to his privacy, but there was no practical need as I found Papa sitting in a wheelchair an inch from the door, squeezed between his bed and the wall. Taking up the majority of the room was a family gathered around a person lying in a second bed.

"Pup," I whispered and tried to smile.

Get me out of here, his eyes suggested and his words intoned.

I struggled to free him from the bed and table, and we wheeled into the hallway.

"Where to?" I asked, hoping for home.

"There's a games room down there," he pointed, and we rolled.

The games room was a sterile box with a large television, plastic couch, a kitchenette, and a couple of laminate tables. There were in fact, no games. We were the only people in it. Here Papa explained to me that he had been trying to find a place to go other than his room. The man in the bed beside him was expected to die at any moment, and he hoped to offer the family some privacy. Thankfully, I thought, my grandfather was a retired physician, well versed in dying people, and better equipped to handle the situation than my grandmother, who had been afraid of the dead ever since her nursing training days when she had turned a corpse and thought it had come to life when the air went out of its lungs. The games room was the only space of respite for Papa except for my grandmother's bedside, but my grandmother's lapses in consciousness and her hearing-impaired roommate's insistence on listening to taped romance novels at maximum volume made for a bit of a difficult situation. As for programming providing Papa an "out," the highlighted options at Greenhills included physiotherapy, occupational therapy, and religious services.

Over the next months, Papa persevered, lived through multiple roommates, and saw my grandmother transferred to a long-term care facility that really seemed no different except that it was uglier, as it was missing the one feature of Greenhills that made me smile: Chagall prints up and down the walls. In the middle of the night, shortly after arriving at the new long-term care facility, my grandmother died. Then, surprise of all surprises, Papa became well enough to leave Greenhills, and he insisted that rather than move to a retirement home, he return to the family home. The retirement homes, he said, sapped him of his privacy and he couldn't have his family around him in the same way. In all this time, and in all the visits with my grandparents, I never once saw a child near all the elders or contemplated even for a moment taking my son to visit them. I worried at dividing my family members into young and old, but these places, the rehabilitation centre and long-term care facility, were not, I felt, good places, not places where people lived and found pleasure in life. They were places where people were stored and death seemed like a reprieve from the monotony.

Through it all, I had visions of Blessed Mother foremost in my mind and wished that this were where my family could be spending their days. Note that Blessed Mother offers a spectrum of care from retirement apartments, to rehabilitation stays, to long-term care.[1] What I wondered at the time of my grandparents' "confinement" and what burned in me ever after, were the questions: Why aren't places like Blessed Mother the norm? Why is the best we can offer elders and their families places like Greenhills?[2] What is lost when people's communication, intellect, and desire for relationship are ignored and learning is shut out of their lives? What are people and society as a whole missing when elder family members are segregated and every hour of their day is medicalized?

While the segregation of young children in early childhood education and care settings is obviously not nearly as problematic as the scene I just painted, and children are provided opportunity for learning in such settings, not just therapy, the notion of bifurcating populations is salient in both situations. This chapter considers the alternative vision. Schwab's (1973) curricular commonplaces call for a consideration of the milieux in which intergenerational learning programs occur. I have interpreted this as requiring a look at the institutional and organizational structures of these programs, like how classes, activities, or even specific programs like the art programs at Blessed Mother and Picasso were situated within the institutions and how issues around personnel requirements and professional development were treated. Because there is no shortage of guides on how to set up a variety of intergenerational programs (e.g., Penn State College of Agricultural Sciences, 2003), this chapter will not try to duplicate the information therein or provide a how-to but rather elucidate some of the structural considerations in which intergenerational curricula are nested. I do this through the illustrations of Picasso, Watersberg, and Blessed Mother as these sites attempted to create and sustain intergenerational shared-site learning programs. The goals of the chapter are to support readers in better understanding the relationship between milieu and its sibling

---

1 The literature identifies social networks and supports as key determinants of health. Relocation of elders, which disrupts these, can have grave physical and psychological effects (Dupuis-Blanchard, Neufeld, & Strang, 2009).

2 I might also add that a spectrum of care such as what is offered at Blessed Mother means that people do not have to move to new facilities, which as mentioned can put stress on people's mental and physical health. Thus, if the structure of Blessed Mother had been an option for my grandmother, she would not have had to endure a move when she was most vulnerable.

commonplaces of learners, educators, and subject matter, as well as their connection to the benefits and opportunities to which intergenerational programs can give rise, as described in the previous chapter. I begin by describing the birth of a shared site through the case of Picasso, then lead into ever more mature intergenerational programs, ending with a discussion of the structures that help to enable the type of intergenerational curriculum that can promote expansive communication and identity options. Of note is that throughout I quote at length from the recreation therapists and educators who participated in the studies. I do this because it can add to the trustworthiness of the studies but also to provide readers, insofar as possible, access to the institutions through the words and perspectives of the people who spend their every day (and sometimes every night) in them.

The Birth of a Shared-Site Intergenerational Program

The literature on intergenerational programming that I introduced in Chapter One itemizes the strengths of the shared-site structure. Ideally such programs are not add-ons to existing programs, but rather by their very physical and curricular natures create opportunities for a diversity of intergenerational learning, interaction, and relationship-building. Picasso, as an emerging intergenerational shared-site program, is a prime illustration of the challenges of establishing a shared site. As mentioned, Picasso, an over twenty-year-old elder care facility, rented space to Picasso Child, a child care centre. Picasso Child was located in a remote part of the building, and no sustained, shared curricular programming had taken place until our research team suggested there was potential for development. I discovered the Picasso centre after looking in vain for many months for a shared-site program in a medium-sized city in southwestern Ontario where I could study intergenerational art curricula. In a region with a population of almost 400,000, we could not find one shared-site program.[3] In fact, my research assistants and I were

---

3 Note that this might be changing since I began this work in 2003. Colleagues and I (Heydon et al., 2011) who are working on establishing a curriculum for intergenerational singing, conducted a systematic study of the intergenerational programs in the same region and our preliminary data analysis showed that while we could find no fully shared sites (i.e., where child and elder care share both space and programming), there were intergenerational activities happening in a number of organizations

shocked to find that the child and elder care organizations we contacted often did not believe that such programs even existed. This was even the case in situations where we spoke with child care centre directors whose centres were located in the same building as elder care. One director mentioned that she would never have the children of her centre interact with the elders in the other part of the building because there were health issues to consider. She explained that children carry germs and could infect vulnerable elders.[4] The lack of shared sites is somewhat shocking given the over forty years of systematically planned intergenerational programs (Larkin & Newman, 1997), the documented growth of such programs (Kuehne & Collins, 1997), and the number of remarkable benefits described in the previous chapter.

In the absence of a pre-existing shared-site program in the target vicinity for a curriculum study, I approached Picasso Child and Picasso to see if they would be interested in having the research team pilot an intergenerational art class. Both sides agreed, eager to see what the

---

that service young and old. Anecdotally, I also noticed an interest in intergenerational learning programs when I published a paper on the topic in the National Association for the Education of Young Children journal, *Young Children* (Heydon & Daly, 2008). Almost every day for months after the paper was published, I received at least one email from educators across the United States asking for more ideas on intergenerational curriculum and testimonials from educators about the wonderful things they had seen since participating in intergenerational learning programs. Moreover, a study of intergenerational programming in Calgary, Alberta (Ayala, Hewson, Bray, Jones, & Hartley, 2007), showed that out of 107 organizations serving "youth" and "seniors" surveyed, one-third reported offering intergenerational programs and there was "significant interesting in and ideas for offering a diverse range of [intergenerational] program in the future" (pp. 45–6).

4 I discussed this misconception with Blessed Mother and Watersberg. In the case of Blessed Mother, Generations Together Learning Center director Jane explained that their facility is accredited by the National Association for the Education of Young children and was thoroughly reviewed to ensure the health and safety of all people. Additionally, there were rigorous processes for licensing on the elder care side of the program. While the regulatory bodies were different in the case of Watersberg, the directors in charge of elder care and child care explained comparable safeguards. All sites, including Picasso, exercised good hygiene standards and in the case of an outbreak in any area of the building, resorted to isolation-type practices. In these situations all visiting and programming was suspended until it was safe to resume it. Jarrott, Gigliotti, and Smock (2006) reported that there is a perceived fear among administrators of adult care sites of young children infecting elders. They recommended measures such as those undertaken at Blessed Mother and also immunizations for all participants.

class could offer to participants. Doctoral candidate Tara-Lynn Scheffel and I acted as the first leaders of the art class and then gradually handed control to the site's practitioners (early childhood educators and recreation staff). Three years after its inception, using the support materials we had developed (e.g., a book of project lesson plans, samples of projects to use as models, art supplies, modelling of teaching, and professional learning workshops), practitioners were organizing and teaching art classes, and the program had begun to lead to other activities for intergenerational relationship-building (e.g., singing). Significantly, these secondary activities would not have been possible outside of a shared site and without the structure of the primary intergenerational art program, and though I here refer to them as secondary to signal to how they were consequences of the art program, the opportunities they created for participants should not be thought of as minor. For instance, educators arranged for children to visit the adults in their rooms. In an interview about how this practice began, educator Sarah explained,

> It was the week after the art [class] ended, and we all ... the kids ... we all just [felt], Oh when is the art class! So I got the room numbers from Mathilde [the recreation therapist] that day, and I said we'd probably come up for a visit a few times, so that the kids don't lose face with them and the seniors don't lose face with them, and we did [the visits]!

Sarah's choice of expression "lose face" is an interesting one. Within the context of the conversation, it was suggestive of maintaining a connection or presence. While Sarah was not referring to Levinas's notion of face, there is something eloquent and fitting about the children and the elders responding to the existence of the other and the draw to be with and for each other.

Not to be missed is that it was the children who drove the response to the face of the elders. In detailing how the visits proceeded, Sarah drew attention to child participant, Anna, saying,

> It's really nice for the kids because like all of the kids come upstairs for the visit, there's like certain ones, like Anna ... we first went to visit Joyce ... and I was like this is the room so we have to go here and after this hall is the – and Anna was like, "We have to go visit Mona! We have to go visit Mona!" Because that was her friend throughout the whole art [class] – that's Mona! – she just needed to visit Mona. Like that was her thing.

When readers meet Mona in Chapter Five, they will see how her face in particular might call for such a connection. Yet all of the adults, as Sarah relayed, appeared to have a thirst quenched by the children's visits. In describing one morning of visiting Sarah said,

> Joyce [an adult participant] was really happy. She was taking a nap and said, "I'll get up! I'll get up!" and was just talking about all her art and all her kids and all the leaves, like you know how she [loves talking with the children]. And Keith was really happy, he was like just [beyond] belief that we went in and visited and he was like come back anytime, and he had tears in his eyes.

Further, although "ethics consists in not thinking [of] reciprocity" (Robbins, 2001, p. 49), no doubt the children's recognition of the faces of the elders in their visits was in turn met with opportunities for pleasure, learning, and relationship-building for them. In Sarah's description of the children's responses to the visits, one can see their exuberance and excitement. When I asked, "What did you notice about the kids when they went into a room?" Sarah answered,

> They were really excited and they were just looking around at [the adults'] stuff, like that's their home and they understood. The kids were like "What's this? And what is this?" They were like "Wow" ... Like at daycare it's just daycare so that's not their home, so like I think that it was just weird for them to see that that's actually where [the adults] lived.

Sarah described the children's response to the visits in positive terms (e.g., "excited") but she also characterized their experience of seeing the elders living in what is essentially an institution as "weird." This term may carry with it some pejorative connotations, but it could also feed into the ethics of the face and provide important learning opportunities for the children.

Anna, Roger, and the other children at Picasso responded to the call of the elders and in so doing came (literally) face-to-face with them. The differences between the children and elders are interesting. On the one hand, they are not so deep or meaningful as to constitute the basis for each person's alterity – they are indeed differences of properties, countenances, and/or dispositions in space (Robbins, 2001). Yet these differences may create an important pedagogical moment that has implications for the ethical relation while begging for Britzman's (1998) notion of *queer pedagogy* –where what is taken to be normal is questioned with implications for people's senses of identity. In the visits, the children encountered what was queer. Levinas (2001) teaches that the "singularity" of the individual, her uniqueness, what makes her *her* and says that even if she "resembles so and so" really, the other "resembles no one but himself [*sic*] and no other can take his place for us," "only appears in extreme and ultimate moments" (p. 127). I wonder if the moment of the queer, the *strangeness* of the other is not one of those times when, if the conditions are right, great opportunities might arise for the founding of an ethical relation and the opening of identities. While this may sound like heady or even dangerous stuff vis-à-vis young children, I must ask at what age a person is a learning subject and thus eligible, if you will, for queer pedagogy? At what age are issues of normalcy, identity, and ethical relations germane to a person? What are the consequences of opting children out?

In less philosophical terms, I might notice how the visiting of the rooms seemed to be an important part of establishing people's connections through the sharing of the adults' intimate spaces, their homes. Children seemed to begin these visits stiffly, formally, then gradually connected to the adults in personal, sometimes familial ways. In her description of the children's easing into the visits, Sarah explained,

> We walked into a few rooms and all the rooms like at first [the children] just would kind of stand around, and just kind of ask questions about the room and then they would be "Whatever!"– like ... Roger just went into Keith's room and sat down next to him on the sofa and was like looking at his teddy bear and it was normal for him, it was as if Keith was his grandpa or something.

In her gestures and intonation, Sarah communicated that eventually the children reached the point where the strangeness become a "whatever!" or no big deal, and the meeting of child participant Roger and adult Keith in Keith's room appeared to be a significant opportunity for them to connect in a personal, familial way. I wonder, however, to what extent the "whatever" and the "normal" are not so much repudiations of alterity or queerness but rather preconditions for the maintenance of the response to the face and in that way opportunities (e.g., as in the notion, I am not shocked by you; I recognize you as a person as I am a person)?

Children visiting elders' rooms was standard practice at Blessed Mother (as Generations Together Learning Center director Jane's interview later in the chapter shows) and such visits were also an important part of the routine at Watersberg. Given that the rooms in the homes were indeed people's private spaces, Watersberg had a clever way of facilitating interaction near the rooms that did not invade people's privacy. They established a routine where the children delivered daily newspapers to rooms. Thus, elders could invite children in or not, and the task of the delivery created an authentic reason for children and elders to be in the same space.

The Difficulty of Establishing Shared Sites

At Picasso, following the room visits, adults were observed dropping by the children's play area, and formal gatherings were held around holidays. Despite these gains, however, three years after the program had begun, the door that connected Picasso with Picasso Child still had a prominent sign posted on it saying "Private," and staff, faculty, and administration still saw the intergenerational component as an add-on. For example, the Picasso administration counted the purchasing of art supplies for the intergenerational art class as extraneous to the core budget for craft supplies for adults-only classes. Picasso Child administrators counted preparation time for intergenerational art class as outside the educator's regular preparation time and thus saw it as an additional expense, and despite two years of successful art shows, under their control, practitioners chose not to hold another one (citing the great amount of work involved as the rationale). These examples demonstrate how intergenerational activities were perceived to be outside the normal course of practice and had not become integrated, regularized parts of practice or policy. This case evidently lies on a different part of the intergenerational spectrum from more established programs like that at Blessed Mother and even the more fledgling program at Watersberg. In the following, I relay some of Watersberg and Blessed Mother's story, but note that all examples, including Picasso's, speak in similar ways to the need for time, leadership, a critical questioning of the social positioning of elder and child care and the people who work within them, and for curricular support in intergenerational programming.

An Example of a Fledgling Shared-Site Intergenerational Learning Program

I first started visiting Watersberg when it was less than five years old. Although its history was not much longer than Picasso's, it was a very different and more mature place. It was built at the outset to accommodate skipped generations, whereas Picasso was a site that we added intergenerational programming to after decades of it having only monogenerational programming. The genesis of intergenerational programming at Watersberg was the genesis of the child and elder care site – neither had existed before the other. This meant that there was an opportunity for even the building to be created from the ground up to be populated by skipped generations. Unlike at Blessed Mother, however, the children's and adult's spaces were still conceived of separately. Laura, the child care director, described the birth of Watersberg in the following way:

> The [child care organization] was approached by [the elder care organization] to take this opportunity and delve into intergenerational programming. [Our] initial meetings were on the structure of the building and how we wanted the child care to look and what kind of requirements we needed, and the [elder care] building was building at the same time so we were under a lot of construction at that point and it was just visits [between the child and elder care organizations], but it was a way to develop a relationship with the [organizations].

Although Watersberg certainly appeared to be one building with separate spaces for children and adults, it is noteworthy that Laura said "buildings" in the plural, as though the child and adult spaces were separate buildings. This, and the fact that the spaces were primarily designed to be monogenerational, suggests a lost opportunity. Still, some space (and the objects within it) conceived with the secondary intent of brining the generations together. When talking about the planning of the physical space of the child care area, I asked Laura if the intergenerational component was part of their considerations and she answered,

> Yeah, we needed to think about that, so there is a space in our book centre so that if a senior wants to come in, they can sit down in an adult-sized chair ... there are some of the more sensory activities that the kids do, some of the sensory toys, like the balls with the bumps on – that you can also use with the seniors and it's a tactile thing for the seniors so some of the equipment that we chose, we chose because of that. We have ... outside we have ... sponge balls and Velcro and then you throw it and hit the Velcro – that was purposely done so that we could take it upstairs [where the elders are]. It's portable enough, we can take it upstairs and do that with the seniors as well.

Even if spaces could have been conceived of in even greater inter-generational terms, there was a definite desire on the parts of both organizations to work intergenerationally. On the elder care side, inter-generational learning was a key component of their operating philoso-phy. Diane, an administrator with the corporate office which runs many homes, described the situation this way,

> The leadership team ... wanted [to] change ... the dynamics of the home[s] and really deinstitutionalize and decrease the stresses that the residents and families face when a loved one comes in to that kind of living environ-ment. Traditionally up until these kinds of philosophies, the homes were very institutional ... a number [of people from the elder care organization] went down to the states and learned about [an] alternative, gentle care and whole bunch of different philosophies and created our own vision and that basically was to create an environment that was more home-like and weaving together all of those things that you and I would experience in life. So, the pets, the plants, the antiques, the types of programming, the partnerships with [the child care organization] or other daycares to cre-ate a more living experience for our residents day-to-day ... the leadership team ... had looked at the dynamics and what would impact the residents' lives, and what was maybe missing in those day-to-day. And they came to the idea of having the children involved in more than just ... visiting. A lot of different places, of course, have the different groups that come to visit ... but we wanted [it] to be integrated into their lives. And so, that partner-ship began, in conversations with the [child care organization].

It is evident that the drive for the intergenerational component came originally from the elder care organization's desire to change the way elder care is traditionally done and to weave children into the fabric of adults' daily lives. From this impetus then came more planning and conversation.

The discussions within the elder care organization then had to be opened up to include the early childhood partners, to consider, as Diane said, the "expectations from both sides" and "the legalities" of running a shared site, which included consulting with different gov-ernment ministries. The conversations resulted in several intergenera-tional shared sites throughout southwestern Ontario[5] that were headed

---

5 At the time of the interview, Diane indicated that her elder care organization was looking at creating approximately 15–16 intergenerational shared sites.

by the elder care organization. The goal with these sites was to create, in Diane's words,

> daycare space on-site and the idea is to have programming both planned but also spontaneous ... and allowing residents who might have been teachers, or involved in children [in] some stages in their life to be able to go down [to the day care] if they wanted to and just read a story or, you know, in one particular site we did have children who actually came up into resident space and had their meals. And residents could join. So they're really integrated and residents had a choice of that level of involvement. So, some would get really involved and some could be just watching from a window while they play outside in their daycare space.

On the child care end of things there was not an organizational philosophy that drove the intergenerational initiative, but as is common in intergenerational share sites and programming more generally, there was a key administrator who was committed to intergenerational learning.[6]

In describing the child care Watersberg offered, child care director Laura explained, "We have 16 [children] in total at this point on any given day ... two staff and me at this site." There was also a school adjacent to Watersberg that had before and after school care run by the same child care organization. Laura explained,

> We also have a [child care organization] childcare over there ... we have 30 [junior kindergarten–senior kindergarten] children and we also support 45 after school children between the ages of 6 and 12, so, we're not just our 16 preschoolers, we're a little bigger than that.

The child care organization had set as a goal for these children to, as Laura put it, "come over at least once a month and do more of the special project[s] or the service learning things with the seniors." That said, the bulk of the children in the shared-site program were as Laura said, "two and a half to about four years of age."

I call Watersberg a fledgling shared-site program, because it was still developing a curricular component. There were some routines at the

---

6 Jarrott, Gigliotti, and Smock (2006) note the commonality of this situation saying that since intergenerational programs often "belong" to a committed staff person like Lisa, "the sustainability of the program is a challenge even at shared site facilities" (p. 76).

site that helped to facilitate intergenerational interaction (e.g., news-paper delivery), but as I mentioned in Chapter One, there seemed to be a dearth of meaningful or challenging programming. In my field research I observed child and adult participants being brought together for a series of disconnected activities that created limited opportunities for the development of communication or even relationship-building, as intergenerational interactions were not fundamental to participating in the activities. For instance, in response to my question, "Can you tell me about some of the different intergenerational activities you plan?" Maxine, a recreation staff member who often led intergenerational activities said,

> Last week we did a teddy bear social. So all the residents and children had a teddy bear. We talked about a teddy bear. We felt all the different teddy bears. Some had lights and some made sounds. (laughter). It was a little different ... and we've done baking, play day, dress up, glamour, teddy bear clinic ... walks ... trying to think ...

Maxine did not elaborate on why she laughed in what seemed like a nervous way and what she meant by "different," but several other people involved in the teddy bear socials and teddy bear clinics (where participants were to play "doctor" with the bears) commented on how the teddy bear activities were not ideal. Educator Alice commented that at first the bears offered a chance for children and adults to bring their "special toys" together. After this, however, another educator commented that the bear activities seemed to be happening because educators and recreation staff had "run out of ideas" and had resulted in people simply "sitting in a circle wondering what to do." Note that play day involved putting out buckets of children's toys on tables for children and adults to play with, and glamour, as mentioned earlier, was a hair and nail time.

Educators and recreation staff were all working hard to create an intergenerational learning program that could provide optimum opportunities for participants. Everyone on the front lines at Watersberg told me, however, that they felt they could do a better job of this. One issue impeding this better job was a lack of what many educators and staff called "training" but what I will call *professional learning opportunities*. Out of all the educators and members of recreation staff only Lisa had any specific, substantive, professed intergenerational knowledge. Lisa had through her own interest, participated in some intergenerational professional learning in the United States and had put together her own intergenerational curriculum with the hopes of having it adopted at the local college in the early childhood education and care courses. Apart from this, Cleo, a recreation supervisor, had the next most experience, which was minimal. She explained, "[I worked at another care facility] although it wasn't a set [intergenerational] program; we had done some intergenerational programming." Cleo also took a "personal interest," and thus had "done some reading and some self-education," and she received "some direction from our head office in terms of what they expected and sort of what had been taking place in other homes where they established these programs already." Included in this direction was a small binder of activities to which Cleo referred. Mostly, however, knowledge of intergenerational curriculum was developed and practised in an ad hoc manner – a learn on the job type of arrangement with little framing for educators and recreation staff. My conversation with Maxine underscores this.

RACHEL: What kind of training was there or introduction was there to intergenerational?
MAXINE: Ah…just these are the type of programs that we do … and then these are the way that they're ran [sic] (the intergenerational sessions) so that we're all doing them as a consistent basis.
RACHEL: So, is all of that material written down somewhere?
MAXINE: Not that I'm aware of.
RACHEL: So it's just another staff member told you about it?
MAXINE: Yeah.

Maxine was, as I mentioned, the person who was largely responsible for running the intergenerational sessions, and I observed her putting great time and effort into her job, yet she did not have any knowledge of there being even the slimmest of resources that might have helped her. When talking about what she would like to get out of my research, Lisa, from the perspective of an educator who wanted to improve practice but had limited resources said,

some best practices for the intergenerational program so are there specific things that we can do to make the program successful and it's just not a trial and error thing anymore. I would like some training and orientation for staff that are coming in that have no idea what this is about as opposed to "come follow me watch what I do."

In the absence of substantive professional learning or knowledge related to intergenerational programs, it seemed that in the early days of the shared site, educators and staff attempted to collaborate on the types of activities to offer, each drawing on their expertise relative to their own population (e.g., child or elder). Cleo described how this early planning proceeded;

We ... sat down with Laura from the daycare and with her experience kind of came up together how we were going to move forward.

RACHEL: And what did you decide through those discussions, like how did you want to see it happen?

CLEO: The structure of it so how often we would have the kids involved, times of day that worked, expectations for daycare and our staff in terms of interacting with the residents and the children, and whose responsibility it was for managing who and the groups ... We decided we were going to have [the children] come [to the elders] on a daily basis when we first opened. Mornings generally worked better for them [the child care centre] so we worked around that ... We also looked at staff. There were some concerns from the daycare staff in terms of their responsibilities of a resident was being inappropriate or for some reason something happened with them with a cognitive impairment, what their role there would be in terms of using the staff and their comfort level. And that was really dependent on the individual and most of the daycare staff really were very eager and involved and we didn't have any problems there. Our staff had some questions about if the children were getting out of hand, what their role there was and for the most part the daycare takes the lead on that ... Training, the daycare staff had asked if they could have some training on what to expect on working with the residents because most of them had never done anything like this before. So we decided that as a group we could probably meet that need by just by having Andre [a recreation person] and I go over, and we sat and talked to them about what to expect in terms the residents that will be here, what to expect in terms of the physical disabilities and cognitive disabilities that you might see, how to answer their questions so that they were more comfortable when they started and I think that made a big difference ... training for our staff, we did as part of our orientation when we opened as well so we did general expectations for what we would like to see in an intergenerational program, basic things that need to take place to make the program successful ... the environment set up for interaction versus having all of the residents on one side and the kids on the other, how to gage attention spans and things like that with the groups, appropriate programming so that [no one] bring[s] in a really complicated program idea. Something else we did with the daycare was determine what kinds of programs we wanted to offer and then divided them up so baking was something we wanted to do with them. And because we have the ability and the resources, we took that on so we bring that program where[as] a craft program that we wanted to do, the daycare would bring that program idea so that the staff didn't have to worry that it was going to be outside the level of ability of the kids.

I have quoted Cleo at length to give a sustained understanding of where the foci of the person in charge of recreation resided. There was so much to plan in the initial stages that in many ways the focus was on management (of participants especially), and the content of the programming beyond level of difficulty and its connection to what the literature says about creating optimal intergenerational programs was lost.

There was an evident loss of momentum now that the program had its legs. Cleo admitted,

The only thing that I would have to say I think we should have done and haven't is we did the initial training with all the staff that started ... When my staff start now, we do some training with them, their part of the orientation is to observe and participate in intergenerational programming with staff that have experience doing them, the expectation on all of those things are laid out but we haven't actually made a point of working with the daycare to go over and educate their new staff on the residents, and Laura has never asked us to because I don't know whether the need has arose [sic], but we've also never asked if they want that either. So that's probably a gap that since opening we haven't really filled.

I wondered too about the gap in Maxine's orientation, which through my observations seemed to be the result of communication difficulties caused by high attrition and people with limited experience and knowledge being responsible for orienting new hires. Changes to the participants and the educator's and staff's abilities to program effectively for them also seemed to be a factor that made intergenerational programming more difficult. Again, Cleo remarked on this point:

When we first opened, we had a greater number of higher functioning residents who were able to remember the kids' names, able to interact with them, and although we do still have a population that's like that, a lot of our residents that are more cognitively impaired are physically declining. We have a greater number of them in the later stages of their diseases and so they're not as interactive ... I think that the staff struggled to find ways to make that interaction happen.

Unfortunately the staff struggled, but without comprehensive professional learning that included at look at the intergenerational literature which documents approaches to this problem, this work was rendered even more difficult. Key to solving many of these problems would be for a person to be on staff who works exclusively in the area of intergenerational programming.[7] Perhaps one of the reasons Susan's intergenerational art class at Blessed Mother worked so well was that she was responsible for the intergenerational programming there and her responsibility and concern was for both generations from the outset.

An Example of a Mature Shared-Site Intergenerational Learning Program

Prior to the 1990s, Blessed Mother was a nursing home with a hospital-like setting. Thereafter, it dispensed with its medical-model approach by, for example, retooling wards to become "neighbourhoods," adopting a resident-directed format (i.e., one in which residents make decisions about their daily living and care), and encouraging intergenerational relationship-building and learning by establishing the Generations Together Learning Center, the child care program that invited intergenerational interaction in all aspects of its structure (both architecture and programming). At the time of the research, more than 400 adults between the ages of 29 and 103 (with an average age of 89) called Blessed Mother home, and the Generations Together Learning Center provided care to 125 children aged 6 weeks to 5 years. Blessed Mother has been long recognized as one of the first shared sites, and continues to lead in innovative child care and elder care .When investigating the context of the intergenerational art class at Blessed Mother, I conducted a number of interviews with Center administrator, Jane. Jane told the following story of the genesis of Blessed Mother's intergenerational program.

---

7 The literature notes that the "ideal" situation with regards to staffing would be to have one person appointed as an intergenerational "program coordinator" (Kaplan et al., 2003, p. 6) who is responsible for both generations.

This building had a new administrator, and he came here from a program in [another state]. And at the program in [that state], they were trying to do more home care environment in an institution. The old model, and the model you still see [in many institutions] is really kind of a hospital model. You come in, we take care of you. We tell you where to go. When I first came here to work, that's what it was like, but its days were already numbered then, because he was here and they were going to make some major changes in how it functioned. So, a part of that is to bring us into the program so that kids could be part of that whole picture of resident-directed care. So residents had the opportunity to say, "I really want to see the babies," or "I don't want to see kids at all." (Laugh) And then that can be respected both ways.

As Jane relayed, there had been child care at Blessed Mother prior to the paradigm change, but this care was separate from the adults and the purpose was really, as she said, "to have an employee benefit for child care." The push for the intergenerational component, like at Waters-berg, came from the adult end of things, "to have all ages represented in the building," Jane said,

so that residents, when they come here to live, aren't totally cut off from the community. They still have the opportunity to see teenagers in different ways and also babies and young children different ways. And of course from the other side, it also gives children the opportunity to be around older people and they may or may not have that opportunity in their lives.

Jane then described how cultural and linguistic diversity were also large parts of the program given the demographics of the people they served, and how this was, as she put it, another "opportunity" provided by the program.

Next, in response to my question about the structure of the program, Jane stated:

We have six rooms. We have one infant room, three toddler rooms, and two preschool rooms, and in each room all the staff are formally connected to other parts of this building. And this, a large building with five floors and a number of number of residents: There's 450 residents or something altogether. The teachers are connected to a particular community, or as we call them neighbourhoods ... other people might know them as units, but it's a living group. It's a group of twenty to twenty-three people who essentially live together in a particular living neighbourhood or community, and a teacher is connected to that community. So, throughout any given week, the teacher takes her group of children and visits with the residents in that community. So that's kind of the quick piece; however, residents also come and visit us, although we're the more mobile part of the program, so we do much more visiting than residents do. Starting with the babies and the youngest toddlers the residents are really just kind of friendly neighbourhood visits. Just as though you were walking down the street and you stopped to chit chat with your neighbour. And it's kind of taken from that point of view. And the teacher is a very primary person in this because she's the one that sort of stays the same. So she has to get to know who some of the residents are, who are very interested in seeing babies or young toddlers as well as, of course, she knows her children very well. As they get a little bit older, the activities can become a little bit more structured, so that a little bit older toddlers might do singing with the group of residents, or they might make something that they can just make and eat – a kind of no bake kind of item that they'll put together, and they can sit around and eat it together, or drink it together – whatever it is. They do exercises where everybody's sitting in a chair. Of course the residents are mostly sitting in wheelchairs, but the kids will bring their own child-sized chairs and sit in those, and then they'll do exercises together. It's range of motion for the resident and exercises for the kids, except the kids don't have to stay in the chairs. They're up and down. They do some kind of systematic things where when you first get together with the group you shake hands and when you leave at the end you wave good-bye and you shake hands if the children feel like it. But they'll begin to learn how say, "Hello, my name is ..." and shake hands with somebody. (Laugh) It's their little ritual that they go through. And then as they get older into the preschool years, they do more complex group times together, some of the classes, one or two classrooms, they will invite residents to come in for special reasons. And it might be to read a story, or to share something about what a holiday was like for them as kids. ... And then there's some extra special programs. We have Susan's Art Studio, and Art Studio in the morning is an intergenerational arts studio with about six residents, six kids, and our two preschool rooms rotate through that studio experience throughout the year, and one room goes on Tuesdays and the other one on Thursdays. Then we had in the fall intergenerational glee club, and it was all signed up on by people who really wanted to be a part of it, so the kids were the kids who just really wanted to be singing, and the residents were residents who really wanted to be singing, and then someplace along the line they co-opted four high school students who come into this building part of the time, too. So it's a very intergenerational group and they sang a few songs they knew, and they all have to learn some new songs, and then they put on a performance, which was very fun and enjoyable, and we may pick that up again in the spring, or maybe not again until next fall.

As Jane's lengthy description shows, Blessed Mother offered many different intergenerational opportunities that themselves offered greater or lesser degrees of structure. The opportunities were scaffolded, in that more formal programming happened when children were older and had already had a variety of informal interactions with the adults.

Recreation therapist Jana also explained in an interview how the adults were able to respond in different ways to this variety in programming. After describing a similar set of programs to those listed by Jane, Jana stated,

> The babies come up in a baby carriage. It attracts a different group than the intergenerational art group. So, almost all of the residents benefit in some way from the intergenerational programming – whether it's holding a baby or actually doing the art work ... It's just awesome the benefits. I remember one lady who can't really hear very well and who can't see very well. And she's really old and just doesn't know who she is anymore, but you put a baby in her lap and she just comes alive. She says, "Oh, I'll take care of you. Your parents are too busy." It's like more words than I've ever heard her say. And she couldn't even see the baby, but she could feel it. That's just one example, but we had the other guy just today ... the 4 year olds' classroom was up here, and he was a man who doesn't speak out. He can't really speak much anymore, just really short words. But these two little boys on each side of him just loved him, and he was kind of smiling all through the whole class, and they did this little finger game together the little boys and the man whose in his late 70s, and he's had a stroke. So he's lost a lot of his capabilities. And they just played, and [the adult participant] smiled the whole time and they had this great interaction, and then when the boys left they waved and he waved which is all just a lot of stuff for him to do 'cause he usually doesn't communicate or engage in activities much at all.

The observational data also contain many examples of the various ways in which the specific structure or type of the program created different kinds of opportunities for interaction and relationship-building. Again, with the unique programming for people from birth through old age, one might think of a scaffolding of intergenerational opportunities where people are providing with a gradual release of support in their programming.

Further, in relation to this notion of scaffolding, volunteer Marianne also made an interesting observation regarding the strengths of ensuring a diversity of programming and interaction which came from the shared-site structure. She offered,

> Sometimes [in art class] I don't see much interaction, but I think this year in particular we're getting ... maybe it's the teachers ... I'm not sure, but I'm seeing more of the kids have met the residents on their floors, on the resident's floors. They go up there for making cookies or for visiting, and the teacher of the children reminds them, "Oh yes, we know this person from that floor. We remember this person; we used to visit that person." And so we're getting more of that interaction, so it kind of tells me that you can't just interact in the art class. It's nice if they can interact throughout the building throughout the week.

Marianne's comment also suggests how the shared site itself was a form of scaffolding, allowing little bits of informal intergenerational interaction that were strongly supported by educators and gradually asking more of participants.

Next, relative to this notion of scaffolding, I asked Jane how the intergenerational element was or was not included in the children's curriculum even when they were in the Generations Together Learning Center without the elders. I posed, "When the children are here and they're working with the teacher, how does the curriculum bridge the different parts of their day in the program and the people that they meet every day?" Jane responded,

> a lot of different ways ... for example, we have wheelchairs that can be in the kids rooms, particularly the preschool children's rooms where they can play with them and ride in them, and figure out how the brakes work and take the footrest on and off and do all those kinds of things ... we make sure that our books are multi-generational books and that there's lots of stories about grandparents, or older people. The dolls and the little people that kids play with always have a range of [ages] ... grandparents are included in those little family sets nowadays. They didn't use to be ... as

well as little wheelchairs that dolls can fit in or glasses to play with ... then the teachers also do some discussion around "What is it like to be older? What does that feel like? What do you think it's like?" and if there's any incident that comes up, there's a time when that gets discussed as well ... if somebody yells at somebody or says something you wish they wouldn't have said in front of the kids, we'll talk about ... to mention what dementia means.

Jane then explicitly linked the intergenerational aspect of the children's program to a social notion of communication and the learning opportunities the Generations Together Learning Center was trying to create by stating,

I think is interesting as part and parcel of our program is [something] we call problem solving, but it's a really language rich program. Part of it is teachers helping kids learn how to solve problems and ... that might be a social relationship or how to talk to another person and that other person could be a kid or it could a resident ... [Sometimes] a child needs to hear what the words are first. The teacher. Say[s], "this is a way to say to such and such, I want that," or "I don't want you to do that," or "can I please have that?" And it's them using language which only gets richer and richer. So those things I think are all overlapping.

I offer this here less to talk about curriculum (which is the topic of the next chapter) and more to show how the mature site tried to have an integration of generations and subject matter related to intergenerational learning throughout its day.

Even in a site as mature as Blessed Mother, there were nonetheless perennial challenges that had to be addressed, and these challenges seem similar to those experienced at Picasso and Watersberg. Next, within the context of a discussion of institutional and related programmatic structures that can be supportive to intergenerational participants and educators, I highlight the challenges that were most salient in the data and link them across sites where applicable.

Structures for Supporting Intergenerational Participants

The studies add to the literature related to the need for intergenerational programs to be structured so that participants can make decisions about their participation (e.g., whether or not to participate and in what ways). More broadly, however, the studies teach that generational diversity brings with it a diversity of needs and respecting participants' personhoods demands flexible, responsive program structures and the necessary institutional supports so that people can participate as they desire. For instance, some older adults at Blessed Mother and at Picasso expressed that they needed to know they could leave art class with no notice to tend to toileting, and the like. To maintain dignity they did not want to have to explain or be excused. As well, at Blessed Mother, I observed that children remained engaged in class with a particular project for differing amounts of time. Although I never observed a child wanting to leave an art class before the one hour mark (the typical length of a class), I found occasions where children did not feel finished by the end of class and wanted to stay to complete their own project or assist an adult with theirs. Art class at Blessed Mother was able to accommodate most of these needs: Susan, the art teacher, stayed with the children and adults who wanted to remain in class, children returned with an educator or volunteer to the Generations Together Learning Center, and volunteers helped any adult who wanted to leave early. Further, the art classes that were held in the neighbourhoods also addressed the adults' needs, most notably those related to mobility.

Blessed Mother's flexibility was largely dependent on volunteers, as there was not enough staff to provide the demanded level of support. For example, Doris, a regular art class adult participant who had mobility issues, was absent from class one day, and I found her crying in her neighbourhood. She told me she was crying because she could not find anyone to take her to class. Usually volunteers helped in situations like this but on this day Doris had missed the volunteer, and although there were support staff (e.g., certified nursing assistants) who theoretically could be recruited for the task, my interviews indicated they generally prioritized more standard care-giving tasks (e.g., changing a soiled bed) above tasks such as helping someone to a class. When I asked Generations Together Learning Center director Jane about this, she offered,

> The issue of ... people being available to help adults get places ... is just ongoing ... part of I think what happens here is that there's a lot that happens here, in this building overall there's a lot of choices and activities for people and only so many folks to help make those happen so some things get prioritized. Like Mass is really important, so there's a big push to have volunteers who will take people to Mass, not necessarily are there that many volunteers to take people to like the Arts Studio or to gather

people together, so the volunteer piece is kind of one piece. Another piece
is the jobs of the [certified nursing assistants] we talk about their job being
to help bring people to a group ... but there's a little bit of a view that it's
really the job of the rec therapist. Now the rec therapist ... [who] works a
40-hour week doesn't necessarily work all 40 hours Monday through Friday between, 8:00 and 4:30 when we're doing our [main intergenerational
programs] or available to do [these programs], so a rec therapist might
work a rotating schedule and they work two weekends a month which
takes them out of the loop for working with the teacher staff.

Jane here pointed to a number of issues having to do with what parts
of the institution and perhaps the volunteers themselves perceived as
most important (e.g., attending Mass within a Catholic institution), the
role of the nursing assistants, and the availability and scheduling of the
recreational therapists.

The data suggest that the institutional definition of the roles and du-
ties of workers needed to be addressed before programs could have
optimum flexibility and intergenerational programming needed to be
seen as a crucial part of people's well-being. With a dearth of staff, it
is obvious that changing a soiled bed is a pressing task that needed to
be completed and could not wait. One must ask, however, what is lost
when the emotional, intellectual, and communicative aspects of people's lives cannot be prioritized in the same way. Relative to the recreational therapists picking up the responsibility, the scheduling issues
Jane mentioned were a huge impediment, as was the surprising mar-
ginalization of the intergenerational component of the programming.
For instance, Aysha, a recreational therapist at Blessed Mother, told me
in an interview that the biggest challenge to the intergenerational art
class was physically assisting people to get to class. She cited that lack
of staff available to do this as a problem, but she also referenced how
the intergenerational art class was an "add-on" to her regular monogenerational programming and thus "added" to her workload rather than
being a regular part or sharing of her workload. She said, for instance,
"On Thursdays, for example, I have three other programs going on
and would have this going on with or without the [intergenerational]
art program." Thus, getting people to four different programs would
understandably be very difficult. Aysha offered that she "appreciates
when program is brought to me and I don't have to do anything for
it, because otherwise it is extra work and too hard to coordinate." She
used when intergenerational art class was held in the neighbourhood

as an example of a program being brought to her. Despite the challenges with flexibility at Blessed Mother, Picasso and Watersberg had nowhere near the level of flexibility as they did. The child to educator ratios in U.S. and Canadian sites were both strict, but in the Canadian sites there was no flexible staff and few volunteers, and Blessed Mother employed Susan as an intergenerational educator, whereas there was no intergenerational staff in the Canadian sites. This prevented many people from making decisions to participate.

Also important in Aysha's comments above was the notion of co-ordination. The data indicate that coordination of the programs was a challenge for all three sites. And this issue, especially as it pertains to communication between all partners (e.g., educators and recreation staff) is key in the literature (e.g., Linkages Society of Alberta, 2008; McDuffe & Testani, 1989). Obviously when educators and staff are supported to do their jobs, the children and elders in their care benefit. The following highlights some key findings from the research related to the structures for educators and staff that may benefit participants in inter-generational programs.

Structures for Supporting Educators

Structures to Enable Intergenerational Curriculum Planning

Intergenerational curricula require intergenerational planning. As mentioned, the intergenerational literature indicates there are benefits to having a staff or faculty member whose responsibilities squarely straddle both generations. At Blessed Mother, Susan the art teacher planned all the intergenerational art classes, and because she was hired to work with both generations, she was required to have knowledge regarding both generations, how to facilitate intergenerational inter-action, relationship-building, and the like, and her curricular planning and pedagogy had to serve both generations. Thus, they could not exclude or lean towards the interests or needs of one generation or the other. Even with an intergenerational educator, however, there could have been increased communication and cooperation between the intergenerational educator and the people responsible for children and elders. For instance, in reference to my asking if there were cur-ricular connections between intergenerational art class and the normal course of the early childhood education and care program, educator Gary suggested,

Just this last Thursday ... a child asked me – and I think it's been asked before but it really stuck out to me yesterday ... "What are we going to do? [in intergenerational art class]" ... That's a good question. I didn't know. I didn't know until we get there. Susan knows ahead of time. And at times she wants to know what I'm doing in the weeks ahead so she can tie in the curriculum. And I was thinking about that a lot as far as I've got to talk to her before the [intergenerational art classes] start again this fall ... [Susan and I] can talk more with each other about what's your ideas, what I am doing in the curriculum. Maybe I can know before I go to class what you are doing and I can get kids excited during the week saying, "Oh, man, we are going to do this on Thursday, it's going to be fun."

This kind of coordination could likely also increase learning opportunities as it would allow all aspects of the program to build on each other. The structures necessary to make this happen, however, were even less pressing than those needed for the coordination of the basic aspects of the program.

In other parts of the program where the structure did not include a designated intergenerational person such as in the art class, there seemed to be some lopsided planning (i.e., where planning was done predominantly or even exclusively by a person or persons primarily responsible for and who had expertise related to one generation rather than both). When interviewing recreation therapist, Jana, she explained the planning in this way,

JANA: I share the planning with the other preschool groups, so she [an educator] plans one time, I plan the next.

RACHEL: So instead of meeting, you take responsibility at different times?

JANA: Yeah, because we don't have a lot of time for planning, it's hard to find time to meet together and do the planning. So we just divide it up. I'll do one week and she does the other.

RACHEL: [Someone else mentioned] how hard it is to plan with the teacher and having planning time, and that if it was a perfect world that relationship would maybe be different.

JANA: Yeah, I agree. I mentioned that earlier. We just don't have the time. And they are very busy, the preschool teachers here. So coordinating our planning time is very difficult, partly because I'm not around that much and partly theirs might be a different time than mine. So I agree with that, and that is why I think we've divided it up, you know, where we take turns doing the planning.

Jana then went on to describe how new recreation therapists in particular were "lost" with the planning for the reasons that she indicated in an excerpt from an interview that I include below related to the need for professional learning.

At Watersberg, the situation of lopsided planning was perhaps even more problematic. It seemed that recreation staff alone was making the curricular decisions related to what activities would be offered. Educator Audrey explained just what I had observed relative to how the planning was done. She stated,

> When I first started [working in the child care centre] [the recreation staff] gave us [educators in the child care centre] calendars and it had various programs listed … like say on the 16th we're doing sing-a-long with the day care … and another day it would be story time with the daycare … and then the only things we had to plan on it was craft. Like if it said craft with the daycare, we usually planned the craft … that was when I started. Now it seems like they've taken over the planning of the crafts as well.

In interviews with Cleo, the recreation supervisor, she did not fully corroborate Audrey's statement. She felt that Audrey and other educators could make suggestions to the calendar, and to do so, all they had to do was approach a recreation person. Audrey felt she was open to educators' suggestions saying, "[educators] have come up with some interesting ideas that we might not have thought of." She did, however, offer that the suggestions did not necessarily make it on to the calendar: "but also too I find that if it's a staff member that's not as comfortable with the daycare programming, they tend to choose those programs that are easier per say to run versus the ones that are more effective." The need for both sides to come together to plan and the opportunity for both sides to feel like equal members of the planning beg for the need for structures to facilitate communication.

Cleo noted the communication issue and pointed to how it might be rearing its head because of new faculty and staff. She said,

> I think we're probably at a stage now where having a regular meeting would be a good idea. Probably it would be Audrey and I and the daycare teachers to determine sort of what's going on and how things are working in terms of planning. We did initially when we first started [the program] … now the time has passed and we've had new teachers and things like that come on … that way in terms of planning and feedback we would have a more formal way to do that.

Cleo went on to describe what she hoped would be the content in those meetings, and I include some of this transcript in the next section related to professional learning. Of note is that Cleo saw the need to hold meetings as coming from the educators' lack of knowledge about the adult participants. When I asked her specifically about the possible need to meet for planning she spoke little and while she agreed to the need, did not elaborate. I wondered if Cleo, who was not an educator, did not fully appreciate the benefit that could be derived from cooperative planning and planning in detail rather than simply coming up with a topic for an activity (e.g., "glamour" or "ice cream social").

Planning and communication take time. At Picasso, we tried to use the knowledge gleaned at Blessed Mother and Watersberg to set up structures to facilitate co-planning. As such, we secured funding for the child care centre so that educators working in the intergenerational art class could be released for planning. We did not seek outside funding to do the same on the elder care end, as Picasso was a for-profit centre, and we therefore felt that if its administration found the intergenerational component to be of value, they needed to build infrastructure to support it. The research team also tried to help facilitate common meeting times between educators and recreation staff. Yet even though we instructed the intergenerational art class for one year of programming and acted as consultants and instructors for strategic chunks of the class thereafter (as described earlier), the data indicate that the twin need to time was professional learning: how do people know what to do with their planning time without the requisite knowledge?[8]

Structures to Enable Intergenerational Professional Learning

The literature suggests the need for what it calls "cross-training" of faculty and staff (i.e., where each side of the intergenerational equation receives training related to the population with whom it does not generally work; Jarrott, 2007). To reflect the complexities of education and care and towards professionalizing the people who do this work, I prefer to think not in terms of training, but rather professional learning. The former suggests a techno-rational, one-size-fits-all approach which does not consider the prior knowledge or experience of the person being

---

8 The question of what this requisite knowledge might be outside the scope of a focus on structures.

trained, while the latter suggests learning opportunities for profession-
als that acknowledge where they are beginning and hope to engender
within them a deliberation on the literature in relation to one's circumstances to discern how best to proceed (e.g., Heydon & Hibbert, 2010).
However, at Blessed Mother and Watersberg, many educators and staff
might have been content with even just training because there was such
a great gap in knowledge.

In my studies, educators and recreation therapists in all sites complained about the lack of intergenerational learning opportunities and/
or gaps in knowledge. This complaint was somewhat surprising to me
at a place as mature as Blessed Mother. Recreation therapist Jana from
Blessed Mother saw her recreation colleagues as having gaps that im-
peded optimal intergenerational curriculum planning and implementation. She explained, "A lot of our rec. therapists might be brand new
out of school, and/or not out of school just transferred in from another
department and don't have any idea what to do." The content of the interviews with recreation therapist Audrey agree with this. Jana wished
for "overall training" in the area for everyone where people "within
our facility" "sat down and just brainstormed and talked" about intergenerational programs.

From the Generations Together Learning Center, the concerns were
similar. Educator Monique said,

> There really hasn't been a lot of training. I mean we were kind of thrown in
> that whole [intergenerational] thing. You were thrown in to see if you sink
> or swim … when I first started here, it was a big change for me because I
> had never worked with the residents or older people, other than my own
> family. And that's a totally different [situation] than coming in with all
> these strangers that I had no idea who they were … so it's just been kind
> of a whole learning process of, you know, watching what the residents are
> doing and also picking up on some of their cues.

When I asked Monique if she and her colleagues were offered in-service professional learning opportunities she responded, "No, we don't
have any in-service days," and then she corrected herself by explaining
that although there were "Professional Development Days" they were
not used for learning but rather they were predominantly devoted to
cleaning the classroom, with some presentations made to them which
were not generally to do with intergenerational learning. Monique
elaborated by saying,

Every once in a while we might have one workshop that has to do with some intergenerational aspects, but pretty much if you want any training we have to go out and search it out ourselves. And there really isn't a whole lot of workshops out there having to do with intergenerational. And usually if they are, they're people having to do with Blessed Mother going out and doing workshops.

While the intergenerational literature is wide and growing and professional learning opportunities do exist (e.g., through the University of Pittsburgh and the Macklin Intergenerational Institute out of Ohio), it did not translate to the sites in the studies and practitioners were at a loss.

One important comment that does need to be made regarding the content of professional learning is that learning opportunities for people who plan and implement intergenerational curricula must relate to all aspects of the curricular commonplaces. Thus, professional learning must include subject matter considerations. As evidenced in the next two chapters, curricula focusing on art or visual texts have great potential to expand communication and identity options within an intergenerational curricular setting. The curriculum at Blessed Mother was amazingly rich as Susan was a practicing artist with a master's degree in sculpture who was continually seeking new learning opportunities related to media, techniques, artists and their work, and the like, and this knowledge and skill were combined with her knowledge of art teaching, particularly in an intergenerational setting. The program thus benefited from what Schulman (1987) called Pedagogical Content Knowledge (PCK), where content and pedagogical knowledge intersect allowing the educator to know how to help learners access the content. Every educator and recreation therapist, and a number of adult participants commented on the benefit of having an art teacher in the program. Jana, for instance, pointed to how the structure of Blessed Mother, by employing such a teacher, allowed these opportunities to be. She remarked about Blessed Mother, "We're just lucky that we have an artist that can come, and we have a budget that can afford her." In the field of early childhood education and care, PCK related to art is recognized as significant and is why, for instance, the centres in Reggio Emilia have as central to their staff an atelierista (art specialist; e.g., Gandini, Hill, Cadwell, & Schwall, 2005).

Unfortunately, not all intergenerational learning programs sufficiently value the arts or in a position to employ an art teacher. Given the possibilities created by expanding people's communication, specifically in this case the making of visual texts, I felt that even sites that did not have an artist could perhaps receive sufficient support (including professional learning) such that they could have this as a component of their curriculum. As such, in consultation with the site, I selected the creation of visual texts as the centrepiece of the intergenerational program at Picasso. One of the major goals of the Picasso project was to create a guidebook of projects that could be implemented if an arts or literacy specialist was not available.

At Picasso, the research team attempted to address the lessons taught by Blessed Mother and Watersberg by

- trying to understand educators and recreation staff's knowledge and experience with intergenerational learning. Bringing Susan in to model a class, conduct a workshop, and be available for questions;
- having the research team lead all aspects of the intergenerational art class until faculty and staff indicated they felt comfortable enough to take over;
- gradually moving the research team into a consultant's role;
- providing a research assistant from my team in the classes thereafter to provide support and be available to offer any other desired supports such as *refresher* times when the research team would teach for weeks at a time to provide a model for educators and recreation staff.

The data indicate that the transition time for handing over the class to the site was much longer than we had anticipated, with the site requiring a full year of programming to be taught by us. Even then the site asked for us to do more of the teaching and for a second visit from Susan. The data suggest one of the key barriers to our professional learning plan operating was attrition of faculty and staff.

The high attrition rate I observed for all practitioners in all sites is important. At Picasso, the recreation person who was assigned to art class, changed three times within one year. With the exception of the Generations Together Learning Center educators, practitioners in all sites mentioned low pay, difficulty of obtaining full-time employment, lack of benefits, undesirable hours, and the desire to upgrade; the reasons they say they left their jobs are all commensurate with the literature as it pertains to early childhood education and care workers (e.g., Doherty, Friendly, & Beach, 2003). Therefore, on-the-job intergenerational professional learning was difficult, and each new year for intergenerational classes was like starting all over again in terms of practitioner knowledge and skill. Although we brought Susan in to help model for practitioners, within months of the visit, a new person would be in place; thus, the learning opportunity was missed. This returns the focus to the earlier discussion of the social positioning of intergenerational participants and raises questions about how people who work with the young and old are valued. Evidently, these issues, which are structural, affect learning and relationship-building opportunities.

Conclusion

The focus of *Learning at the Ends of Life* is intergenerational curriculum. As this chapter attempts to demonstrate, however, curricular conversations cannot be independent of the considerations of milieu. Thus, to ground the conversations to come in the chapters concerning what was taught, how it was taught, and with what implications, I have here related the building of three different intergenerational shared-site programs, ranging from immature to mature, their challenges and the supports that the cases taught may be needed to be in place to enable children, elders, recreation therapists, and educators to participate fully in curriculum that can create optimum learning opportunities and communication and identity options. The findings corroborate the literature related to intergenerational curriculum and program and include the need for:

- informal and more formal opportunities for being together
- opportunities for participants to respond to each other's faces, understand each person's personhood, and respect each other's alterity
- the normalization of intergenerational programming so that it becomes a regular part of the site in all senses (including budgeting) and so that it does not become an add-on or extra burden for institutions or the people who work in them
- structures to facilitate conversation, planning, and mutual responsibility for intergenerational programming between people who have expertise dealing with particular populations
- wherever possible the creation of true intergenerational spaces that consider at the outset the different populations who will be inhabiting them

- ongoing professional learning opportunities for all educators and staff, which include all elements of the curricular commonplaces and where allowable, subject matter specialists (e.g., art educators)
- the scaffolding of participants' interaction and relationship-building with each other through, for example, multiple and varied types of programming
- curricular connections to enhance or facilitate intergenerational programs even when children and elders are not together (e.g., the use of children's toys in the children's program such as dolls that represent different generations; helping participants to learn how to use language that can, for instance, facilitate relationship-building)
- flexibility in staffing to allow, insofar as possible, children and elders to participate in intergenerational programming on their own terms
- making intergenerational participation a priority
- the coordination of programming through, for example, a person who is responsible for intergenerational programming
- measures to address educator and staff attrition

At first glance the list above may seem quite instrumental and dry. If looked at another way, however, it can be seen to carry the traces of lives lived in isolation and segregation as well as the possibility for something different. The list is a link between people – children and elders, educators and recreation therapists – and institutions. It is what can help create opportunities for people who may be at vulnerable places in their lives to be connected, well, fulfilled, and happy. It is the list that was nowhere for my grandparents and that I hope will be everywhere one day. It is also the list that can hold the more micro aspects of intergenerational programming – curricular questions like what to teach and how to teach (Egan, 1978) which additionally concern the subject matter of the curricular commonplaces and pedagogy. It is to these concerns that I turn in the next chapters.

Chapter Four

Literacy Learning Opportunities in Intergenerational Curricula

The literature indicates the need for a curricular component in intergenerational programs (Friedman, 1997), which is likely a recommendation for the inclusion of subject matter learning opportunities. This chapter provides a rationale for a curriculum centred on the creation and viewing of visual texts; it attempts to demonstrate the myriad learning opportunities related to literacy within the intergenerational art programs at Blessed Mother and Picasso. Through the lens of the theoretical framework identified in Chapter One I will show how particular forms of art curricula offered numerous opportunities for the expansion of people's communication and identity options. Before getting to the specifics of the findings of the studies, I first pause in the next section to explain the subject matter I am advocating and clarify my understandings of art education and visual texts.

Art Education and Visual Texts

The studies at Blessed Mother and Picasso involved what was termed *art class*, with the viewing and making of visual texts through a variety of media being the primary concern. That said, Blessed Mother's program was concerned with art as a subject; as mentioned, this was less the focus at Picasso. One of the key reasons I attempted to open up art class to look beyond art as a subject was in the hope of making it more accessible to educators, recreation staff, and, by extension, participants. Art education definitely has a place in intergenerational learning programs. Intergenerational art researcher Angela La Porte (2004a) has documented the history of intergenerational art programs in the United States and reports that one of the first recorded programs was developed in the 1970s and "involved using studio instruction in arts and crafts" (p. 6) in a 5-month program at the Hebrew Home for the Aged in New York City. The program paired "troubled adolescents" (p. 6) with the residents of the home with the effect of improving the adults' self-esteem. La Porte argues that intergenerational art programs today are "well established and growing across the United States" (p. 6) and her edited collection of papers describing various intergenerational art initiatives across the country demonstrates this (La Porte, 2004b).

The educators, volunteers, and recreation staff at Blessed Mother all commented that art class was special because it was "real art,"[1] which they distinguished from other visual practices that went on in other parts of the programming at Blessed Mother like "crafts"[2] and participants being given opportunities to work with crayons and paint but without any substantive instructional framing.[3] Given that many educators in particular feel "inadequately prepared in art," in general, even outside of intergenerational programs, art education is often marginalized at best. Children in schools, for example, tend to receive an art curriculum that is "often reduced to 'formulaic, craft-like activities' ... iconic images, and symbols that accompany holidays and are created to decorate classrooms and hallways" (Cowan & Albers, 2006, p. 125). Thankfully, at Blessed Mother, opportunities for the creation and contemplation of visual texts within an art frame were possible, but relegated specifically to the art class.

In a bid to make the visual accessible more broadly, my concern in the studies and this book is not for art education per se. Rather, I would like to see all educators, in intergenerational settings or otherwise, take up the opportunities that education in a variety of semiotic modes and media can offer to learners of all ages. Art educators like Susan are in a prime position to help people with their visual communication, but all educators who are interested in teaching literacy must take seriously their responsibility to teach *literacies* which include the visual.

Visual Texts

In Chapter One I announced that I would be referring to what might be thought of as participants' *artwork* as *visual texts* instead. I borrow

---

1 Statement from volunteer Marianne, recreation therapist Jana, and early childhood educator Monique.
2 Statement from Marianne and Jana.
3 This distinction was made by educator Monique.

the term visual text from Peggy Albers (2007) who writes about art as literacy. I do so to signal the theoretical frame of the studies (e.g., multimodal social semiotic theory) and to indicate that I am interested in the texts not as they might refer to the specific knowledge domain or discipline of art but as *semiotic texts*. A semiotic text, "contains a number of signs that when created or read collectively are known as a semiotic system ... Each element (individual images, words, color ... so on) with [a] text is a sign that has meaning for both the signmaker and the reader of the text, through these meanings will necessarily be different because of the signmaker's or readers' experiences and backgrounds" (Cowan & Albers, 2006, p. 125). Cowan and Albers make note of some important points relative to semiotic texts that hearken back to the discussion of the literacy-related theoretical framework of Chapter One. These are:

- a semiotic text is "recognizable to the larger community" when a signmaker chooses "signs that have common cultural meanings" (p. 125);
- "signs are not constructed independently but are ideological and carry the beliefs" of the signmaker's "community and culture" (p. 126);
- "semiotic texts are always generative" in that when they are read, this act has "the potential to extend the initial meaning of the signmaker" (p. 126).

Having access to a variety of sign systems and opportunities to use and develop these systems is what helps to expand people's communication options. Indeed signs of all kinds "help" people to "create meaning" because there is no "direct access to" the "world" except through signs (Albers, 2001, p. 3). Sign systems, like visual art and language, "allow humans to communicate, interpret, and represent meaning" (Cowan & Albers, 2006, p. 125). Consistent with the discussion in Chapter One of what constitutes literacy, researchers working in multimodal literacy and other theoretical approaches to literacy that involve expansive definitions see that it "involves experience with a variety of semiotic or communication systems" (p. 124); it is not language plus other sign systems" (Harste in Cowan & Albers, 2006, p. 516). Literacy then is "the ease with which" people "can create and interpret the signs of one or more semiotic systems through shared meanings with others" (Albers, 2001, p. 4). Thus, visual texts created within the context of an art class are semiotic texts, and curricula that support the use and development of a variety of sign systems, including art, are crucial for supporting expansive communication options.

Education in the visual as a form of literacy is of particular importance for at least the following reasons. First, similar to foundational multimodal literacy research and theorizing (e.g., Jewitt & Kress, 2003), Albers (2008) notes that "image, as well as other visual modes, is fast becoming *the* source through which many read, experience, and build beliefs about the world ... understanding the visual structures that exist within images is as important to the shaping of eliefs as is the written word" (p. 165, emphasis mine). Albers elaborates that images in the form of picture book illustrations, for example, are mainstays of many children's experiences, and older people "often depen[d] on image for content information, clarification, confirmation, and/or symbolic connections" (p. 166) with these images taking the form of, for example, maps, diagrams, and the like. Moreover, I would submit that electronic images are perhaps even more ubiquitous and salient for all generations than the images just mentioned. Importantly akin to print literacy being an ideological practice (e.g., Luke & Freebody, 1999), "readers for the 21st century must be able to interrogate the assumptions that are embedded in visual ... text" (Albers, 2008, p. 165). People need also to develop a critical disposition towards the visual texts they themselves create, that is, to develop the ability to question what they have represented, how, why, and with what implications (e.g., Kamler, 2001).

Second, based on the work of art education advocates such as Maxine Greene (1995; 2001) and Eliot Eisner (2003a; 2003b), Albers (2008) argues that art can be valued as "an aesthetic object" *and* "as an object created from social practices" (p. 166). In the former instance, art education can create new possibilities for people's perceptions, understandings of the world, and what they create. People educated in the visual may therefore "notice the noticeable, become appreciative and reflective, and understand the role of the arts in making life meaningful"; in turn, "new understandings are made in experience, and new ways of working in the world are opened" (p. 166). In the first mentioned instance, people educated in the visual can attend to the social practice of visual text-making and viewing and "learn to notice and identify relationships across visual texts and begin to internalize how these relationships function and what they come to mean" (p. 166). I would also say that thinking of art and visual text-making and viewing as social practices alerts people to the innumerable ways in which one's social positioning informs visual texts and their making, thus awakening people to the possibilities for critiquing this positioning, these texts, and their readings.

To reach the goal of providing people with learning opportunities in a wide array of sign systems, specific multimodal pedagogies (e.g., Stein, 2008) and multimodal curriculum designs (e.g., Albers, 2006) have been proposed. Following in this vein, the emphasis in my studies, including the Picasso curriculum, was on visual texts, communication, and identity and not on art as a content area. In the following, I therefore focus on the multimodal literacy learning opportunities and identity options provided in the intergenerational art programs and try to show how they were enabled and/or constrained by the curriculum. I have structured this discussion through the general components of an average art class at Blessed Mother, because I noted in my research there and in our attempts to build a similar program at Picasso that these components held key pedagogic functions. Foremost was the components' ability to support participants to work through the semiotic decisions Kress and Jewitt (2003) list as significant:

- what is to be signified;
- what is the apt signifier; and
- how the sign is made most suitable for the occasion of its communication. (p. 11)

No doubt these decisions are interrelated and do not necessarily occur in lock-step; however, the data suggest that different components of the class emphasized different decisions. Also, I must stress that all decisions were made within a context that emphasized the social nature of communication.

To avoid the need for absolute consistency in participation from week to week in the art classes, to help mitigate any memory difficulties, and to keep up momentum, Susan at Blessed Mother designed the art class curriculum so that a different project would be introduced and finished in the same session. We continued this pattern at the Picasso and included Blessed Mother's caveat that participants could stay to work on their project until they felt it was done. Because of this one project per session format, classes could proceed in a fairly predictable manner. The following highlights the key structures of class: orientation, catalyst, technical focus, working on the project, and completion. The remainder of the chapter illustrates each in turn and explains the opportunities they created for literacy learning, relationship-building, and identity options.

Orientations

There were informal and formal starts to classes, which were key in supporting the relational aspects of communication. Even before what might thought of as the official start of class, the entrance into the room and the coming together of the generations were moments of intense beauty, anticipation, and possibility. I have caught on video, for instance, the children running into the room to greet the adults with cheers and hellos and great excitement, children and adults embracing after an adult had been away because of illness, adults being still and quiet only to be awakened by the presence of the children, and the moment of contact, through multiple senses, as a moment of energy. As participants settled after the arrival to class, educators and staff used this time in informal ways to facilitate connections and orient participants. For instance, when research assistant Tara-Lynn Scheffel taught at Picasso, she would set up the room such that a sample of the previous week's visual texts would be on display, and she would direct people to view them, which would inevitably spark discussion and an eagerness to make something new. On one occasion, after everyone had sat down somewhat formally at their seats, Tara-Lynn invited participants to move around if they liked to view the bulletin board that displayed the previous week's self-portraits. Everyone smiled and laughed, deciding who was who in the portraits. When they finally sat back down, Tara-Lynn asked child participant Madeline and adult participant Nora, who were sitting beside each other, if they knew each other's names. Nora turned to Madeline, "What's your name?" Madeline answered and Nora gushed, "That's my granddaughter's name!" Madeline then began to list all of the Madelines she knew, even commenting on how she had been named (the early childhood educator clarified that Madeline had been named after the book of the same name). The entire group then began to talk about the Madeline books, the cartoon, and the live action movie. This prompted Gregory, who two weeks before would not even share his name, to offer a story of his own. In this way, the early moments in the class could be structured to allow wonderful, important opportunities for connection-making and the easing of anxieties.

Even further, Chapter Two relays the orientation component of one of the intergenerational art classes at Picasso and Blessed Mother. Recall the examples of child participant Carl playing with adult Frieda in the sharing of their names and at Picasso, the less formal sharing of names through interaction with materials and the support of the teacher. In the examples a variety of learning opportunities were created which relate specifically to literacy and even identity. Introductions set the stage for all subsequent interactions, including working with signs. Naming is an important semiotic practice, and the children were invited to understand and develop connections between the signified (e.g., the person) and the signifier (e.g., the person's N-A-M-E). They were also invited to think about what is in a name. For instance, at Blessed Mother, an adult participant had the same name as a famous painting. Once when this participant was introduced, art teacher Susan held up a picture of the painting and invited the class to consider the connections. Adult participants like Frieda often commented on the beauty of the children's names, and they compared the types of names common to different generations. Frieda, too, often spoke of her own naming. I witnessed her several times telling the story of how her father named her, and how she hated her name because it rhymed with a "naughty" word. She often followed this story by rhyming off the words F-R-I-E-D-A can make and laughing that none represented her.

Through the introductions, participants were also given the opportunity to see each other's names in print or at least hear the spellings of their names. In the examples, people heard their names spelled or the initial phoneme emphasized. Similarly, another time at Blessed Mother child participant Brittany told her name to adult participant Annie, and Susan reminded Brittany that Annie could probably have guessed her name, because it was hanging from Brittany's necklace. Susan suggested that Brittany show her necklace to Annie. Brittany then took her necklace off and spread the letters out on the table. She spent several minutes going through each of the letters that made up her name while Annie looked on. Annie did not usually speak or move her arms, but she communicated with Brittany through laughter as well as facial expressions (smiles) and by gesturing with her head (nods, shakes, and pointing with her chin). Annie was an audience for whom Brittany could explain her understanding of her name and its letters, and this speaking aloud about an otherwise silent understanding was a potentially powerful learning opportunity for Brittany.

Educators running the classes had a variety of pedagogical strategies to create sound/symbol connections which are pertinent for print literacy development. Wendy, the research assistant who taught at Picasso, would sometimes enthusiastically ask of the group, "Who is here today?!" and then provide the initial phoneme of people's names to assist them in responding to the question. This strategy helped to jog people's memories and tune them in. A similar instance happened with Susan at Blessed Mother in the following narrative:

The M Room

"This seems to be the M room," Susan announces to the group, "Every resident so far today starts with an M!" Susan then repeats all the adult M names. The children begin to coax her to recognize their M names. As a class, they pick out the children's M names and state them proudly.

"Wow, there are lots of M names today," Susan reinforces.

Volunteer Marianne seizes on this learning opportunity as a way of being playful. After reinforcing that her own name starts with an M, she says, "I think everyone whose name starts with a different letter than M should leave."

The children laugh and immediately start to categorize the names in the class according to their initial letter. One of the children then deduces, "But then Susan would have to leave!" The episode ends with more laughter and everyone deciding that non-M-name people would have to stay if they were going to get to make any art. The class chose inclusion and, in so doing, indicated that it was ready to start making art together.

Catalyst

The beginning of classes at Blessed Mother and Picasso also provided catalysts for the day's texts. I use the term catalyst to suggest actions that call for reactions, a creation of momentum in the form of activating participants' schema related to content and/or media for the texts, piquing interest and curiosity, and (sometimes) helping to create purpose. A variety of pedagogical strategies were used at this point in class. In this section I will highlight three which were often used together: participants sharing ideas sparked by educator-led questions or puzzles, the use of visual texts, and the use of picture books or other texts.

Participants were often first invited to think about a problem or theme which would be pertinent to both generations and then asked to interact with each other to produce ideas. This strategy highlighted the social component of the classes and encouraged participants to create signs that they would not have generated on their own. An example of this was in a class one April run by Tara-Lynn at Picasso where the project theme was *Holiday Meal* (for lesson plan details see Appendix III) and the medium was watercolour.

Holiday Meal

The Holiday Meal class directly followed Easter, which all the participants in the class celebrated. After decking out the room in artwork depicting food, Tara-Lynn introduces herself and mentions her favourite food. She then signals for participants to go around and do the same. Gregory, who had heretofore been too shy to push his chair up to the table, raises his head when it's his turn and rather confidently states his name and that he likes "spaghetti and meatballs!"

Child participant Carrie likes "scrambled eggs with sausage when Grandma and Grandpa come over," at which all the adults smile, and Anna also "likes spaghetti!"

Until this point three of the adult participants did not add in their food likes. Aurora was too concerned about Gregory not being close enough to the table to respond; Isla smiled but didn't talk; and Elaine preferred to say, "I'm Elaine. I'm an old woman and I love children, and I can tell you anything you want to know! I like to join with the children" although she did not join in the food naming. Beatrice, however, breaks the pattern by saying, "I'm Beatrice, and I seem to be eating all the time. For Easter I went to a friend's house and had a roast lamb carved so beautifully ... it was a masterpiece." This leads to a rich discussion of what people ate on the holiday. Child participant Oscar says, "I had a big feast just like Alex!" to which child participant Alan replies, "me too!" Oscar then describes the feast of "turkey, potatoes, and apples," with all participants in the background getting exciting and saying "Woohoo!"

Projects were also often introduced through images of artwork or examples of participants' or instructors' art.

Holiday Meal II

Tara-Lynn follows-up the talk about food with a viewing of art depicting food and great feasts. Child participant Connor is the last person to share his name and favourite food. He says, "My name is Connor, and I like apples."

Tara-Lynn replies, "I have a picture of apples," and she pulls out an expressionist painting of apples while explaining that people will today be invited to create a visual text of a special meal they have had with their family.

Connor stares at the painting and asks, "How do you paint apples?" He then asks Tara-Lynn to put the painting right in front of him.

Gregory sees a series of magic realist paintings of donuts, puts his hand up and says, "I like donuts!" Carrie agrees.

Child participant Alex says he wants "to try to make that one!" referring to a painting of powdered donuts. Tara-Lynn is holding this painting and bringing attention to the detail.

Beatrice exclaims, "Oh my!" and there is so much excitement with all the participants, but especially the children, eager to get to work. Tara-Lynn goes through a number of images, drawing attention to how the subject matter refers to the food the participants have just mentioned and hearkening to the foods they might like to express in their visual texts. Even more than just bringing about interest and activating schema related to subject matter, this pedagogical strategy also helps participants consider the technical aspects of the mode. For instance, when Tara-Lynn shows the magic realist paintings that depict the same scene from different perspectives (from close up to further away), without prompting Alex remarks, "That must be a farther picture out," referring to image that is at the greatest distance. Finally, Tara-Lynn invites Megan Merrifield, the artist we have hired as a consultant, to exhibit her visual text of a holiday meal. Megan talks aloud about what she has depicted, how, and why. The participants are transfixed and interacting greatly with the viewing. Alex exclaims, "Squash and carrots!" and Gregory joyfully makes a "bleck" sound and a face showing that he does not like these vegetables.

This viewing of multiple texts also created opportunities for intertextual discussions which generated opportunities for better understanding how meaning is created within and across sign systems; at Blessed Mother, for example, Susan showed a variety of images in a book on Matisse to demonstrate how to create prints with simple lines. She supplemented these images with prints she had made of her cat. The juxtaposition of Matisse and the cat led one child participant to cry, "I have a book and there's a cow named Mootisse! There's even a pig called Pigcasso!" Susan knew the book, *When Pigcasso Met Mootisse* (Laden, 1998), and was able to accommodate a short conversation that included the whole class on the text and its potential links to the project they were about to undertake.

Educators also used picture books as catalysts for making art. When they did so, they selected texts that could be related to previous lessons or to the participants' own experiences and would be meaningful and engaging and/or provocative to both young and old. In a sculpture project of a special place, entitled *Community Structures* (for lesson plan details see Appendix IV), Wendy introduced the project, in part, through the book *Iggy Peck, Architect* (Beaty, 2007), a witty picture book full of verse and line drawings about Iggy, a child who has a penchant for building great structures out of ordinary objects (e.g., a tower out of diapers). Following in the intertextual vein, at Blessed Mother in a textile project with the subject of summer, Susan began the class by reminding participants of a special family quilt, which most participants had seen, that hung in adult participant Frieda's room. She used this to begin a discussion of how quilts can tell stories. Having before in class used American artist Faith Ringgold's (1991) book *Tar Beach,* Susan conducted a picture walk through her (1998) *Dancing at the Louvre: Faith Ringgold's French Collection and Other Story Quilts.* Ringgold is known for her beautiful painting on fabric to create story quilts, and this book shows many images of quilts depicting aspects of summer. After the picture walk, Susan asked the participants, "What do you do in the summer? Tell the person beside you what you do in summer." Conversations then ensued, allowing for the generation of ideas for making art. These conversations could be seen as important literacy practices in their own right, not just as precursors for creating images. This was the case with a story told by adult participant Frieda that was a repeated classic in the class. I next present this narrative.

Flour Bin Days

Susan is leading a lesson on printmaking where the subject is to be a funny story experienced by the participants. She has already modeled her own story and demonstrated how to make a print to go with it. She now asks participants to tell the person beside them a funny story. She prompts the participants by saying, "This can be something that happened in your family, say with your brother or sister."

Child participant Arthur has difficulty generalizing and immediately cries out, "But I don't have a brother or sister!"

Educator Gary steps in and tells a funny story to support Arthur's understanding. He selects a story the children have heard before, and the room becomes abuzz with responses to the storytelling. Child participants Carl and Brittany, who are twins, tell a story together about their dog. Each plays expertly off the other, and their story continues the laughter. This prompts Frieda to tell her story. As she begins, the room becomes quiet and all eyes and ears are tuned to her. She is a natural storyteller, with her expressive face and bold gestures:

"My father, he was a baker in England, and he had those big ..." Frieda struggles momentarily for the words, all the while maintaining the story with her hands.

"Flour carts," adult participant Rebecca offers, having heard this one before.

Frieda nods, happy for the support and continues, "A barrel of flour." She pauses for effect. "He took me down to sit on the edge, and whoa! I fell in the flour!" Frieda throws her arms up as though she is falling.

The room laughs, and laughs even harder once Susan helps Frieda add the visual details, "Did you come out all white, covered in flour?"

Frieda nods and says, "From head to toe!" She leans close to the child beside her and wistfully adds, "That's been so many years ago."

Frieda's story is an example of text-making within a social context. In having an opportunity to tell her story, Frieda is able to share her history and amuse and connect with the other participants. Although there were points where she struggled to pull the necessary signs together to serve her narrative purpose, as is common both at Blessed Mother and Picasso, where participants are used to supporting each other, other participants (e.g., Rebecca) helped Frieda by providing vocabulary and encouraging responses (e.g., with attentiveness and laughter). Susan also helped Frieda. She supported her to elaborate the visual details of the story that aided its aesthetics, and these details also facilitated the visual arts project that followed.

The opportunities for shared storytelling and idea-swapping were crucial for helping participants with their semiotic decisions (especially those related to the content of their texts). These opportunities, however, also had an added bonus for the children in that they were able to witness people of all ages engaged in semiotic practices; they indeed witnessed the authentic making of signs in adults' reading of visual images and print texts, visual expression through a variety of modes and media such as oral storytelling. Children were also exposed to the content of these productions. In Flour Bin Days, child participant Taylor had never before heard of flour. Frieda's story provided an introduction to the term. Later, when Taylor met the word F-L-O-U-R on the image of the flour bin that Frieda created, she had a better chance of understanding the sign. For the rest of the children, the story allowed a demonstration of one way of telling a funny story, but also of how life was lived about a century ago. All had questions about why flour was stored in bins, and conversation was generated around how people in different eras procured their bread. Children were, therefore, invited to juxtapose their own experiences with those of people who were different from them, thereby opening up possibilities for creating new schemata.

Technical Aspects

Classes always included time concentrated on the technical aspects of media and how to carry out the project, thus providing learning op-

Figure 4.1 Community Structures Media

portunities germane, in particular, to the second and third semiotic considerations outlined by Jewitt & Kress (2003), where participants were to consider the signifiers and the occasion of their use relative to what they wanted to communicate. For the *Community Structures* project, for example, research assistant Wendy, who was teaching the class, raised people's interests by organizing the seating so that tables and chairs were placed in a horseshoe around a huge mountain of building materials which included cardboard boxes and tubes (see Figure 4.1). Children and adults alike enjoyed exploring this pile prior to class, and its presence provided building options to participants so that they could consider together what to signify and how to signify it. Finally, after informal exploration, Wendy began to focus participants on the project at hand.

Community Structures
Wendy holds up an Eggo waffle box and looks at it quizzically. Child participant Aaron giggles, "Leggo my Eggo," referring to the slogan for the waffle

company. Wendy smiles and continues, "We've done drawing. We've done collage. We've done collograph with ink. This week we get to do sculpture. And sculpture's different, because we don't get to glue it down on the paper to look at it. How is it different, Lina?" Wendy asks a child who is paying close attention.

"It is different, because you don't need gluing, you can just put it on top of each other."

Wendy attends to the notion of putting things on top of each other by saying, "That's right. And it sticks up, doesn't it? So sculpture is three-dimensional."

"Just like my hair," Lina answers, while pointing to her head which is covered in little pony tails sticking up all over. At this, adult participant Nora smiles and laughs.

"So instead of gluing something down on a piece of paper that's flat like this ..." Wendy puts a fold in a piece of paper to make a tent-like form, "sculpture would stick up like this."

Within the studies the data suggest that the notion of three-dimensionality was particularly challenging for all participants. Thanks to the experiences at Blessed Mother, which preceded our attempts to create an intergenerational art curriculum at Picasso, we were able to anticipate the need to support participants and adjust our pedagogy accordingly. One of Susan's favourite ways of introducing sculpture and three-dimensionality was to invite participants to consider a sheet of paper and how they might make it stand up. In an interview, Susan explained that by experimenting with the paper and working with the people around them, participants figured out that if they folded the paper or crumpled it, it would stand and in fact become three-dimensional. As the next narrative shows, in the Community Structures project at Picasso, after demonstrating for participants, Wendy opted to unite the subject matter with the technical matter to offer support.

Community Structures II
"Now last week we did collographs of our special places, remember? And we had to put our special place in our mind and think about it. Then we had to ..." Wendy elaborates on what the class did to make their Collographs of Home project (see Appendix V for lesson plan details). "If you were going to make that [special] place into a sculpture so that it stood up? What would that look like? Talk with your table ... What if your special place could stand up?"

Lina immediately springs into conceptualizing this, stating, "I know! I would just move the things together like ..." and with this, Lina puts her hands *together in the shape of a triangle. She leans over to the pile of materials and points, "I could use a cereal box."*

Pushing her to consider more options, Wendy asks, "What about these cookie boxes? Would they make good sculptures like a building?"

"Yeah," answers Lina, "I would put them on top of each other."

Encouraging her to problem solve with her table, Wendy advises, "Good idea. So talk to Mina and Nora and see how we're going to get these to stick together if we put these on top of each other."

When Wendy checks on the conversation between Aaron and adult Keith's table, equally enthusiastic problem solving is going on. Wendy inquires, "What are you and your friends talking about?"

"Buildings" answers Aaron.

"Now how are you going to make your sculpture look like a building?"

"It helps cutting out the windows and the doors."

"What other parts of your building will be like a sculpture?"

"A chimney ... I will have to glue it to make a chimney."

Not knowing to what "it" refers, Wendy poses, "Will you be able to use any of these boxes or tubes or trays or things that we brought today to help make your building a sculpture?"

"Tubes. It would work for the chimney."

Returning to Lina's group, Wendy notices a challenge and asks Lina what is troubling the table.

"The roof," answers a frustrated Lina.

Offering options, Wendy directs, "We have Styrofoam trays. We have corrugated – that means it's bumpy – paper. We have cardboard. We have all kinds of things that you may choose for your roof." And with that, Wendy turns the class's attention to Iggy Peck, Architect, *so they can see how the character Iggy solved his design dilemmas. Following the reading of the book during which all participants engaged in a lively conversation, Lina asks, "May I just tell you something?" After getting the okay, Lina connects to the book and the material problems they are discussing by explaining, "One time I had some cups that were plastic and I made a building out of the cups ... I didn't use glue. I didn't use water. It just stayed." Together everyone continues to converse and problem solve around the project, what would they build? How would they build it?*

In this example, the technical aspects of sign-making are critical problem-solving opportunities for people and vital to their communication. This has been noted in the early years art education literature, where it has been said that when making art, children are confronted with "problems ... related to materials and their physical properties" in relation to their "initial difficulty in using the materials due to undeveloped sensory/motor skills or unfamiliarity with new objects and situations" (Pitri, 2001, p. 50). I wonder too at what these opportunities allow adults, for as evidenced in Chapter Five, when creating visual texts, the adult participants exhibited some challenges related to the technical and conceptual aspects of the mode which had the potential to limit their communication options. Thus, for all participants, explicit or *overt instruction* (New London Group, 2000) regarding how to work in various media within the visual mode (and others) allowed opportunities to acquire the necessary physical, mental, and creative dexterity for diverse sign-making. It also offered people the opportunity to develop an awareness of the possibilities of mode and media. This can expand their sign-making options so that people may select the mode and media that best suit their communication needs/desires. In all aspects of the intergenerational art classes, participants were invited to view and create images and to interrogate critically what affects images (e.g., media and composition) and with what effects (i.e., how do the media and composition of an image affect the way that the image communicates its subject and is read or viewed?). This *critical framing* of the communication might allow *transformed practice* such that participants might be able to carry out their new literacy practices in ways that are keeping with their "own goals and values" (p. 33).

What perhaps allowed the technical component to create so many learning opportunities was that they were couched within a meaningful whole. Literacy researcher Victoria Purcell-Gates (2001) recommends a "whole-part-whole" structure for teaching print literacy whereby learners are provided with a context with a focus on meaning-making from which educators can provide overt instruction regarding how a part of language, or in this case an aspect of visual communication functions or how to perform a specific skill. The part is then related to the whole of meaning-making. An example of this would be where at Picasso, Tara-Lynn used a whole or complete visual text (e.g., a series of paintings) from which the participants were introduced to perspective as an element of that whole, and then participants were invited to attempt to use perspective within their own texts.

Also helping to bring about learning opportunities was that the entirety of making visual texts was embedded in a meaningful, social whole or *situated practice* (New London Group, 2000). Situating literacy practices can be addressed in a number of ways. Educators can

- invite learners to participate in practices that are meaningful to them;
- help learners to feel safe, like part of a community, and as though the learning is in their "interest" (p. 33);
- encourage learners to play multiple and different roles in the learning community based on their "backgrounds and experiences" (p. 33);
- ensure that the community includes "experts" or "people who have mastered" the practices the learners are expected to develop (p. 33);
- carefully consider learners' "affective and sociocultural needs and identities" (p. 33); and
- use evaluation to guide learners not to make harsh judgments.

To help situate the multimodal literacy practices in intergenerational art class, educators did the following: Before launching into the technical aspects of the project, participants were provided with a catalyst to help engage them with the project and infuse it with meaning. Structuring class so that each day a project would be started and finished provided opportunities for engagement with the project as participants knew that there would be a product to share. In all, there was something to communicate and a reason for communicating it. Also, the media and the subject of the project were engineered to work well together and promote intergenerational interaction and relationship building. An interview where Susan explained how she planned for class provides insight into how this happened:

SUSAN: I think when I first started [at Blessed Mother], I didn't always know the limitations ... I had mostly worked with kindergartners through 6th-graders, all of whom can typically use scissors or glue things. And so, from experience now I find ... what kind of things that most seniors or most preschoolers are able to do, and then there's always exceptions to that. There are some residents that can only move one hand. So what I do is I design projects, and I research [around that] ... and ... the media ... is one thing. There's also what kind of theme or subject can we put into it. There are some [subject matter] ... where it's kind of built into the project ... for example, if we were doing collographs... there are subject matter that can work and some work better than others ... I am interested in the product in the sense that if you get a good product, people will come back, and they'll feel good ... they have a good self-esteem about completing it, and pride. So, there is that. That's not always important, but it's important at least to have that sometimes. But then the subject matter, too, I like to have things that they can talk about, especially things that spark memory in the residents, because if you can spark some memory and get them talking to the kids, then there's a conversation. And some good, valid subject matter ... just aren't conducive to having conversations. So I try and choose that kind of thing, like, for example, what do you think about when you think about home? And that's a subject ... that comes up often ... with the ... residents is that they miss their houses, they miss their pets or their garden.

RACHEL: And ... the kids resonate with that one as well?

SUSAN: I think they do, especially because as a preschooler, you know, a lot of their [foci] are around home, and some of them have a hard time leaving home to come into a facility like [this]. So, you know, that's something they can talk about. Another thing might be a pet that you really loved, and both the kids and the residents, if the kids don't have a pet, the grandmother might have, or they might wish they did, or sometimes they see little kittens,[4] so they both have a response to that. So I try and choose some things like that. Even sometimes things like weather ... I've done this one project once, where we talk about what kinds of lines describe weather. And we can talk about where people come from, what kind of weather they have there, because a lot of the residents come from different places. And ... there's a lot of diversity in the kids and the staff, too – a lot of Asian or Hawaiian, Cambodian. So talking about the weather where people come from can be, is a part of us having a frame, that's not just the media, it's also what subject.

The above transcript suggests how Susan carefully balanced subject matter with media and modes so that participants had something meaningful to express and equally meaningful ways of expressing it.

Focusing on the technical aspects of communication also entailed immersing participants in the language of styles of art (e.g., terms like surrealism, abstract expressionism), art-making (e.g., names of tools, colours), and the visual (e.g., terms like composition, tone, and scale). The following narrative from Blessed Mother during a class on *Amate* (see Appendix VI for lesson plan details and Figure 4.2 for a sample from a child participant at Picasso), a symmetrical paper cutting project, demonstrates a characteristic opportunity for language learn-

---

4 Animals lived at and were brought into Blessed Mother.

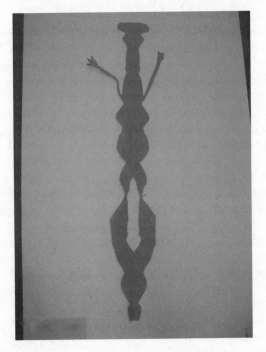

Figure 4.2 Child's Amate

ing and concept development (the signifier and the signified coalescing into the sign).

Symmetry All Around: Amate at Blessed Mother
"Remember we talked about symmetry?" Susan asks the participants as she draws attention to the technical component of the class.

"That's when one thing is the same on both sides!" Child participant Chloe immediately exclaims.

"Yes!" The other children chime in.

"What is something that is symmetrical?" Susan prods further.

One of the children yells, "Your head!" The child then draws a finger down the middle of her face. Susan agrees, then demonstrates what the class will do in class today with this concept of symmetry.

While the children work on their projects, I notice that they return again and again to the concept of symmetry. Child participant Mimi turns to peer Clara and asks to see her work. She announces, "Look, it has squares."

Child participant Barry adds, "It's symmetrical."

Clara turns to an adult participant and says, "Yes, and I have a heart in the middle. [It's] symmetrical."

Towards the end of class, Clara notices a painting hanging on the bulletin board that was created in the adult class. She correctly says to the adult participant near her, "This is almost like what we're doing, because this is symmetry, too." Although she is currently working on a project in a different medium from the painting, Clara is able to take her new vocabulary to help her perceive a concept that is common across media.

This ability to link concepts, language, and visual grammar (e.g., visual symmetry) across projects and situations was not unique to Blessed Mother. In the same project at Picasso, child participant Aaron could not wait to share during the technical component of class that he had done a similar art project in "a different art class!" He explained a project where, "The page looks see-through, then it gets taped with an animal print on the window to look like a stained-glass window." Symmetry, it seemed, was the link. I frequently observed when the participants were in the phase of class in which they were intently working on their projects this coming together of subject matter and media and signified and signifier into a sign, together with the enhancement of this process through the intergenerational component.

Working on the Project

Although I have belaboured the catalyst and explanation portions of class to focus readers on their important pedagogical functions, these components of class usually took up no more than about 15 minutes of class time. Susan noted in our interviews that the children were generally so eager to get started that they could not wait much longer. That said, the instruction and demonstration of the project often did allow participants to be physically engaged with the lesson even if they were not yet actively working on the project. For instance, at Picasso, Tara-Lynn invited participants to sketch symmetrical shapes on their own paper while she was performing her own demonstration of symmetry. All participants, but especially the children, seemed so excited by the tactile stimulation of the projects that they demonstrated a great desire to interact physically with the media (e.g., through touch and even sound). Readers will note in the passport section of the book the children's fascination with opening and closing scissors – hearing, feeling, and seeing them work. With the Amate, during the demonstration where Tara-Lynn crumpled the paper, the participants were transfixed with the transformation of the medium. Aaron was wide-eyed and gasped; Gregory immediately wanted to feel the paper after it had been crumpled to see the difference; and all the participants could not wait to feel the paper after Tara-Lynn ironed it, with child participant Courtney exclaiming, "Oh that's cool!" when she was offered the chance to feel the melted wax on the sample. One might also ask what opportunities were created for the adults to engage in this highly sensual experience. The data for this portion of the classes were replete with examples of smiling, touching, laughing, nods to other adults, and talking with the children about what was happening.

Discussions about subject matter and technique continued throughout the making of the art as participants worked through what to express and how to express it (Kress and Jewitt's [2003] decisions 2 and 3). True to the nature of early literacy with its emphasis on children as capable producers of signs, educators in the classes prompted participants to solve problems and experiment together. The social process of collaboratively figuring out how to work through the project was an important feature in this component of the classes. Note, however, that it did not necessarily just happen on its own, but was related to the conditions that had been created through the structure of the classes (e.g., introductions) and in on-the-spot support from the people working in the classes (e.g., educators). The following example from Blessed Mother demonstrates how such interaction can be facilitated:

A House for a Dog:
An Example of Facilitating Intergenerational Collaboration

Adult participant Alma is beautiful in her shawl but is so low in her wheelchair that she's struggling to make contact with child participant Mimi, who is sitting beside her. The class is working on a Styrofoam Print *(see Appendix VII for lesson plan details) with the subject matter being home. Alma is struggling to draw on her piece of Styrofoam, which will be used as the plate for the print, and she is looking around, presumably for some support. Susan notices Alma's attempts at catching the attention of Mimi, who is sitting beside her, so she goes over to facilitate the interaction and the sign-making.*

Susan crouches down between Alma and Mimi and stretches her arms out to invite the two to lean in closer to each other. She is careful to repeat everything that's said so that nothing is missed. She speaks in a loud, clear voice, and begins with Mimi, "Alma's trying to think of what to draw. What do you think she should draw?' Susan then says to them both, "Remember, we're trying to think of things that remind you of home. What would remind Alma of home?"

"A house," Mimi offers.

Alma can't hear Mimi, so Susan inquires of Alma, "Would you think of a house?"

Alma looks at Mimi, and although I've seen Alma draw numerous times, she pleads to Mimi, "I don't know if I can make a house. Can you make a house?" Mimi nods and looks as though she's considering what to draw.

Susan then provokes more conversation, which creates an opportunity for the participants to consider more deeply what they are communicating. She directs this conversation towards information that will help Mimi draw a house for Alma. "Did you have a big house, Alma?"

"Not too big, no."

"Not too hard to clean!" Susan enthuses.

Mimi offers something about her own house, but it's too quiet for the rest of us to hear. Susan encourages Mimi to speak some more, "Do you have a big house?" Mimi says no. Susan notices that Mimi still hasn't even picked up a pen. She lights a fire for this and makes a new connection between Alma and Mimi. "So we can draw a little house."

"We can draw a little dog house," Alma offers with a great, big grin.

Mimi likes this idea, but is still unsure of how to proceed. Susan now focuses on the technical. She breaks the image of a house down into its essential shapes, saying, "It seems that the bottom of a little dog house would be a square." Susan forms a square with her fingers. Alma nods and Mimi leans closer to Alma. She takes the pen from Alma's hands, pulls the piece of Styrofoam closer to herself and starts copying the shape that Susan is modelling. When she is finished, Mimi asks for help with the roof. Susan directs her response to both Mimi and Alma, "What would the top part look like?" She puts her fingers in the shape of a triangle. Mimi then draws on the roof.

Following this is a discussion among the three about the dog that needs to go in the picture. Alma explains that she used to have a little "mutt." Mimi passes her the pen so that she can draw it in.

In this example, Susan invites Mimi and Alma to work collectively through several struggles: first, how to conceptualize home and to translate it into a mental image; second, how to turn technically that mental image into a concrete, exterior image; and third, how to communicate across the barriers of hearing impairment and different generations to make meaning in a dialogic fashion. Susan acts as support for participants through all of these struggles and pushes participants to use each other as resources insofar as possible. The lessons of representation and communication appeared to pay dividends. For example, in the same Styrofoam Print class, I witnessed Mimi transfer the notion of fundamental shapes and metaphor (e.g., the top of a house as a triangle) in her interaction with adult participant Manon. Mimi was showing Manon a drawing she had done.

Styrofoam Print II

"Can you tell me what is this?" Manon asks as she points to one part of the drawing. She receives no response, so as she points to a big triangle she offers, "This looks like a sail."

Mimi counters, "That's like a big A."

Manon looks impressed, "That's a big A. That's very good."

The lesson of collaborating to create signs was also evident when later in the class a volunteer, Fiona, brought Mimi and Alma back together so that Mimi could help Alma print her name on her artwork. Mimi held the pen, and the three of them problem-solved through spelling Alma's first and second names.

Of course there were many times at all the study sites when educators could not be directly scaffolding or facilitating interactions, but the data suggest that the setting of ground rules for interaction and monitoring what was happening during the interactions was critical to positive relationship building. Consider the following instance at Picasso, in a class where participants were to create miniature drawings of a spring theme which would later form a composite from class (see Appendix VIII for lesson plan details). Note that this class happened in the first year of the study and shortly after we had implemented the program when we still had much to learn.

Missed Opportunities

Child participant Rudy is looking at his drawing and seems very unhappy. Adult participant Elly is sitting beside him and offering what seems to be encouraging words, "That looks great! It has petals and leaves."

Child participant Noel is sitting across from the duo and she rises up on her knees to look over at Rudy's drawing, perhaps in response to Elly's glowing comments. Noel concurs with Elly and says to Rudy, "That looks very nice."

But Rudy is silent and his facial expression suggests he is unhappy. Rudy picks up a black marker and begins to draw a border. Elly is now fully engaged in Rudy's drawing and asks, "What about the sunshine?" She takes out an orange pencil crayon and adds orange to Rudy's yellow drawing of the sun. Rudy seems a bit agitated and puts his hand to his head to lean on it while Elly draws on his text. When Elly puts down the orange pencil, Rudy picks it up and continues to add to the sun. Without invitation, Elly then holds up a green pencil and says to Rudy, "Make your leaves darker." He does. Elly appears a bit impatient. Before Rudy is even finished with the leaves she remarks, "You don't have any people in your picture." When Rudy is finished with the leaves, Elly looks at it again and advises, "You need to add more colour." Rudy remains silent, but follows her directions. Now Elly begins anew to add orange to Rudy's sun.

Rudy finally speaks and seems to be accepting of Elly's help: "Why not a mix of colour?" He then pulls out the yellow again, works on the sun, and when Elly is finished with the orange, he takes that up. Rudy's body language suggests he is beginning to relax and now he invites interaction with Elly asking, "What colour should I do for a bird?" Elly looks to ponder the question while in the interim, Rudy reaches for the dark brown. Elly begins to draw the outline of a bird on the table for Rudy. In response, without speaking, his body language seems to invite her into the bird making and he draws a bit, turns to look at her, then when she responds in the positive, "Yes, it's good," he continues to draw, checking in with her every so often. Rudy next adds a tree and Elly, ever direcing the making of this text, prompts Rudy to write his name on the bottom of the picture.

She finishes by saying, "That's beautiful. Next time you can put more colour. But it's a real picture, and you will have to bring it to your mommy when you go home." Rudy turns his face away, begins to draw on top of his tree and says, "I don't live with my mom." Elly looks a bit sad and says, "It's beautiful. It's beautiful." And she continues this way, with Rudy drawing and neither looking at each other.

Life is messy, and if relationships are to be built, then uncomfortable conversations may sometimes be had. There is no real way that any facilitator could have (or perhaps should have) shielded a child like Rudy from having to confront the troubling question of his mother. Yet there are a number of problematic elements in the above interaction that might have been prevented or at least minimized by the laying down of some ground rules. At Blessed Mother, Susan early on established that no person should make a mark on another person's text without the prior permission of that person. Even then, she dissuaded participants from marking on each other's texts, reminding all that they could make suggestions or model a technique beside a person's text, but that a person's text is his or her own. There were, however, specific projects where the "authorship" of the text was collective[5] that were the exceptions to this rule. Susan pointed out that she felt it equally important for adults not to write children's names on their texts because the mark then became part of the visual field. Children were encouraged to decide where and how they wanted their names included, with occasionally an adult writing in light pencil a name on the back of a text.

Elly was somewhat critical of Rudy's text, which she perhaps attempted to temper with non-specific compliments (e.g., "That's beautiful"). Unfortunately even these compliments were not structured in a way to be helpful. Susan counseled people working in the art class and participants to curtail their use of generalized evaluative comments (e.g., "I like that"). Creating opportunities to engender feedback where participants recognized a reading of a text and where it came from, and to recognize that no text was either all good or all bad, but that the value was in the reading, Susan advised specific feedback like, "I think it's beautiful the way that you *used the purple in this part of the picture*, it makes me feel ..."

• In addition, rather than supporting Rudy's text-making in a collaborative way where both were equally participating in the project, Elly took on the role of *managing* Rudy's text, speaking in imperatives. Elly, because she was not working on her own project, took on the role of director of Rudy's text and was not his equal. When classes were structured and participants supported to all be text-makers and responsible for their own work, this seemed to give each participant a purpose. Had this been the case with Rudy and Elly, her sole purpose at the table would not have been to take over Rudy's text. Also, the studies show that having educators and recreation staff closely monitor interactions helped redirect participants when needed. An important offshoot of having all participants responsible for creating their own texts was that it created opportunities for people's texts to be positively affected. The following example from a Picasso class based on a *Mobiles on Twigs*

---

5 Note that in a subsequent intergenerational art and singing program I ran with colleagues (Beynon et al., 2011), we noted the need for more intensive strategies to facilitate intergenerational interaction, and thus we invited participants to create most texts in pairs.

project (see Appendix X for lesson plan details) concerning things participants loved, is a prime example of how participants benefited when they were equally working through the demands of a project.

Struggling Together: Hearts on Branches

It's very near Valentine's day and I'm a participant observer at the point in class where people are working on their projects. I'm standing near adult participant Nora and child participant Anna, watching Anna attempting to cut a heart from construction paper. She looks at Nora and asks, "Is that how?"

Nora, who is struggling with her own cutting, says, "Here, turn your paper over." Together, the two begin advising each other on the cutting, and I turn to child participant Aaron to help him with his creation of a cat. Once Aaron is away and finishing his cat, I hear Anna tell Nora she wants to make a cat to go inside her heart, which she has finally completed. Nora looks over at me and appeals to me by laughing, "Well, I am trying to make a cat!" She is attempting to navigate cutting out a tiny cat from the midst of a huge piece of paper. I have just modelled for Aaron how to cut away the excess from around what he is trying to cut out to make it easier. Nora requires the same lesson.

"Yup, you're trying to cut out that little piece. You know if you cut around the cat like that ... you can get rid of all this extra paper and then you cut," I suggest.

"Nora does this then asks of the table, "Is that pretty good? Is that pretty good?" She's laughing and then says of her cat, which is a bit fat and misshapen, "It's a boat!"

Wanting to re-engage Anna and have her and Nora work collaboratively, I ask Anna, "Does Nora's cat look like a boat?"

Anna smiles and jokes, "That's a boat, that's not a cat!"

Bringing it back to solving the technical problem I inquire, "What do we need to do to that to make it look more like a cat?"

Anna offers, "Put legs and a tail."

Louder, so she could hear the advice, I say, "We need legs and a tail on that Nora."

"Oh, okay." Nora smiles and laughs.

"Anna told you there!" I say directing Nora to the source.

"Four legs" Anna counsels.

"Four legs. You put four legs on and put a tail on the kitty," Nora instructs. Anna does, and then Nora asks, "Now about some eyes. Are you going to put some eyes on him?" Anna affixes eyes, to which Nora laughs, "That's his ears! We put his eyes ... where do you want to put his eyes?"

"On top of his ears" states Anna.

"Not on top of his ears" Nora jokes.

"Where are your eyes, Anna?" I wonder.

Anna, smiling, puts the eyes on the cat, and Nora asks proudly, "Is that okay now? Does it still look like a boat?"

Aaron joins in the fun and says he thinks the cat looks like a dog. I suggest, "I know one thing that a cat needs. Do you know what a cat needs?"

"Whiskers!" shouts Anna.

"Whiskers! That's what really makes a cat look like a cat, doesn't it?" I declare as the gang gets ready to work on the whiskers, and we continue until the whiskers are safely on and what began as a boat is now a cat, so the group can turn their energy towards making that dog Aaron mentioned.

This example speaks to how when everyone making texts was supported in their interaction, participants were provided with opportunities to solve problems and work through communicational decisions. The children and Nora each had something to contribute and no one was in authority over another.

A final example of the working on the project component of class that highlights the importance of all participants making texts that are meaningful and challenging to them involves an *Accordion Book* project (see Appendix IX for lesson plan details) at Blessed Mother. This one also demonstrates how the dialogic entered the text.

Making Meaning Together:
Betty's Book at Blessed Mother

I am standing in a neighbourhood where I see many children and adults sitting around large tables that have been pushed together to make one enormous table. Surrounding this are dozens of people in wheelchairs who are participating through observation. The class is about three-quarters of the way through, and although adult participant Betty shakes whenever she tries to employ her fine motor skills, she has finished making her book.

Recreation therapist Jana approaches child participant Carol, who is sitting next to Betty. She squats down between the two and looks at the drawing Carol is completing.

"I like the colours." Jana then turns her attention to uniting Betty and Carol. She asks Carol, "Do you want to show Betty your picture there?" Carol folds up her accordion book so that a picture she created earlier is showing.

Betty holds the book with her hands fluttering like butterfly wings, "Oh what a pretty picture!"

"It's a princess," clarifies Carol. "It's a princess. Yes, a pretty princess."

Child participant Betty Lou, who is sitting across from the two gets right up on the table excitedly yells, "Let me see!"

Betty hands Betty Lou the book. "It's a princess." Betty Lou considers the image and looks unimpressed. "Yah. It's hers." She hands the book back to Carol.

Carol takes her book back and looks down. Jana tries to smooth things over. "Is there another picture there that you have?"

"No," Carol says, then turns to do more work on her princess.

Jana tries a new approach. She asks Carol, "Do you want to see Betty's pictures?" This seems to work well. Carol immediately turns to Betty to look at her book.

Betty shows Carol the book. She points at the images and the print. She also adds her own commentary: "See, this is a doggie, my little doggie. The best pet I ever had." Betty reads this last sentence carefully, as it is the caption. She then comes to the page that says, "My friend." She points to her drawing and says, "This is Mina. That's Mina across the way." Betty points to adult participant Mina, who is sitting on the other side of the table working on her own book. "So here's her blonde hair. She has blonde hair on her." I notice that Mina's hair in "real life" is about as grey as hair can come. I also notice that Carol's princess, who sits above the caption, "This is me," is fair-skinned, blonde-haired and blue-eyed, while Carol is African-American. Betty continues, "And this is my ice cream. I love ice cream!"

With that, Betty Lou yells, "I want to see! I want to see!"

Betty shows her, "See," she points to each picture and phrase, "There's a doggie, there's Mina, there's Mina sitting next to you [Betty Lou turns and looks at Mina who is smiling], there's ice cream ... I love ice cream, and there's '7 North'" Betty reads the phrase, "This is where I live."

Jana elaborates on this last point, "We call this neighbourhood '7 North,' so she [Betty] drew the orange beams there." Jana motions to the ceiling where there indeed are beams. Betty holds the book up so that Betty Lou can see better. In the process, Mina is able to see it.

Susan brings a smile to Mina by saying, "She [Betty] had the words, 'My friend,' and she drew a picture of you!"

"Oh!" Mina grins.

Betty is now off showing her book to child participant Kurt, and the sharing continues.

The book project created many opportunities for making signs from print (i.e., reading) and incorporating print within a larger meaning-making scheme (i.e., using print with other modalities such as drawing). As usual, all sign-making was dialogic and tied to the presence of significant others. Through Betty's book, Carol and Betty Lou were given opportunities to understand signs better; they saw Mina in the book and Mina at the table; 7 *North* in the book and 7 *North* as the place where they were sitting. They also were provided with links between print and illustration, thus exposing them to the idea that the two should have a relationship. They also witnessed Betty's investment in her signs: her dog, her Mina, and her ice cream. There was affect, meaning, and value ascribed by Betty to every aspect of her text. It may be that this was a lesson Carol had already learned – her princess was obviously very dear to her. The next step would be to consider how to support participants to consider the relationship between their texts and desires (e.g., what were the conditions in which Carol figured herself as the pink princess and Mina's hair was blonde?).

When structured and monitored in particular ways, the completion component of class allowed cooperative completion of people's texts. Examples of this cooperative spirit and what was required to help bring it about were also strikingly apparent in this component.

Completion

Typically, at Blessed Mother and Picasso classes would last for about 1 hour. At Picasso, children were then told they had to leave to return to their classroom. At Blessed Mother, participants could stay a bit longer if they so chose, and the number of participants would dwindle until people felt finished. The abrupt versus staggered ending to class created different opportunities.

At Picasso, because people needed the whole session to complete their texts, there was often insufficient time for much of a showing and discussion of them. Therefore, the program attempted within its structure to provide time for a formal audience of the texts. This was provided by hanging texts on the bulletin board in the classroom and through the art show in the spring. To make good on the notion that people's text-making is social, to recognize that the texts were all important in their own right and that effort and meaning had gone into them, we ensured that each piece was framed and that the show had food and beverages for all. The effect was gorgeous, and participants brought friends, family, dressed up, took photographs, and generally seemed to have a wonderful time.

Blessed Mother also had an annual art show and the benefit of the staggered exit; thus, the end of class would sometimes contain only a handful of participants finishing their projects. This was often the ripest time for conversation and collaboration. The following narrative tells of when child participant Tim was encouraged by volunteer Marianne to assist adult participant Alma in completing a project entitled *Crowns* (see Appendix XI for lesson plan details).

Crowns

Child participant Tim seems to be very interested in the project for this class, which invites participants to create a multi-media crown (using kraft paper, cut-outs, glitter, markers, coloured pencils, coloured paper, and plastic garland) that represents an imaginary country. Back in his classroom, Tim and his group have been learning about chickens, and Tim decides he will create a chicken country where he is "king" of the chickens. When he finishes his crown, Tim begins to dance. When I ask him about this, he shows me how he has drawn dancing chickens on his crown. When he is finished dancing and showing his crown to other participants, volunteer Marianne invites Tim to assist her and adult participant Alma on adult participant Millie's crown.

Millie is having trouble finishing her crown. She knows what she wants, but in the aftermath of a stroke, she is physically unable to carry it out. She is also limited in her speech. Nonetheless, she, Marianne, and Alma communicate through word and gesture what should go on the crown. After Tim decides he will help them, Marianne places the kraft paper for the crown between them and in front of Tim. This way they can all see the paper and each other.

Tim draws a chain of people across the paper while the group discusses what he's doing.

"I love watching him make people," Marianne remarks of Tim.

Alma turns to Susan, who is walking by, "We love watching him make people." Alma then turns back to watch Tim. As Tim draws, Alma asks as she points, "Who's that there?" Tim doesn't answer. He seems too engrossed in drawing.

When he's finished drawing, he stands back and contemplates his work. Alma encourages him to take the drawing further, "They'd look better with ears, though," she suggests.

Tim smiles, is silent for a moment as if he's considering the suggestion, and then walks back up to the paper and says, "I'll make blue ears." Tim struggles to make the ears. He discusses with the others that this difficulty might be because the heads he's made are small.

After minutes of drawing, the conversation turns to the weather in Millie's imaginary country. Millie can say only that she wants the weather to be nice. Alma decides, "It should be partly hot and partly cold."

Tim takes this to mean that all forms of weather should be represented on the crown. He lists the weather elements, including sun, rain, snow, and wind, and draws them, each in a different point on the crown. While he draws, he discusses aloud what he is doing. When he chooses to draw hail, as he draws he explains, "You need some darker white so that it will show up." And he compliments himself on a well-crafted image, "That's a nice shape."

This example foregrounds what it means to create text in a supportive environment. Surrounded by persons who valued and even depended on his skills and knowledge, Tim was encouraged to create signs that could communicate the group's ideas. Tim had already demonstrated that he was a proficient user of multiple modes. In his own crown and performance of the crown, he created signs in two different visual modes to communicate the concept of the country in which he would like to live, and he drew on texts of the classroom (oral and print) to inform his artwork. When he worked on Millie's crown, he pulled from his knowledge of the media (e.g., how to use the colour white) and subject matter (e.g., forms of weather) to create a text that was agreeable to all. In this way, Tim used his sign-making proficiency to mediate Millie's disability, and in so doing, the product is, in Bakhtin's (1981) terms, quintessentially heteroglossic. The coming together of the disparate to make a comprehensible whole is again present in this last example, again taken from the end of class. The example took place at Blessed Mother and involved a *Chalk on Cloth* (see Appendix XII for lesson plan details) project focusing on summer.

Frieda's Husband

It is towards the end of class. Adult participant Frieda has been one of art classes' most regular attendees, and she has come back to class after a hiatus because of illness. She is very happy to be back, but is in a difficult physical state. She is using an oxygen tank and struggles to breathe and to speak. She is also today struggling to complete her project. Many of the other participants have left the room, but Susan, volunteer Marianne, educator Gary, and child participants Arthur and Jimmy remain and help her to complete it. Susan leans over Frieda's cloth and with permission adds something to her drawing. Arthur and Jimmy stand slightly back, watching.

Susan tries to engage the boys. She explains, "Her husband was an artist. Right, Frieda?" Frieda smiles.

Susan has told me that Frieda enjoys remembering her late husband. "Ah huh!" responds Frieda with a giant nod of her head. Susan needs to leave to at-

tend to something else, so Marianne enters the scene. She squats beside Frieda and rubs her back to calm and help her breathe. Jimmy watches behind Arthur.

Gary, who is paying attention from across the room, exclaims in reference to Frieda's husband having been an artist, "I didn't know that!"

Frieda turns to Jimmy and points to him and touches him on the nose playfully, "And you, too!" Earlier in the class, Frieda informed Jimmy that she thought him an artist. Jimmy now makes a funny face, as if he's ill at ease accepting the compliment.

While this interaction is taking place, Arthur has taken the pastel from Susan and is now completing his contribution to Frieda's cloth. Once he is finished, Marianne says, "Hey that's nice!" She then adds, "Jimmy, would you like to put something on Frieda's picture too?" Jimmy steps closer. "What could you put on it?" Marianne asks.

Frieda points to Jimmy and Arthur moves back. Marianne begins to point to everything that's in the picture and labels it, "There's a beautiful flower, there's Frieda's husband, there's a house. What else could we put on this picture?"

Before she even finishes, Jimmy says gleefully, "Beach ball!"

"A beach ball?" Marianne turns to Frieda who nods, "Of course, we need a beach ball!"

Frieda calls, "Hey," and points to child participant Taylor, who is at another part of the table, to join in. "I love beach balls."

Jimmy draws a shape, stands back, and announces, "It's an oval."

"It's a good shape, and now he's colouring it," Marianne says to Frieda, keeping her up to date on what's happening.

"Look at that, it's a beach ball that you take down to …" Frieda barely squeaks out the name of a local beach before she is interrupted by Jimmy.

"Actually, it's an egg," Jimmy clarifies.

Marianne moves again to get the participants back together, "Frieda says, is that a beach ball you'd take down to [the beach]?"

Jimmy, however, has made up his mind, "It's an egg."

"Oh no, it's turned into an egg!" Marianne lets Frieda in on the change.

"What?" Frieda is confused.

"It's turned into an egg," Marianne helps.

"It's a snake egg," states Jimmy.

With this, Frieda takes Jimmy's hand and kisses it as though she's punctuating the moment. "Oh, good for you!" Frieda then tweaks Jimmy's nose.

"Oh, Susan was ready to eat it." Marianne begins a new leg of the narrative.

Susan picks up on this, even though she's ironing cloth for the project in another part of the room. She asks, "Where is the snake? Where is the mama snake?"

Jimmy points to the egg, "That's where the baby is." He smiles, enjoying the story, "It's a rattlesnake."

"Uh ho," Marianne pronounces, "Are they born with the rattler already?"

All the while this conversation is going on, Jimmy continues to work on Frieda's text. "Actually, it's a poisonous one."

Frieda looks right at Jimmy and seems to be taking it all in.

"Like a black snake. It's a black snake." Jimmy seems to decide that the story is complete, because he moves away from the text. Marianne holds the cloth up so that it is clearly visible to Frieda.

"Oh!" Frieda starts to name the elements in the image, "There's my flower, my husband, an egg, and my house." Marianne, Susan, Arthur, Jimmy, and Frieda then each add their names to the text, making it a collective work.

In this closing to the class, the participants and educators' valuing of each other and communication provided opportunity for each participant to feel important enough to have something to convey and capable enough actually to convey it. Susan and Marianne scaffolded the participants' text-making and interactions. They demonstrated their own enthusiasm for taking risks in sign-making; Susan and educator Gary explained in their interviews that this modelling of initiative and lack of fear helps to create a climate of risk-taking necessary for communication. Moreover, in this episode Susan and Marianne demonstrated a calm and lack of fear in the face of serious illness, allowing the importance of text-making and being with and for each other to focus their attention. As is typical for the classes, they also used talk to promote the creation of texts, and they moved Jimmy to be thoughtful in his narrative. As in the examples related to *Crowns*, the children were invited to be equal partners to the adults in creating signs and to contribute collectively to the communication of a collective message. The final text in this example reflects a shared effort and a vision that could never have been made possible without everyone who participated. The signing of each person's name reflected the contributionsof each.

Conclusion

This chapter considered the literacy learning opportunities that were created by the curricula in the intergenerational art classes at Blessed Mother and Picasso. My ability to identify these opportunities comes from an understanding of visual texts within a broad definition of literacy informed by theories such as multimodal literacy (e.g., Jewitt

& Kress, 2003). In part by providing opportunities to explore a sign system in detail and its relationship to other sign systems, curricula that include the visual provide many literacy learning opportunities as, for example, identified by Albers (e.g., Albers, 2001; Cowan & Albers, 2006). This learning is connected to expanded communication options, which have a number of potential implications including developing new ways of perceiving and being in the world (e.g., Albers, 2008). One might ask what can be created in the world when people's access to sign systems are enabled and expanded.

The art classes at Picasso were in large part modelled after those at Blessed Mother. Thus, all classes tended to follow the format of orientation, a catalyst for the day's project, a focus on technical elements, time to work on the project, and a completion component. Each interrelated component of class served a specific pedagogical purpose and engendered various learning opportunities germane to different communicational decisions (e.g., Jewitt & Kress, 2003). Also, the social nature of literacy was highlighted. Besides creating avenues for participants to witness the communicational possibilities of visual texts, they were invited to broaden and improve their communication: They were invited to consider the content of their communication, to learn and practise expressing themselves in a variety of ways, and to view or read other's ideas in visual form. Thus, visual texts provided a vehicle for participants to get to know each other and the world around them and beyond them. Also, because class insisted on production and on participants assisting each other with idea formation and technical tasks (e.g., cutting), participants explored their own and each other's strengths and worked with a common purpose. The projects were also inherently differentiated, as people with differing levels of skill and knowledge could participate and be challenged by the technical and subject matter aspects of the creation of text. Last, the public display of products in the building and in art shows gave purpose and audience to participants' work and solidified relationships by providing opportunities for family and friends to bear witness to the participants' relationships.

While this chapter has focused on components of a class, the next chapter considers how curricula built over a number of classes related to participants' communication and identity options.

Chapter Five

Opportunities Created by a Semiotic Chain in an Intergenerational Art Curriculum

The previous chapter considered learning opportunities in the art classes at Blessed Mother and Picasso and gave some understanding of the structure of a class that might optimize them. This chapter pushes the notion of multimodal pedagogy further by addressing a sequence of lessons in Picasso's art curriculum and what participants were able to do when they moved an idea from medium to medium. Specifically, the purpose of this chapter is to report insights gleaned from studying the curriculum, pedagogies, and practices of one aspect of a series of lessons within the novel circumstance of the art class at Picasso. The chapter narrows in on a chain of four lessons where participants were invited to communicate what they felt was special to them through various media. It addresses questions about the learning opportunities that were created in the class and what the fixing of participants' ideas within a semiotic chain said about their facility with communicative modes and media, interests, and identity options. Key findings include: when compared to the adults' work, the children's use of media was more elaborate, experimental, and less inhibited and their designs more complex; the content of the children's communication was multifaceted, and looked to the future while some of the adults' communication was constrained by limited identity options related to their position in the life course; and the class's multimodal pedagogies provided occasion for the exploration of modes and media with support for working through key communicational decisions.

Theoretical Framework Revisited

As discussed in Chapter One, multimodal social semiotic theory teaches that modes (i.e., "set[s] of resources people in a given culture can use to communicate" (Bainbridge, Heydon, & Malicky, 2009, p. 4)) each have their own *affordances* (Kress & Jewitt, 2003) or possibilities regarding what they can most easily express and how. For instance, in Chapter Four, I relayed how at Blessed Mother, adult participant Frieda told a story about being a child many years ago and falling into a flour bin. She followed up this story with a print, a visual text, of the event. Although the linguistic and visual modes each expressed the same story, a listener's or viewer's experience of the story would be different given the affordances of the modes.[1] There would be, for example, variations in terms of temporal experience: With oral storytelling, a tale cannot be experienced all at once, it must follow the temporally linear path of, for example, the syntax of the English language, and the experience is a cumulative one. In contrast, the visual mode allows an apprehension of a whole text at once, even if the viewer may choose at various points to zero in on a particular aspect of the print. Similar to the affordances of modes are the "facilities of media," which refer to "what is readily and easily possible to do with [a] medium" (Kress & Jewitt, 2003, p. 16). Thus, even within the same mode, the media will affect the communication, creating certain semiotic possibilities and restricting others. In sum, different modes and media afford different things, and these affordances affect the kinds of expressions people can produce and the meanings they can make from the expressions of others. Many multimodal literacy researchers (e.g., Pahl, 1999; Stein, 2008) have remarked on the numerous communicational possibilities provided by moving an idea across modes and media. The following narrative that I wrote when my son was twenty-eight months old illustrates some of these possibilities.

Skateboard Crash Scene:
A Spontaneous Semiotic Chain
My two-year-old son and I are making a puzzle containing intricate images forming a streetscape. When finished, Oliver zeroes in on a tiny scene of a boy on a skateboard colliding with a man carrying groceries; an apple from the grocery bag is mid-air. Oliver asks, "What happened, mum?" I explain in a

---

1 I do recognize that communication is multimodal. Thus, even in the oral story there is still a visual component in Frieda's use of gesture, but within the expression there was a dominant mode and for clarity it is on this my discussion focuses.

perfunctory way what I see, and Oliver presses me further: "Why, mum?"
In asking this question, Oliver invites an expansion of what we can see in the
puzzle. I tell a story of a boy skateboarding down the road minding his own
business when all of a sudden a man whose vision is obscured by a big grocery
bag runs into him. Both people go "crash," and an apple flies out of the bag. Ol-
iver asks me to repeat this story as he studies the image. He implores, "More!"
and he poses the questions he knows how to ask, "Why?" and "What?" which
I've sometimes taken, given the context and the limits of Oliver's language, to
mean "How?" After I tell the story numerous times, Oliver stands up, pre-
tends to skateboard and purposely bumps into me. I take this as another invi-
tation, this time to act out the collision scene. Taking Oliver's lead, I become
the grocery-carrying man who lands on the ground. After many goes, Oliver
runs to the door and says, "Need my skateboard." I bring the board in from the
porch then Oliver runs to the kitchen and says, "Need apple." We return to the
living room with these props and resume the drama, but the storyline becomes
more sustained with Oliver asking after my fall, "You okay?" The first time
he asks I say, "Yes," and we repeat the scene. The second time he pauses after
the question and asks, "You scrape your knee?" When I answer, "Yes," Oliver
responds with "Need bandaid!" Then he looks around and seems not to know
how to proceed. I mime opening and applying a bandaid, which he accepts and
repeats in the next iterations of the drama. All of this takes approximately an
hour, and my two-year old would have continued had his exhausted mother not
called for bedtime.

The preceding narrative contains some key observations from educational research about children and communication which I have discussed in Chapter One; namely, that children "research," make meaning
from, and express the world in myriad ways. Their exploration and
communication are "deliberate" and open to possibilities, because children have "not yet settled into the fairly narrow range of methods of
communication used by the adults around them" (Fraser & Gestwicki,
2002, p. 249). Language, it seems, is the culprit here. Thus, Oliver was
relatively free to move from mode to mode (e.g., image, gesture, and
language) in his receptive and expressive communication and could
take advantage of what each mode afforded. When Oliver, for instance,
wanted to expand the crash story from the visual information the puzzle provided, he turned to language, and when he reached the limits
of what this could do for him, he combined it with gesture with and
without props, rendering the communication multimodal. With each
new mode, the story became longer and more elaborate and showed

possible antecedents and consequences of the crash. This is an example of "transformation" (Pahl, 1999) or "transduction" (Kress, 1997) where the linked, collective literacy practices and products create a "semiotic chain" (Stein, 2008). As mentioned earlier, semiotic chains create important spaces for learning, creativity, and concept development (e.g., Kress, 1997; Pahl, 1999; Stein, 2008). Further, as in the instance with Oliver, they can help people to express themselves better, and they might also help people make better sense of others' expressions of others. Finally, given the link between literacy and identity as described in Chapter One, an increase in communication options is linked to an increase in identity options.

Context of the Semiotic Chain Curriculum

The study that undergirds this chapter was designed to "identify and gain analytic insight into the dimensions, dynamics" (Dyson & Genishi, 2005, p. 81) and consequences of the processes and products of an attempt to create expanded communication and identity options within the intergenerational art class at Picasso. Spotlighting four lessons that formed a semiotic chain, the study asked: What did participants do within the multimodal learning opportunities that were created by the class? What does the way participants chose to fix their ideas say about their facility with the various modes and media, their interests, and identity options? What are the consequences for educators hoping to offer children and older adults expanded communication and identity options?

The focal lessons centred on different media and all pertained to content that asked participants to draw on their "funds of knowledge" (Moll, 1992; i.e., the communicative and epistemic resources they brought with them to class) to represent visually what was special to them, moving from themselves to further out into the world:

- an ink and pencil on paper *Heartmap* (Bainbridge, Heydon, & Malicky, 2009) of what was figuratively in their hearts (as mentioned in Chapter Two, with lesson plan details in Appendix II);
- a collage and digital photography *Passport* to bridge a version of the self and the outside world (see Appendix XIII for lesson plan details);
- a *Collograph* of a home (See Appendix V for lesson plan details);
- a *Community Structures* project, which was a collective, three-di-

mensional, mixed-media construction of a special place in the community (as discussed in Chapter Four, with lesson plan details in Appendix IV).

In addition to the data collection methods that I employed in all the studies, which, I discuss in Chapter One, within the specific focus on the semiotic chain at Picasso, data collection attended to textual "processes and practices" (Pahl, 2009, p. 193) with me attempting to document participants' talk about what they were making as it was being made. I conducted short reflective interviews with the adults about their texts just following class or at the next class when reviewing the last day's projects. I held reflective interviews with the children towards the end of class as soon as they completed their texts. To begin the interviews I asked, "Please tell me about what you made," and then posed questions related to choices in materials, design, and content. Children in particular seemed eager to hold up their work and talk about what they had created. I also created reflective field notes (Dyson & Genishi, 2005) by audiotaping conversations I had with Wendy Crocker, the experienced early years teacher and research assistant who taught the semiotic chain lessons (and who attended all classes the art class during the year the semiotic chain lessons were taught).

The classes were based on the literacy theoretical framework and findings from the intergenerational learning literature and the previous intergenerational art class studies. Foremost:

• The semiotic chain lessons were couched in the overall intergenerational art class, because learning opportunities are most prevalent in contexts that support intergenerational *programming* rather than *activities* (see Chapter One).
• As intergenerational learning programming has been found to be most beneficial when participants are supported to cooperate and work towards "common goals" (Jarrott, 2007, p. 5), and programming should be "beneficial" and challenging to both generations (Friedman, 1997, p. 107), the lessons were designed so that participants with differing levels of skill and knowledge could be challenged.
• Classes capitalized on findings from earlier phases of the study (e.g., Heydon, 2007), including the benefits of supporting participants in their communicational decisions by organizing classes around the five main components outlined in the previous chapter.

- Finally, classes took advantage of strategies to expand identity options and depathologize old age and childhood by "focusing on what individuals contributed to the collective" and their "quality of life," insisting on "meaningfulness in interaction" and that those who worked in the program "confront their biases," and making "good on the notion that learning is lifelong" (Heydon, 2005, pp. 265–6).

Participants

Because this chapter focuses closely on specific participants, it is important here to introduce aspects of the people who were part of the class. Seven adults (six women; one man; mean age >80) and eight children (six girls; two boys; ages four–five years) participated. No participants identified themselves as part of a minoritized linguistic or ethnic group. No child's care costs were subsidized,[2] and all children attended the half-day kindergarten program at the neighbourhood school when they were not at Picasso. Most of the adults had been part of the class for three years and the children for two.

Learning Opportunities

To consider what participants did within the learning opportunities that were created in the class, I first had to consider what the actual opportunities were and how they were generated. In general, I found the opportunities to be similar to those detailed in the last chapter, in that they addressed all aspects of the communicational trajectory.

Given the plethora of data and the need to provide ample contextualization for it, the following discussion of learning opportunities primarily spotlights the second project in the semiotic chain, the passports, which invited participants to create a collage from digital photographs they took of each other, travel images, brochures, and coloured and textured paper. Participants were invited to represent themselves as well as a place somewhere outside in the world to signify the moving from self to the world.

---

2 Due to the stringent requirements for subsidies and the small number of them available, the fact that the children did not hold these spots does not necessarily mean that they were of high SES. Many lower income families did not have subsidized spaces.

Pedagogies for Passports Narrative

The tables in the classroom are placed in a large square, awaiting the participants for intergenerational art class. Several women arrive first, take their
seats, and look excitedly at the travel brochures that Wendy is placing on the
tables. Despite their enthusiasm, the women look at but do not touch the images. Wendy instigates interaction by picking up an image and joking to the
woman beside her, "You love Hawaii, Nora. There you are in Maui, or maybe
it's Oahu. I'd like to see you in one of those [grass] skirts." Nora laughs and the
women dig through the images, rejecting some, holding others up. The discussion bubbles, and once the children come they quickly join in on the talk. After
allowing time for interest to build, Wendy calls the class to order.

"Hello everyone ... Are you curious about what all of these pictures might be
for?" Everyone answers, "Yes!"

"Last week we travelled inside ourselves to think about maps of our heart.
This week we're going to be travelling in our imagination anywhere you would
like to go. So ... turn and look at the partner you'll be working with today. ...
Does everyone have a big partner to work with? Does everyone have a little
partner to work with?"

Next, child participant Lina points to a brochure and informs Wendy, "This
is where I'm going – to Disney World!"

"Where do you think that is, Lina?" asks Wendy.

When Lina looks as though she isn't sure, Wendy guides her to her partner.
This had the effect of building intergenerational conversation and allows Lina
to peruse more options before settling on Disney World. "So you and your
partner need to have some time looking at all of the things on the table and then
we'll talk about our job today," Wendy directs.

The partners continue the conversation. Lina notices the Eiffel Tower and
says, "I've been there!"

Nora looks at an image that she knows but cannot name. I whisper it to her
and she proudly instructs her partner, "The Taj Mahal, that's what that is."

Child participant Cara asks Wendy to explain the term "ball" as she looks
at an image of people dancing. She knows she had heard the word before but
wants to know more. Wendy responds with, "Ask your partner where that
might be."

Next, Wendy introduces the concept of passports by showing her Canadian
passport and a British passport for comparison. When one participant says she
was born in the United States, the talk turns to people's citizenships and where
they were born. Following this, Wendy gears the class to the media people will
be offered that day. She shares the term collage and gives examples.

"I have a very famous collage called The Snail," explains Wendy. "Do you *see the kind of snail shell that is curling around in this picture? This is by an artist named Matisse. Do you see how in collage we cut out pieces of paper and put them on top of each other? ... There are also some very famous artists that do illustrations for books and one is called Eric Carle. Eric Carle (1998) wrote a book called,* Catch Me a Star. *He actually teaches us not how to catch them, but how to [make] them. How many pieces do you think Eric Carle used to make his collage star? When you think you know, talk to your partner and see if that's what they got."*

In unison participants call "Five!"

After more viewing and discussing of collages, with many of the children stating they have Eric Carle books at home or school, Wendy models the creation of her own passport collage. She explains, "I had a chance to go through all of these pictures when I was at home, and I chose the place that I would love to go out of all of these." Wendy introduces the Kentucky Derby and discusses why it is special to her. She then helps people view the photo she has selected for the foundation of her collage.

"I just love this picture because it looked like the horse was coming right at me ... and look, there is even another horse coming up here second place." Wendy then offers that in her passport she will put a photograph of herself with the horse. She next helps the class think about the photo they will be taking of each other later to use in their own collages by saying, "[When I'm getting ready to go to the Kentucky Derby] do you think that I am going to have a grumpy face like [I do] in this passport? No! This is the kind of face that I am going to have!" Wendy pulls out a digital photo: "There I am ... big happy smile, cheering hooray because of course my horse is the one that is in first place."

Next, Wendy talks aloud about the decisions she needs to make and the process she will take to create her collage. She says she wants to dress her photograph and invites participants to witness how she considers context and the facilities of the media to do this. "I am going to put clothes on using collage ... So I found a beautiful dress," Wendy holds up a picture of a dress. "I really liked the colours that were in this dress, and I thought I would make myself some pants using that pattern. May I please have my glue stick there, Mr Roger? Are you the keeper of the glue stick?"

Child participant Roger laughs and passes over the tool. "I am making pants," Wendy explains as she cut. "Now you are going to take a lot more time than I am doing this, you are going to be careful and it will be so beautiful. Are you going to wear a skirt?" Wendy asks adult Bonnie, connecting what she was doing to what Bonnie would be doing. "You have to think about where you are going to be." Bonnie and her young partner whisper about where they might go. "There are my beautiful pants," announces Wendy as she turns her attention to another essential item for the Kentucky Derby, "What about a hat? Why would I need a hat? The Queen could be at this horse race and everyone at this horse race always wears a hat." Then Wendy models a design choice: "I found a hat, so I could wear that," she muses and shows an image of a hat. "Or I could make a hat, and I thought that this fabric was beautiful because I want everybody to see me at the horse race. So if I used this fabric for a hat ..."

Bonnie now asserts herself and nods, "You've GOT to wear a hat!"

Wendy next goes through every aspect of her wardrobe, including sunglasses, until her passport is finished, and it is time for the participants to create their own.

"So here is your job," Wendy declares. "Number one: Pick out where you are going to go." Wendy advises participants to work together to look at different options. "Then, [the practitioners] and I are going to come and tap you on the shoulder for taking pictures ... you can still have a look at all of these different things that are her to start to cut." Wendy signals to all of the available media (travel magazines and brochures, construction paper, and heavy white paper). "Okay, here we go!"

The passport narrative demonstrates how participants were prepared for the carrying out of the project: They were prompted to think about subject matter (e.g., self and the world) and provided catalysts for contemplating this, yet they could interpret the content in their own ways. Wasting no chance, the classes set out opportunities to consider the content even before the official start of class, invited exploration, and focused on the technical aspects necessary to carry out the creation of the texts that dealt with a variety of media (e.g., photography, collage). Further, what and how to communicate were grounded in context (e.g., what would be suitable to wear in a particular situation?).[3] The lesson took advantage of learning from other intergenerational art classes including those at Blessed Mother. For instance, Susan at Blessed Mother and our research team at Picasso had noticed that in collage projects many participants used images in literal ways (e.g., for a self-portrait project participants chose actual images of mouths to signify their own mouths in the collage). While the literal use of image could be the most

---

3 A critical reading of the situation would find that the context in the example and the particular notion of travel in the opening narrative refer to somewhat high socioeconomic status practices.

apt signifier in some instances, it might not be in all. Thus, to expand participants' options, Wendy modelled how an interesting texture in an image of a dress could be translated into a pair of pants which better suited her interests, and she showed how she could create a hat rather than use a premade one.

Learning opportunities were generated both from the intended curriculum and the participants themselves. For instance, one day the children were waiting for the adults to arrive, and the tables were covered in protective newsprint. One of the children started to "read" the news and the practice caught on. The children called to each other about what they had found in the paper and noticing the teachable moment, Wendy began a game of *I Spy* with images and features from the print.

Learning opportunities were also heightened by participants' curiosity about and engagement with the project tools and materials. The children in particular were fascinated by scissors. In their research Kress (1997) and Pahl (1999) identified the importance of cutting in early literacy and each time the children in the study were offered scissors I was reminded of this. At the beginning of the *Collograph* class, for example, the children were asked to go to the supply table and to return with materials for the adults. The children squealed with glee when they saw the scissors. They hurriedly returned to the tables and immediately started to play with them. Roger made cutting gestures in the air, and this caught on with all the other children doing similarly. Another child pretended to cut the newspaper covering the table. This started a new game with the children calling to each other, "Don't cut that!" and then pretending to cut things. Anna, another child participant, seemed mesmerized by her scissors, cutting in the air with her right hand, feeling the blades opening and closing with her left, and holding the scissors next to her ear to hear their movement. The scissors were so fascinating to the children that this was the first time in art class that I witnessed a participant's interest diverted from the project. Roger, for example, quickly cut out heavy paper to create a plate of a house for his collograph and then, finding that the negative space made the paper look like a pair of pants, he danced around holding them in front of his legs showing everyone. That cutting could create something unexpected was an interesting learning opportunity for Roger and not one I could have predicted.

Given the learning opportunities that were created when the intended curriculum was operationalized, key questions emerged regarding what participants choose to fix in their semiotic chains and how they choose to do this.

Fixing in the Semiotic Chain

Although within the studies as a whole captured many examples of
the different generations cooperating with each other in the process of
text-making (e.g., Heydon & Daly, 2008), many of which are recounted
in these pages, in closely reading the practices and products of the four-
lesson chain, there appeared to be a split between generations in relation to the communicational and identity options that they took up.
To illustrate, I turn to all of the semiotic chain study data and their
relationship to, in particular, the intentionality of the children and the
ways in which particular design characteristics in the products seemed
germane to the children and others to the adults.

Complex Interests

The children most dramatically demonstrated that they had interests
they wanted to communicate. The seriousness with which they approached their projects and the extent of the motivation of their signs
was obvious by how intensely they worked and how much they per-
sisted even when they had difficulty. Creating signs that could communicate their interests presented many design and technical challenges;
Anna's case is a good example of this.

In the *Passport* project Anna took great care in cutting out the digital
photograph of herself. The photograph was black and white, and her
long dark hair blended in with the background. In cutting out her photograph, Anna inadvertently sheared off some of the hair in the image
and did not like the results. Consequently, she tried to cut out the hair
that remained with the background and then glue it back on her head.
She attempted this in the air rather than putting the pieces down on the
background and assembling them that way. The result was thus like the
process, awkward. I watched Anna become increasingly frustrated and
asked, "What do you think?"

"It doesn't look good!" she answered with a frown and threw the
paper across the table.

"Well it's a good thing we have more than one copy of your picture,"
I offered and pointed to where she could get one. I reconnected Anna
with her adult partner, and we talked her through the cutting. She suc-
cessfully remedied the problem and was elated with the product.

In the *Collograph* project, Anna exhibited a similar interest in getting
the cutting right. She tried to cut a triangle whose base could exactly
match the side of a square she had cut, to fashion a plate that would

print the image of a house. The more the base of the triangle did not fit, the more she cut from it. Tongue sticking out of the corner of her mouth, brow furrowed, Anna concentrated deeply and became agitated by the challenge. Eventually, I demonstrated how Anna might solve the problem. As we worked together, I noticed Anna's desire to remedy the mismatch between the vision of what she wanted to create and her own facility with the materials. Other children exhibited a similar commitment to their projects and an interest in working through challenges. In contrast, the adults did not get visibly frustrated when they could not carry out a task such as cutting. When they reached an impasse with their work, the adults usually put their tools down, watched what the others were doing, and waited for assistance. Adults rarely appealed for help directly but rather, like participant Nora, simply laughed until someone (adult or child) responded. There seemed to be less of an attempt by adults to push the boundaries of their facility with the modes and media, although the data certainly support that they were interested in communicating; for instance, as mentioned, it was not rare for adults to stay after class to finish their texts. While there were differences in the way the generations demonstrated their interests and motivations in the creation of their texts, there were also differences in their products.

Complex Texts

In terms of visual grammars and complexity, there were no major discernible differences between children's and adult's texts in the *Collograph* and *Heartmap* projects.[4] With the collographs, every participant interpreted the theme of home by creating a house that was largely signified through a triangular roof and rectangular base (see Figures 5.1 and 5.2 for examples from child participant Sarah, and adult participant, Noreen). This shape for a house is definitely iconic and participants might have been referring to the example they were shown.

Participants also drew on iconic signs in their heartmaps. The figures of Roger's and Keith's maps in Chapter Two demonstrate an iconic heart shape which was used in all participants' texts, and the cluster

---

4 I could not make a comparison in the *Community Structures* project, given that it was a group project.

Figure 5.1 Sarah's Collograph

Figure 5. 2 Noreen's Collograph

of faces in Roger's heart is reminiscent in form of Keith's faces, all of which are also iconic within Western visual grammar (Fei, 2004).

Despite these similarities, the data indicate a definite divide in the *Passport* project between the visual aspects of the children's and adults' texts, with the children's texts appearing to be more visually complex. This seemed to be the result of the children pushing through the limits of their facility with the media to experiment and communicate interests. For example, perhaps as a response to Wendy's passport including sunglasses, many children wanted this accessory in their texts. This required a high degree of ingenuity. To make his sunglasses, Aaron glued two small, round pieces of white paper to the eyes of his photograph (see Figure 5.3). Making the circles was a task he struggled through. Before creating his "lenses," Aaron noticed that Roger had cut some circles: "Oh you made circles!" he exclaimed. Roger showed them off, and Aaron was intrigued, perhaps because making circles was difficult for him. Aaron tried to cut circles repeating, "I can't cut circles!" but with perseverance and using Roger's text as an example, he was finally successful. Aaron's lenses were followed by two large rectangles signifying the arms of the glasses: "They're the parts that go over your ears," he explained to Roger, who had asked what they were. Aaron extended the arms beyond the boundaries of the background so they were one of the most prominent aspects of the text and created an irregular border for the text as a whole.

Cara's text (Figure 5.4) was also the result of experimentation and challenging her facility with the media. Like the other children's texts, Cara's incorporated sunglasses. Adept at cutting triangles, Cara created lenses from two small triangles of dark, opaque paper, and she dealt with the problem of how one might "see" through opaque paper by locating the lenses at the corners of her eyes. In this way, she could signify sunglasses while allowing her eyes to still show. Cara further experimented with triangles by including two white triangles at her chin to denote the collar of a shirt. Cara was not wearing a shirt with a collar in her photograph, but she went up to Wendy, pointed at her collared shirt, and asked, "What is that?" Wendy explained that it was a collar, after which Cara promptly added the triangles to her text and then proudly showed Wendy.

Child participant Eden found a different way to fashion eyewear (see Figure 5.5) by placing one small square and triangle, each its own colour, on top of her eyes with a sliver of paper glued between to form a bridge. The complexity of Eden's text continued. Rather than build her

Figure 5.3 Aaron's Passport

Figure 5.4 Cara's Passport

Figure 5.5 Eden's Passport

Figure 5.6 Lina's Passport

collage on top of a standard sheet of rectangular paper, Eden cut multiple pieces of paper and glued them together to create an irregularly shaped background. She then superimposed the image of a hula dancer over a surfer on the top piece and carried cut-out images in a downward direction with her own portrait sticking out to the left.

Other details that added complexity to the children's texts included that all the children dressed their photographs. To do this, they chose textured rather than literal images: Aaron created a psychedelic shirt and red hat, Cara fashioned a little body jutting from the side of her head so as not to disrupt the background image, and Eden made herself a hat reminiscent of what one might wear to a birthday party. Other details included were a small suitcase Cara made from textured paper and a shirt decorated with a cut-out of husky dogs which gave Lina's text (see Figure 5.6) another layer of intricacy, as the northern dogs were not immediately semantically compatible with her surroundings. Also interesting is that Lina explained that when she was dressing the arm in her photograph, she made the sleeve too short, so she superimposed a long arm over it and extended it beyond the frame of the passport. Her solution to this design and facility problem resulted in an increased visual complexity to her text.

In sum, the children's interests drove their text-making. They all, for instance, shared an interest in communicating themselves with sunglasses, and they solved the quandary of how to do this in unique ways. Further, in the absence and sometimes eschewing of literal details (e.g., with psychedelic shirts and suitcases), the children chose to experiment, thereby pushing the boundaries of their facilities with the media. The children's inventive practices resulted in their texts sharing particular qualities such as visual complexity.

Conventional Texts (?)

In the *Passport* project, the children's texts when compared to the adults' demonstrated more overlapping of materials and images, more cutting, less literal use of images, and more experimentation with the media. The designs were more elaborate, resulting in more visually intricate texts. In contrast, the adults' texts seemed more conventional. They mostly avoided finicky cutting and overlays, opting instead for large images laid beside each other (e.g., Mona's Passport, Figure 5.7). The exception to this was Nora, who chose to intricately cut out trees, a hula dancer, and her own image (see Figure 5.8). Still, the cut-outs were different from those of the children in that they followed more conventional design elements. For example, the boundaries of the images dictated where Nora cut (e.g., the palms of the tree were each cut along the line of the image). Also, like all the other adult texts, Nora selected a frame for her text that was predetermined by the borders of the standard piece of paper she used (rectangular-shaped; 8½" × 11").

While the adults' decision to avoid cutting could have been the result of fine motor limitations, participants were used to receiving help from each other and the instructors to solve conceptual or technical problems (e.g., Heydon, 2005). Additionally, even in the face of technical limitations, the children's texts were more complex. Thus, the relative simplicity of the adults' texts could have been a design choice, perhaps connected to conventionality as a degree of socialization or even as an outcome of a lack of experimentation as they had more experience with perspective, proportion, and manipulating the media. Also, as mentioned, adults were less inclined to push beyond their facility with the media.

Figure 5.7. Mona's Passport

Figure 5.8 Nora's Passport

Collective Visuals

The *Community Structures* project where children and adults worked together in groups to create one text per group is interesting to consider juxtaposed against what might be thought of as single-authored texts like the passports. The two groups on which I had permission to report[5] consisted of child participant Lina and adults Nora and Mona (Group 1) and child participants Lauren and Aaron and adult Keith (Group 2). Group 1 collectively decided that the special community structure they wanted to build was Picasso (see Figure 5.9), and Group 2, with the decision coming from Aaron, decided to build the neighbourhood school where Aaron and the other children attended half-day kindergarten (see Figure 5.10). Trends I identified were that all the participants seemed particularly challenged by the media and the attempt to create a text in three dimensions, which coincided with their struggles to work together in a group in a way where all participants were equal, contributing members.

Group 1

Group 1 begins their work in collegial, cooperative terms with Lina being somewhat in charge given her ownership of the pen she is using to draw a blueprint. Lina easily draws a blueprint of Picasso after the group decides this is what they want to build and then asks Nora and Mona to spell their names so that she could write them all on the print signaling that this is a collective.[6] Lina makes the decision to put the women's names first. She requests that Mona spell her name and when she is finished with the writing, she turns to Nora and matter of factly states, "How do you spell your name?"

When Nora's name is down Nora responds with, "Right! Now what about your name? Yours goes next."

Lina responds by writing her name and spelling it out loudly so the women know how to spell it. In this early time all participants smile and seem to be enjoying themselves. This overall easiness and good mood, however, does not seem to extend into the three-dimensional component of the project. In the next

---

5 Note that there were four groups, but on this day I did not have permissions for the children in two of the groups.

6 For anonymity's sake, I had to block out the names on the image of the plan in Figure 5.9, but they were prominently written in black marker on the upper left side of the paper with Lina's being last.

Figure 5.9 Lina, Nora, and Mona's Picasso Building

Figure 5.10 Aaron, Lauren, and Keith's School

phase of constructing the text, all participants struggle with the media, and the group dynamics change to being more of a push and pull of labour with decisions and the physical responsibilities for the making of the text belonging to individuals rather than the collective.

At first, Lina seems to claim the project but also expresses confusion as to exactly how to proceed. After the blueprint, Lina stares at the pile of materials but doesn't move and neither does either of the women do anything except smile and giggle.

Wendy tries to light a fire under the group, "Oh, look at your blueprint! So have you architects talked about the kinds of things that you need to build that?"

"No" answers Lina.

"Okay. What's the next step?" Wendy poses to the group. Nora laughs.

Wendy is in high demand by all participants in the class and is being asked questions by two other groups while trying to support Group 1. Perhaps one of these interruptions prompts Nora to finally realize they need to do some problem solving on their own, and she asks Lina, "What colour do you want it [the roof]? There is paper over there that you can get – some different coloured paper if that's what you want." And with this comment, she demonstrates that the text at this point is about what Lina wants.

Lina in turn takes up the ownership and rather than work with her group approaches Wendy, "I want a colour of paper for my roof."

Wendy helps but then redirects Lina to her group, saying to them all "Did you show Nora and Mona – a red roof, is that okay?"

Mona reinforces Lina as director: "Is that what you want Lina? Okay."

When Lina finally returns to her group with her paper, the three cannot figure out how to make a three-dimensional roof from a flat piece of construction paper. Mona finally suggests Lina cut a triangle out of the paper, but when this is done, they are as unhappy as the roof is flat. Eventually, the women start to provide more direction to Lina, in fact bordering on ordering her what to do. They request that Lina go to the material pile and collect some boxes which, unlike the construction paper that they cannot get to work, are already three-dimensional. Lina consents but is obviously getting frustrated.

From the table, Nora directs Lina in the collection of boxes: "There ... for the chimney. Bring one over for the chimney." When Lina returns with the box, there is a piece sticking off about which Nora asks Lina, "Do you want to cut [it]?"

Lina is not in a good mood and is not taking direction well. "It's supposed to be on there."

Mona says to Lina, "You should put the roof on."

"That's the roof" Nora answers laughing… How do you put the chimney on?"

Mona answers, "Use the box. See you put the chimney on there," and she directed Lina where to locate the chimney.

Exasperated, Lina replies, "Oh, I don't know!"

Nora says, "See it's the chimney … it don't go on the bottom of the house. It goes on the roof. The chimney goes on the roof. So how big do you want the chimney?"

"I don't know," Lina whines.

Mona selects a little gift box which is smaller than the box Lina is working with. Norma laughs, "Oh that's better! That's better – yeah." Mona laughs too, though Lina frowns.

Overall the trio struggles with their text and how to negotiate working together. At one point the group succeeds in piling boxes on top of each other unfastened. Wendy comes and suggests, "There are all kinds of things on that table that you might want to use to stick them together. There's elastics, there's paperclips, there's glue … all kinds of things."

Lina is obviously frustrated. She appeals to Wendy, "Don't really like it … I don't really like it."

Wendy asks, "So it there a way to change it?" Perhaps without realizing the extent of Lina's frustration and the limits of Mona and Nora's ability to work with the media, Wendy redirects Lina to the women, "So talk to the architects … how could you change that?"

Lina explains her dissatisfaction to her group, maybe referring to the piling of boxes: "You just put different things on it."

Eventually, together, although not smoothly, the group finishes the text. Mona takes over the scissors and makes a door, Lina adds a birdbath, and Nora adds a patio (which is signified by a small box wedged under the bottom of the overall building). While the text is complete, it is a hard-won battle. Nora and Mona laughed throughout the process, which is reminiscent of the kind of fun I have documented in the other projects, but Lina did not smile or laugh and displayed her frustration with the process.

Group 2

As the following narrative suggests, Group 2 also struggled with the media and did not take up wholly cooperative and egalitarian roles in the creation of the text.

Child Aaron immediately takes on or is designated by adult Keith to take on the dominant role in the group, deciding on the subject matter for the text (his school), how construction will go, and who will do what.

Immediately on being set off to work, Keith looks at Aaron and says, "So what are we building, Aaron?"

Aaron is already underway designing a school without consulting any of his group members, "It is a school building." Perhaps not understanding that this is to be a collectively owned text, Aaron invites Keith in to what he positions as his project, "Want to help me make a building? Now it's time for the door."

At this point child participant Lauren has been completely excluded. Keith seeks to remedy this, although not to ascribe co-ownership over the project, "Can Lauren help?" Noticing that Lauren is not even fully positioned at the table where the project is happening, I intervene and set her up physically.

Aaron consents to Lauren's involvement with the directive to her, "You can make a window."

When Lauren doesn't move, Keith seeks clarification from Aaron, again bowing to his authority, "You want to make a window up here?"

Aaron answers, "Hey, that's not a window!

Keith follows through with making a window where he thinks one should go, challenging Aaron's absolute authority, and I get involved to try to help with the hoped for collaborative nature of the project, inviting Lauren in and asking what everyone thinks needs to be included. Aaron immediately responds with, "I think we should have a water fountain."

Keith offers, "I think that we should have a flagpole."

Aaron rejects this and asserts his knowledge of the school over Keith's saying, "Hey, you haven't seen in it!"

Figuring that in this close-knit community where people usually spend their lives in the neighbourhood, I say, "I bet Keith's seen [the school]."

Adrian retorts, "But he hasn't gone in it."

"I don't know... ask him" I suggest.

Aaron turns to Keith, "Have you gone into [the] school? What does it look like? I know what it has in... a water fountain!" Aaron's tone at this point is more astonishment at the notion that Keith might know what he perceives to be his school and is less autocratic. Keith laughs.

I now asked of the group, "Well what do you think of Keith's suggestion of the flagpole?"

Aaron insists on the importance of the water fountain, but once he sees there is room for both, he wants that plus a chimney. He cannot, however, figure out how to attach the long fountain, flagpole, and chimney tubes to the pizza box he is using for the frame of the school without the whole building toppling over. He puts the tubes in place, directs Keith to hold on to them, then proceeds to work on the rest of the structure. When Keith cannot convince Aaron that he needs to create a proper base for the school (in response to this suggestion, Aaron cries, "Nooooo!"), he spends the rest of the class holding on to these tubes, which he does with a good-natured spirit and a smile on his face. Lauren, however, has no input into any of the building at any point. When the school finally goes on display in the room, Aaron props it up against the window so that it will not fall over.

What to Signify

Within and across all projects in the semiotic chain, I identified certain trends in terms of what participants chose to signify in the points of fixing in the chains. With the exception of the passports, elements common to people's immediate environments generally figured prominently (e.g., Aaron's structure signifying his school; the children's collographs being their houses; the adults referring to the children in their heartmaps) with some adults having more difficulty than other participants in knowing what to include.

Regarding content choices, the *Heartmap* project was the class's first invitation to express their attachments and funds of knowledge. As mentioned, children and adults both included each other in their texts, with Keith and Roger being an excellent example. Despite the thoughtfulness and quickness with which Roger and Keith decided how to fill their maps, a couple of the adults in particular found what to signify difficult. During the process of creating the maps, I noticed the children were talking far more than the adults. After a child told her adult partner, Mona, that she was putting her family in her map, Mona said, "I don't know who would be on my map, because I live alone." Mona, who lived at Picasso with over one hundred other people, was obviously speaking figuratively. Even following the catalyst portion of class that had addressed the question of what to signify, Wendy noticed that some adults needed prompting and indicated that chocolate had a special place in her heart. She turned to Mona and adult participant Beth and said, "There is chocolate in my heart."

Beth quickly turned to her heart saying, "Oh, I like that one!" and child participant Samantha followed suit with, "Yeah, me too!"

Mona still sat, searching for something to include. I asked, "How about you, Mona, what will be in your heart?"

She chuckled nervously and said, "Not much these days ... Well, I enjoy going out for a walk, and I enjoy coming down here to draw with the children."

Figure 5.11 Mona's Heartmap

"There you go, that will be in your heart, eh?" I offered.

"And calls from my son ... which are rare," followed by another nervous laugh.

I then turned to the child working beside Mona and sought to make a connection: "Mona said that you're going to be in her heart." When Mona's map (see Figure 5.11) was completed, the children were not included, and most of the contents were solitary activities: the word "TV" held one of the prime areas of the heart (the upper left corner), with a single chair beside it; followed by "reading" with an image of a book; "sleeping," with the image of a single bed and one pair of slippers beside it; "walking," accompanied by a single person; a visual and written list of food, culminating in "dinner," with a single place setting represented; "family," which was the only inclusion of others with the space the item occupied on par with the other elements; and "car ride."

Nora's affect during the creation of the heartmaps definitely seemed more jovial than Mona's (i.e., more smiling, laughing, talking, and interacting with everyone), but when I asked her, "Tell me what's in your

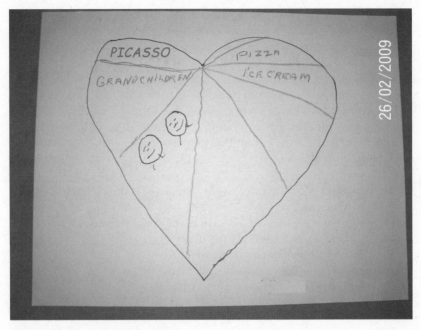

Figure 5.12 Nora's Heartmap

heart," she replied, "Just my grandchildren, that's about it. Everybody else is dead."

"But I see Picasso in your heart too" I mentioned (which was a simple word written in red in capital letters on the upper left side of the heart).

Nora responded, "Uh huh," but did not elaborate.

In the end, Nora's map (Figure 5.12) showed an array of divisions radiating from the peak of the heart with the words, "PICASSO,"[7] "GRAND-CHILDREN," "PIZZA," and "ICE CREAM" in each. Two sections were entirely blank and a fifth showed two smiling faces, the children from the art class who had worked with Nora that day.

The difficulty these women had with their heartmaps raised many questions for me, such as: What is the connection between the women's difficulties with what to signify and their own identities as older adults

---

7 Note that the actual site name is blocked out for anonymity.

living in a retirement home? Were their identity options restricted with their options of what to signify? On a positive note, though, that the children and adults chose to call on their community of friends from art class to fill their hearts showed the importance of the project in their lives, gave them something to signify, and we hoped allowed them identities they might not otherwise have been able to access. It is telling too, that even though they experienced a great challenge with the community structures project, Group 2 opted to signify Picasso. In the debriefing about the project and their structure, Nora, Mona, and Lina said the following:

RACHEL: So, Nora, Mona, and Lina ... can I ask what is this building? Tell me about your building.
LINA: This is Picasso. This is her house (indicating Nora) and this is her house (indicating Mona), and this is my day care.
RACHEL: So ... everybody is part of this building.
LINA: And Art Class! (Lina signals to a part of the structure.)
RACHEL: And Art Class ... right there in the middle window.
Nora and Mona laugh and laugh.

Passports

The Passport project was designed for participants to move from themselves outward into the world and provided some of the most interesting data related to participants' interests and identity options. For this reason, this section deals with this project in some detail. Participants' initial interests from the catalyst portion of class were present in the products although sometimes in unexpected ways. In the passports, Nora's text highlighted Hawaii, the first place she talked about in class. While the children were originally intent on Disney World as they were perhaps drawing on ubiquitous Disney Discourses, they did not move this interest directly into their final texts. Instead, as Wohlwend (2009) found to be the case when the girls in one kindergarten classroom were allowed to play with the idea of Disney across modes and media, the original relationship that existed between their identities and Disney morphed into new storylines and possibilities. In the intergenerational art class the girls' early, literal interest in Disney World became a more generalized interest in palaces, castles, and balls: Cara superimposed her image over Buckingham Palace; Lina, who had a discussion with Cara and adult participant Noreen about balls and who had initially

been interested in the Eiffel Tower, did include the tower in her passport, but the most prominent image in her text became an ancient castle.
This transformation of interests followed its own microsemiotic chain.
Interests began as stories of travelling to Disney World between participants, became visual texts in the passports, then following the creation
of the passports, Lina, Cara, and Eden told elaborate stories to each other about their texts, and these stories featured them as princesses. The
translation of interests across modes also happened in other instances
when, for example, Cara told a story about the woman in the grass skirt
in Eden's text. This woman was the same person, she said, as the one
who was scuba diving and then playing volleyball. The woman, Cara
explained, just kept "falling down the page" moving from activity to
activity. The images in Eden's text were indeed organized vertically in
this order.

The children enthusiastically chose multiple places to represent in
their passports, places that were not random but could, as demonstrated through their storytelling, form a coherent narrative. Children
also used constructs in their narratives like, "I am going to go" and "I
will go," suggesting looking towards the future. Hence, the children's
texts communicated identities of possibility and perhaps "hope" as
they were a "predisposition toward action" (Simon, 1992, p. 4). In their
narratives the children additionally highlighted what they knew about
the images (e.g., Lina's naming of the Eiffel Tower), and they sought
detailed information about what they did not know (e.g., Roger highlighted L'Arc de Triomphe in his passport, and he wanted to know the
structure's exact name and where it was; Cara was similarly interested
in Buckingham Palace). The concern over detail is understandable if the
children interpreted the project as being a plan for action.

Some of the adults, however, seemed to interpret the project as being
about reminiscences or wishes related to unfulfilled desires. In contrast
to identities of possibility, many of the adults communicated identities
based on "wishes," which are impotent in that they do not include "the
dimension of activity" (Simon, 1992, p. 3). Adult participant Mona's
passport is such an example (see Figure 5.7).[8] During the making of her
text Mona interacted little with her child partner. When I asked about
her passport, she told me about life on the prairies in the 1920s.

---

8 Although Mona gave me permission to use her data, I have blacked out the eyes on
   her image due to the sensitive nature of her narrative.

"The roads were just tracks ... and we had a car, you had to put it up on blocks over the winter, and [use a] horse and buggy, and my aunt and uncles' family lived not too far from us, and they used to bring the kids to school in a sleigh. They used to pick my sister and I up and we'd go to the little one room school, but my mother didn't like out West. She didn't like the wind and the dust so she talked my father into coming back east. I was eight years old at the time, but I remember lots of it ... my one sister went back and saw the old place, and I have a cousin that goes back every so often and visits."

"You've left a little piece of your heart out West?" I wondered.

"Well, I suppose. I was just young then, and it was home to me."

Shortly thereafter, I spoke with Noreen about her passport and its images of Venice. Mona listened in and said to Noreen, who was in her sixties, "You're still young; you can do it." Mona then became sad as she talked about how she had liked to travel until her husband became ill and they had to abandon trips they had planned.

I read in Mona's collage her interest in her past with the lupines and hydro wires which she identified with western Canada. In reference to her text, Mona said she wanted to be drinking wine on the deck of a boat looking at beautiful flowers, all reminiscent of her travel days with her husband. She also explained that she included the train, because it was "going fast." Mona then became teary saying she "never got to go anywhere anymore." There is a tension in trying to read Mona's texts semiotically; there is at once optimism and sadness. The optimism is communicated through the vertical orientation to her design, which is reinforced by the tall hydro tower, building on the top of a mountain, and upright lupines, the smile on her face, the sunny scene in the bottom left corner, and the speed of the train. The sadness is communicated by the fact that Mona faces to the left, her back turned against the tower of her childhood memory. Also, the verticality of the text could be challenged by a horizontal orientation that is created by a left to right lying down of the cut-out pieces. Sadly, the sense of an identity of loss wins out when one considers the narrative that surrounds Mona's text. This example speaks to the need to consider the practice *and* product of a text in its reading.

Other adults negotiated the identity issues associated with aging in different, more explicitly hopeful ways. Noreen, the youngest adult in the class, likely interpreted the project in a similar way to the children. When I asked her to tell me about her passport she said, "It is Italy that I *want* to go to." Noreen interacted a great deal with others during class and worked intensely on her text, even opting to stay late to finish. Like Mona, Bonnie expressed that she would not be travelling anymore because of her age; however, akin to the children's texts, hers was a plan for the future. Bonnie's passport included young, smiling people frolicking in the water, a train signifying the trip she would like to take "through the Rockies to British Columbia," and a ship to travel to "the glaciers," with a photo of her smiling towards the top right of the layout: "These are the places," Bonnie told Wendy, "that I'll have to leave for the *next* time." Bonnie laughed throughout the entire class and like Noreen interacted with others and took care in the making of her passport. Thus, dissimilar to Mona's experience, Bonnie's text-making was joyous, and the identity she communicated was forward-looking.

Conclusion

The literature relates some of the opportunities for creativity, expression, and concept-development that can come from the process of transduction, the movement of an idea across semiotic modes and/or media. Pedagogies designed to capitalize on this process are still in a nascent stage; so too is the understanding of what children and adults do within them. This chapter provided some analytic insights into what participants did within the multimodal learning opportunities that were created by specific intergenerational art class, how they chose to fix their ideas within the semiotic chain, and what this says about their facility with various modes and media, interests, and identity options. A key finding was that where participants were in the life course affected their texts in terms of what they intended to signify and how they signified it. The notion that children may be more open to communicative possibilities than adults was reinforced as some of the children's texts were more visually complex than the adult's. Moreover, the children experimented far more with the media. This is an important observation that rejects an emergent literacy framework that sees children's meaning-making as a lesser version of adult meaning-making. Instead, it gives substance to an early literacy perspective where children's literacies are "valid in their own right" (Gillen & Hall, 2003, p. 10). Finally, the children appeared to have expansive identity options with texts that communicate a forward movement and looking. This was not always the case with some of the adults, whose practices and texts instead showed fewer attempts to push the boundaries of their facility with the media, more conventionality, and somewhat more restrictive identities.

Despite these last findings, the data do indicate that the semiotic chain lessons created learning opportunities and are potentially fertile examples for the development of other multimodal pedagogies. Key is exposure to and occasion for the exploration of diverse modes and media with support for working through the communicational trajectory. Future inquiries, however, might consider how to foster children's hundred languages while keeping their facility with various modes and media active through the life course so that adults too may have broad communicative options and opportunities for the creativity that can be fostered through multimodal communication. Given the reciprocal relationship between communication and identity, one might also inquire if and how increased communication options might open up identity options, so that aging need not be equated with narrowed identities. This question of opening possibilities for people as they are confronted with the limits of the life is the subject of the next chapter.

Chapter Six

Living, Death, and Dying in Intergenerational Learning Programs

A Narrative Introduction

The intergenerational art class at Picasso is now over. The supplies are packed away and all the children and adult participants have left, yet June remains. Well into her eighth decade, June sits in her shorts, with snow falling behind her outside the window. Always an active person, June prefers shorts even in cold weather because they allow her, as she's explained to me, to be unencumbered. One of her daily rituals involves moving, these days with more difficulty than she'd like, around the grounds of Picasso where she can access Picasso Child's playground. On these walks June is able to observe and talk with the children who share art class with her every Thursday. I've witnessed the children on the playground spot June in the cold weather in her shorts, and children like Ethan and Amber have triumphantly cried her name as they smiled big, excited grins, then giggled at her bare legs while comparing them to their own covered ones.

On this particular Thursday, in the wake of art class, June looks at a line drawing she's just finished (see Figure 6.1), and she begins to explain it. Pointing to the small smiling faces that she's tucked into corners throughout her drawing, June names them her "voices" and says: "These are the voices from my past and those of the children who call to me from the play area. I am very aware of how limited our time is and how we are connected to the past and to the future. These are the voices that surround me and remind me that we are here for just a brief time."

Shortly after this exchange, June did not arrive with the others for art class, and the children repeatedly asked where she was. As June had been ill, I wondered if today was the day June would finally not make it to class. Then, relief: Greeted with smiles all around, June entered the room, took her seat, and joined in the text-making.

Figure 6.1 June's Drawing

Whenever I have been a witness to young and old coming together for learning – formally, as in the case of intergenerational art class or informally, such as when I learned at my Nonna's knee--I have been reminded of the Japanese aesthetic of *mono no aware*. Introduced by eighteenth-century Japanese scholar Motoori Norinaga, mono no aware has been translated as "the sorrow of human existence," and as "a sensitivity to things" (Keene, 1988, p. 86), meaning an apprehension of "the simultaneous existence of beauty and sadness in life" (Dodson, 1993, p. 2). This sensitivity "usually takes the form of realizing the transience of something beautiful" or responding to "the beauty of forms" that are "poised on the brink of dissolution" (Berry, cited in Dodson, 1993, p. 3). The cherry blossom is the quintessential motif of mono no aware.

While mono no aware is indeed a very Japanese aesthetic, it is not "uniquely a Japanese sensibility" (Hirakawa, 2005, p. 496); many cultures have ways of describing the poignancy of the transient or the impermanent. It is this aesthetic that strikes me every time I am witness to young and old together, particularly within the context of an intergenerational learning program. The power of this aesthetic and related truth, that learning in an intergenerational situation is literally learning at the ends of life, shadows the visual texts and relations in the previous five chapters, and it is in search of bringing this into view that I now turn to wonder about the place of death and dying, as elements of life, within intergenerational curricula. Further, the contemplation of life, dying, and death is of critical importance in any curriculum, perhaps most evidently in a curriculum built around visual text, where there is an emphasis on relationship building and an attempt to expand people's communication and identity options. Thus, this chapter contemplates the treatment of death and dying in the programs as they may be related to people's communication and in turn their identity options and abilities and desires to forge relationships within and across generations.

Death and Dying in the Literature

One of the cornerstones of intergenerational learning curricula is the need to teach children about aging (Basman et al., n.d.; Lyons, Newman, & Vasudev, 1984; Newman, 1985). There is very little mention, however, of *how* or even *if* such curricula should approach the topic of death and dying. In a literature review of death and dying and intergenerational learning curricula, research assistant, Wendy Crocker and I were only able to find cursory mention of the topic. Hawkins & McGuire (1999) referred to the need to educate adolescent participants on "dealing with loss and grief" (p. 24), although Seefelt (1989) found "lessons on death and dying designed to change adolescents' attitudes toward older adults did not appear to be effective" (p. 190). Nothing was mentioned in these publications about the topic and young children. As for young children, McDuffie (1989), in a one-page entry in an intergenerational handbook entitled *What If Someone Dies?* recommended that when talking to children about death and dying one should not use theology, religion, or euphemisms. She then suggested some children's literature on the topic. Nothing was mentioned beyond this, including how to frame the literature. In the same handbook, Cook (1989) addressed the question of whether young children should be shielded from knowledge about death. Again, in just a one-page entry, she surmised that children should be given some facts about death within their developmental level "since death is a part of life ... [and] it may actually be easier for a child to first learn about [death] during an IG visit than to suddenly be faced with the loss of a close loved one" (p. 25). What these facts were, however, was not included. Barring any sustained or in-depth discussion of children and death and dying in intergenerational curricula, there was some scant discussion in an intergenerational guidebook by one of the leaders in the field. This was perhaps the most substantive statement on the topic we could find:

> Don't worry about sparking children's questions on the topic of illness or death, because at the preschool age, their interest is typically matter-of-fact and not fraught with emotional distress. They are curious and the images that surround them on a daily basis should reflect the outside world as realistically as possible so that they can ask questions and become comfortable with individuals who are physically different than themselves. (Kaplan et al., 2003, p. 20)

In another literature review focusing on curriculum on death and dying for young children in general, Wendy and I noticed that sparse attention was given to the subject from the field of education with most authors and publications being from health-related disciplines (e.g., nursing and medicine; e.g., Cole, 2001; MacGregor, 2007; Zolten & Long, 2006). Additionally, the bulk of attention to the topic happened at least twenty years ago (e.g, Childs & Wimmer, 1971; Moseley, 1976; Ryerson, 1977; Hare, Sugawara, & Pratt, 1986; Hare & Cunningham, 1988). In the professional literature in education the question of death and dying and young children is most obviously on the minds of educators *when* someone dies, as evidenced by a day care centre director who wrote in to the teachers' "lounge" in the journal *Young Children* (Turcin, 2009) to ask how to deal with the death of a child in her centre. Two other educators were invited to respond to the question through short, three-paragraph letters that provided advice from their own practice. This included the recommendations to bring in a counselor, offer opportunities for texts of remembering such as the making and viewing of scrapbooks, cards, and posters, and to avoid one's personal views on what happens after life (Kraut, 2009; Seachrist, 2009). Of the seven related *Young Children* articles linked to the lounge (Christian, 1997; Cummins, 2004; Essa & Murray, 1994; Greenberg, 1996; Hopkins, 2002; Sandstrom, 1999; Wood, 2008) all offer sound support for children's grief and/or responses to the loss of a loved one (including a pet). The link to children's literature contains suggested picture books that similarly confront the issue of death as a special event or topic;

that is, the majority of books contain stories about when a particular person dies (e.g., *The Tenth Good Thing About Barney*, Viorst, 1971). The exceptions are books like *Lifetimes: The Beautiful Way to Explain Death to Children* (Mellonie & Ingpen, 1983) and *The Fall of Freddie the Leaf: A Story of Life for All Ages* (Buscaglia, 1982) which chronicle the lifecycles of aspects of the natural world so that death is positioned as a normal, natural part of life. Most of the books and articles, however, with their focus on grief and response, do not offer recommendations for how death might be positioned within early childhood education and care curricula in general.

Given the gap in the literature, that intergenerational programming happens with people who are at the ends of life, and that the data from the studies presented up to this chapter hint that issues around death and dying, in particular in relation to adults' identity options might affect curriculum and relationship-building, I felt a need to revisit the data from the intergenerational studies to consider this particular topic. For this chapter I therefore returned to the studies at Blessed Mother, Watersberg, and Picasso to ask:

- In what ways (if any) did the intended curriculum (i.e., what was planned to be taught) of the intergenerational programs in all three sites represent or deal with death and dying?
- In what ways (if any) did issues related to death and dying enter the operational curriculum (i.e., what actually got taught)?
- How do the findings relate to the children's learning opportunities, opportunities for interaction with the elders, and in the ways in which they were positioned?

Findings

The Intended and Operational Curricula

The intended intergenerational learning curricula at Blessed Mother, Picasso, and Watersberg were developed by various parties. Generally, at Blessed Mother, the early childhood educators were responsible for the curriculum with the exception of art class which was taught by the intergenerational art teacher. Recreation therapists and educators were expected to assist during class. At Watersberg and Picasso, educators and recreation therapists were supposed to share the development and implementation of intergenerational curricula. The intended curricula of the programs in all three sites did not deal in any way with death and dying. These topics, however, did enter the operational curricula through adult participants dying, the ways the institutions dealt with the deaths, and by the faculty and elders' own thoughts, feelings, and sense of preparedness for the topic.

There were elders in all three sites who did die. The greatest number of deaths occurred at Blessed Mother, with eight participating elders dead by the second year of the study. Only this site told the children when an elder died, although there was no consistent protocol. Educator Gary explained what happened when two residents died and the deaths were included in the building's general morning announcements over the loudspeaker.

This week, eight o'clock [a.m.], we're starting breakfast ... and they start the prayers, which is fine, you know, but they get into this we need to pray for two residents who just died. And that's great. Kids need to know about death, but now on the breakfast conversation table one kid says, "They died. Did you hear that? They died. Oh, no!" when they heard the persons' names. Now, what if it was like Frieda [a favourite adult participant] or someone really dear to us. And that was the first thing they heard? Not through us or a parent or someone telling them through compassion. What if we are sitting and all of a sudden, "We are going to pray for Frieda who just died"? So I went to Jane [the Generations Together Learning Center director] and Sister Mary and Sister is touchy because she ... was in that broadcasting. And I'm sitting with Sister and telling Jane the story. And Sister hadn't heard the story yet, and I'm telling Jane. The first thing, Jane is like laughing, thinking, "Oh, that's funny," and Sister's like, "Oh, that's OK. Kids need to know about death." You're right, Sister they do need to know. Now, Jane help me here. Stop your laughing, 'cause you think you put me in a funny situation for the moment. Kids need to learn things, but in the proper way and time. And I was trying to ask Jane, could you please talk to that person who does the announcements, and please ask them to use a word like deceased, passed, something to where if I choose to explain a situation it'll be my choice at that time in the morning. And I can't tell the [institution] you have to do this, but it'll sure help me as an educator if they could use a different word. If the kids are smart enough to figure it out – great. But just that they [on the loudspeaker] scream "DIED"!

The inclusion of the children in this announcement did not appear to have forethought, and it did not spark any change in the intended curriculum. The data from Blessed Mother do not include any further announcements of this kind, and in fact, volunteers, educators, and the art teacher all complained later that they frequently did not hear of elders' deaths until well after the fact.

The lack of a plan for how to proceed with the children following a death was echoed in Jane's telling of the announcement story that she raised when I asked her about the professional development she felt the educators needed to do a good job in intergenerational programming. Note that in Jane's response, she signals that there was great emotion around the topic.

> I honestly don't have a real good view of what [professional development for teaching intergenerational] might look like, 'cause I have some ideas of some things, but I don't know if that's really the stuff that people want. Can I just do a little [illustration] of that? ... I have a new PA speaker right outside the office, and ... we've been complaining about not having it for about a year and a half, and by golly, they've fixed it. Now, at 8 o'clock in the morning and at 5 o'clock in the afternoon there's a prayer, which is fine, but Gary, who's in the classroom right next to me was so upset last night with me and the new speaker, because, he says, "Now, while I'm sitting here having breakfast," he said, "I don't mind the prayer. What I mind is when the Sister who's giving the prayer says, 'It's time for us to pray for the two residents who died last night.'" And he doesn't want to have to talk about that over breakfast. That was upsetting to him. And I was kind of laughing at him a little bit about it, 'cause [of] the intensity. But I understand that he wasn't prepared for that to happen, and that maybe he could be prepared better, I guess is why I thought of that story in relationship to your question. That's the sort of topic that, now that we have a speaker, is going to come up much more often as kids hear the word, and they know [what] the word "died" means in preschool, and then they want a teacher who can just have a conversation with them about that.

Despite Jane's observation that the educators could benefit from professional development on the topic of death and dying, none of the sites in the study offered any. As mentioned in Chapter Three, staff, faculty, and administrators at Blessed Mother and Watersberg remarked that because intergenerational programming was relatively new in North America, they were the ones who were usually asked to conduct in-service professional development for other educators – a job a number of them expressed they did not feel prepared for.

Further to the theme of preparedness was Gary's response to my question, "Have you as a staff talked about how to talk with kids about [death and dying] or when to do it?"

Actually we haven't had that sit down conversation as a group [of educators] or anything. I've had it with Tammy, a teacher in my room, because she's had a couple of residents on her floor that she visits die, and the kids were close [to the residents], and they talked about it. So we do, but I don't think it's ever been as a group thing. I can't remember ever a group talk about it. But when we do [talk to the children about death and dying], we keep it simple as everything we try to do.

Jane and Gary, over the course of the study, also spoke about some reluctance on the part of many educators to fully engage with intergenerational programming, an observation that I had also made at Picasso. Following one of our conversations where death and dying emerged, I tentatively forwarded to Jane a hypothesis about this reluctance which suggested that the null curriculum (i.e., what is not taught) affected the operational curriculum:

The more interaction you have, the more questions will emerge, and the more minimal that conversation, the more sanitized everything can be. So that may explain some of the reluctance, even, to enter into those stronger relationships with the other parts of the building [i.e., where young and old meet] ... today during class, one of the residents was, she's been ill, and she really had a strong coughing spell ... And again, I can see how those kinds of issues are things that people, need to be prepared for. But in terms of ... facilitating [intergenerational] interaction, I have noticed also that there are some [educators and recreation therapists] who may be not quite as comfortable moving between the two populations and focused on just the one that they feel responsible for. And sometimes when that happened, we ended up with ... what looks like what I might call parallel play.

In response, Jane smiled sadly, shook her head and said, "And never the two shall meet. Yes."

Recreation therapists at all three sites did talk about not being trained to work specifically with children which could, at least in part, account for the "parallel play" (i.e., the sense that people were working *beside* each other but not *together*). Some data, however, point to educators' fears also potentially being a factor in the ways they operationalized curricula. At Picasso, educators Penelope and Sandra, in a year and a year and a half of observation, respectively, were never seen to initiate conversation or touch an adult participant during intergenerational art class, and the study documented at length Gary's struggles to become comfortable around adult participants given his own fears of death and dying in his personal battle with cancer. Despite talking of himself as finally finding a level of comfort with the adults, when I asked, "You had spoken in these interviews of being a little apprehensive at first of working with the residents, and then you became more comfortable. And I wondered what you thought made you more comfortable and did your illness affect your perception of your job?" Gary raised a recent incident during an intergenerational activity where he clearly equated elders with death. He explained that his group of children was giving a performance in chapel, and he was crouching behind some pews directing the children:

> I wanted the kids to see me ... so I could go, "Louder! Louder!" and I'm lying there and all of a sudden this pressure is hitting my spot where I got my radiation [a cancer treatment] ... I don't want to move around to sit up, because I'm blocking up the aisle. I'm going wow what's that? I'm torturing myself just lying [there]. I feel my brain start pulsing. I'm like, no, I don't want to be caught dead here with the kids like a resident. I better get up.

The suggestion that one's comfort with a population affected the intergenerational operational curriculum is also something that was hinted at in the example of art class volunteer Marianne. While Marianne was observed to frequently facilitate intergenerational interaction, she was also recorded as paying particular attention to the adults. She explained this behaviour in an interview, saying that she often focused on the adults because they were not educators' first choice of people to work with given that they were often sick and not "cute." Yet Marianne's support of the adults seemed also to support the children. Recall in Chapter Two the situation where Frieda, an adult the children knew well, who had been having breathing problems, had a coughing spell while she was completing a visual text with two children. Frieda was already carting around an oxygen tank with a tube in her nose, and this coughing could have been scary for the children (as well as for herself); yet during the attack Marianne calmly stroked Frieda's back and spoke to her softly about the text. In the presence of Marianne's calm demean-

or, the children stood by Frieda's side and when the attack subsided, the team went back to their collective work.

The faculty's perceptions also seemed to affect the intended and operational curricula in other ways. For instance, despite Jane's reference to the need for professional development related to death and dying, there were many inconsistencies in the data about whether faculty, staff, and administration thought there was a need for the topic to enter the intended curriculum. Jane, for instance, talked about how there was perhaps no need to educate children about death and dying, because they did not "really" bond with the adults anyway. Talking about her intergenerational program and the difference between expectations and "reality," she said,

> It seems like a really warm, fuzzy environment, and [educators] might feel disappointed sometimes ... people think every child that comes through this program is going to meet somebody they connect with and love and you'll want to adopt for life, and it isn't going to happen that way, but sometimes it does. And when it does, it's really wonderful. But I'll say in the thirteen years, I can count on one hand the number of individuals that just moved in with us, adopted the kids, kids have loved to see, when that person passed on many people came to their service because they were so much a part of us. So it's not even one a year ... But on the other hand, on a day-to-day basis, you see many lovely little things happen between residents and kids, and you see a kids' development ... when they can spontaneously say, "I'll get this for you," or "Let me pick that up and hand it to you," or "I hear somebody's sad. Let's go see what's wrong." Those kinds of things are just a joy.

Wondering if the perceived lack of a number of strong connections between children and adults was reason to negate death and dying in the curriculum, I asked, "You were saying before about that those incredible attachments only happen every now and again, but what do you have to build in, in terms of the death and dying aspects?" Jane replied,

> That ... is maybe less than you think it might be ... Kids will change groups, maybe every year or every other year. Residents turn over fairly fast. The average age here is about 87, if you can believe it. So only occasionally have we really had that sort of discussion where we talked about a resident [dying] with a group of kids. And a lot of [the children's] families came to say goodbye to that person when they passed away ... More often

than that, a person declines and withdraws from us and our kids grow older and they leave before that person passes away. Does that make any sense? It just doesn't happen that often as even I thought it would when I first started here.

Also at Blessed Mother, recreation therapist Anna seemed to support Jane's view. When I asked her, "What happens when a resident dies?" she answered, "I haven't really had the chance or observed anything happening with that. I mean a lot of my residents die but none of them have ... I don't think the children were that bonded to certain people who have died." "So they don't notice when residents are gone?" I wondered to Anna, to which she replied,

> I've never observed it, but I have heard someone else say that it was hard 'cause there was one particular lady who just loved kids. So when she was gone there's been people who experienced that, but no, no one has passed away that's been really close to the kids that I've noticed ... I do think one thing to work on is maybe to find out how to bond more ... But it's really amazing how fast the time goes and how short a school year is. I mean they just start coming and it really is hard to find, to get that bond going. Like even our weekly group, it just seems like at the end of the year, it's just when your kids start to make headway and getting to know that particular group [then it's over] ... [We do have] babies up to preschool, but the groups all move around ... I think for most of the residents they don't remember. They can't remember well enough to know ... it's great for them [the kids and adults], and they enjoy it, but they can't exactly remember a certain person and know that that's the same person every week.

Anna then said something somewhat incongruous. When I asked if the children knew the adults' names, she emphatically announced, "They do. They do. They have good memories. They don't remember everyone, but most of the people that come a lot they know. They know that that's Jennifer and that's Barbara."

The idea that children did know the adults was substantiated by the study's documentation of some very rich interaction, particularly during art classes (Heydon, 2005; 2007; 2008b). This whole book in fact, is abounding with evidence of intergenerational relationships. Consequently, there is ample evidence to support the notion that children and adult participants formed relationships that appeared to hold meaning for them, rendering the death of the adults potentially significant or at least noticeable to the children: Witness alone, for instance, the hands in Figure 2.1. Another photograph from that day shows June, from the opening vignette, looking into the eyes of child participant Robbie, with her hand laid over his in anticipation of working on the *Intergenerational Hands* project. This is the project where participants were invited to work together to create a representation of an old and young hand together holding flowers (which were on the tables). The image shows the meeting of hands and eyes in the midst of mutual cooperation and text-making. This is not an image of strangers. Further, the figure on the cover of this book, which shows a product from the *Intergenerational Hands* project, also states that there is a connection. Note again that this visual text became the image for an invitation for an annual intergenerational art show. The artists had signed their names together on this work signaling further to the connection and cooperation in the project.

There is more evidence of relationship: staff and faculty, in particular, talked about key adults with whom classes of children formed a bond. In Watersberg, Maureen, a recreation therapist, replied as follows when I asked if she had seen the children get to know the adults well: "I do 'cause I work on the second floor and a lot of them get to know Grandma Jaquie.[1] And [the children] ask about her if she's not there ... so they really do get connected." Grandma Jaquie attended as many intergenerational programs as possible, and the children were seen to hug, kiss, and greet her at her every arrival and departure. Additionally, the observational data, some of which are included in earlier sections of the book, are replete with examples of relationships being built between participants at Blessed Mother and Picasso. Participants showed pleasure in seeing each other by giving each other big smiles, saving seats for each other, being disappointed when someone was absent, and chiming out each others' names during the orientation component of classes. In the art classes at Picasso, we also observed children and adult participants influencing the images that each made. One such instance involved elder Beatrice and child participant, Sarah, and this was a catalyst for death to enter the operational curriculum. Unprompted by anyone other than each other, the participants together

---

1 At Watersberg, children were encouraged to refer to all residents as Grandma or Grandpa.

chose to create visual texts of rabbits during a lesson on texture. Sadly, Beatrice died later that spring before she could see her artwork displayed in the annual art show alongside her friend's. After we packed up Beatrice's piece and sent it to her daughter in another province, her daughter contacted us to say,

> It is ... very sweet to know about the companion rabbit piece that was made in response to my mom's image ... it seems comforting, now that she has passed away, to think of the idea of a companion for her! ... My mom used to call the 6 of us ... her "little bunnies" right up until her passing so it is rather ironic to hear that her last piece was called the Rabbit! ... I was also born on the first day of spring and always felt it was a special time. The day of my mom's funeral, I walked by myself from the funeral home to the reception to just enjoy the sunshine. I realized that all the blossoms were in full bloom ... not a petal had yet fallen ... I felt it was significant that my mom would choose this to be the time to depart.

The staff and faculty did not explicitly refer to Beatrice's death in front of the children. Her rabbit hung beside its companion at the artshow, yet Beatrice's real life child companion, Sarah, stood in front of the artwork by herself with no explanation.

Thus, in all circumstances the intended curriculum omitted death and dying, and there was discomfort on the part of the educators when the topic entered the operational curriculum. The only exception to this was an incident that occurred at Watersberg. In an interview, educator Amelia talked about her contact with elders and how this affected her personally and professionally. She talked about this in relation to the adult participants being close to the ends of their lives:

> [Intergenerational programs have] enhanced my own philosophy about [early childhood education], about bridging that gap between the seniors and the children, 'cause as an adult, we forget that oh yeah, we will get to be that age one time and what we are going to have to look forward to ... seeing how they light up with the kids ... when I get to be eighty or ninety and I can't stay at home anymore, I would love to be at a place like this where I can see children and youth ... see them growing up again, and going okay, there is our future after I'm gone ... for me, it's sort of sentimental too, just to see my uncle ... having him pass, and then going oh well, I can see the benefit from having these children with the seniors – they make them happy. Like, we'll go and deliver papers in the morning and we'll

see a few of the grandparents and the kids will be like, "Hi Grandpa." They'll sing a song in the dining room in the morning or they'll go in and they'll say, "Hi, have a good day," "How are you?" and you can just see the smiles light up in the seniors' faces first thing in the morning.

I later learned the following about Amelia's group of children from recreation therapist Maureen:

> A couple of months ago, we had a resident that passed away, and the daycare actually went into the room, the resident's room while she was in bed. She was palliative; they went in to visit her. She only, I think she only lived two days after that. So they d[id] build a relationship with her ... They went in knowing she was sick.

Watersberg officially followed an emergent curriculum design where any intended curriculum stemmed from what the educators perceived as emerging from the children's lives and interests. The data do not suggest that the visit to the dying woman was a planned lesson in death and dying, but more of a chance situation as the children daily walked through where the adults lived delivering newspapers and greeting everyone they met. The woman was dying, and the educators did not see this as a reason to stop delivering a paper to her. There was no formal lesson or debriefing, however, on death or dying after the woman's death.

Finally, it bears mentioning that the data propose at least some of the adults thought about death and dying and that this may have had an influence on the operational curriculum. Specifically, only one participant at Blessed Mother in the adults-only art class also attended the intergenerational art class. When I asked the adults-only class participants why they did not attend the intergenerational class, elders who the data said liked children stated things like, "It doesn't fit my schedule." When elder Irene said this, I thought it seemed like an excuse, as it was not necessarily true. She then began to speak of her cancer and how it would finally "get her," and she initiated a whole class discussion on death. In this discussion, she said, "They [Blessed Mother] never want you to know who's died. When I die I want them to send out the trumpets so everyone knows. I want to go out with the trumpets!" After this, in reference to the intergenerational class, Irene looked sad and said, "Some children think we're monsters." The data are very complicated in this area. It appeared that Irene, who made me pause every day when I would wheel her back to her room so that she could watch the children play, counted herself out of intergenerational programming. She did not want to scare the children, and she herself was scared and uncomfortable being so close to death. The environment that kept death a secret did not seem to help. Sadly, when Irene died, I learned that her death had not been announced, and there had been no service at Blessed Mother. I was told this was because Irene was a "private person" and she would not have wanted anything broadcast.

Discussion and Recommendations

One cannot help but be touched by the moments in the data: Beatrice's child companion standing alone beside their rabbits at the spring art-show and Irene, loving children but staying away from them for fear they would find her a monster. The sadness of these events is countered in intensity only by the extreme beauty and hopefulness of the juxtaposition of youth and old age, life and death in the day-to-day encounters of the children and elders in the intergenerational learning programs. This is the aesthetic of *mono no aware* (sensitivity to the transience of life and youth) that punctuates educator Amelia's description of her intergenerational learning program. And in the face of all of this, questions resound about the place of death and dying in intergenerational learning curricula. In this chapter I have asked about death and dying and the intended and operational curricula and how the findings to these questions relate to the children's learning opportunities, opportunities for forging relationships with elders, and the ways in which the children were positioned (thus connecting to their identity options and in turn their text-making).

The data are clear that the intended curricula did not deal with death and dying, although they entered the operational curricula. Children were sometimes positioned by their educators and the curricula as not bonding with elders and not noticing when elders were absent. If one were to use the same scenarios and replace the children and elders with middle-aged adults, would the reading be the same? The data that demonstrate the links between the children and elders in the programs suggest that the children in the study were not given sufficient credit for being able to build relationships and recognize elders as people in their own right. The children were also generally constructed as being unable to understand or in need of protecting against troubling information such as death and dying. Elders themselves were even sometimes treated in ways similar to the children and as in need of protection from discussions of death, as in the case of there being inconsistent or no protocols for informing even them of the death of a peer. While it is outside the scope of this chapter and the intergenerational studies to say how children and elders deal with knowledge of death and precisely how they should be educated on the topic or assisted to deal with it, it seems that the null curriculum did little to enhance learning opportunities or opportunities for interaction between the generations. Note, for instance, the hesitancy that arose for some educators in facilitating intergenerational interaction or even participating in intergenerational learning programs, because they were uncomfortable or afraid, the subsequent lost "teachable" moments such as when the announcement of the deaths of the elders went out over the loudspeaker, and the case of elders who had much to teach and give to children but stayed away because they did not feel comfortable with their own stage of life. Further, with such treatment of death and dying, it is not, therefore, surprising that some of the adults had restricted communication and identity options, as evidenced in the passport and heartmap projects described in the previous chapter.

Given the presence of death and dying in the operational curriculum and the negative relationship its omission had to learning and relationship-building opportunities and identity options, it is safe to say that death and dying must be part of the intended intergenerational learning curricula. Data suggest that the topic of death and dying and the reasons for its current treatment in intergenerational curricula are very complex. Indeed, the nature of the topic is difficult, particularly given that it is tied tightly to personal fears and belief systems and is perhaps one of the most intimate and important topics that exist yet also one that is somewhat "taboo" (Northcott & Wilson, 2008, p. 20). Consequently, any response to how death and dying should be treated in intergenerational learning programs must itself account for this complexity. The study implies that for any treatment of death and dying in intergenerational curriculum to be helpful vis-à-vis learning and relationship-building opportunities and identity options, the following issues at least must be addressed:

• Educators must recognize how they and the curriculum position children and elders, including how they reckon with children's and elders' abilities to deal with difficult knowledge.
• Educators must recognize child and adult participants in intergen-

erational programs as full persons and thus as people who might ostensibly have relationships with each other.

- These relationships must be respected.
- Educators must also recognize their own feelings towards death and dying and elders.
- There must be a comprehensive curricular plan in place for educating children on the topic and supporting adult participants before and after people die.
- All parties involved in intergenerational learning programs must be part of this education and the culture of the institution must support open dialogue on the topic.
- Given the charged nature of the topic and its connection to people's belief systems, families of the young and the old should be part of any discussion regarding the approach to take.
- There is a need for current and interdisciplinary studies into educating children about death and dying, including studies that consider the sociocultural contexts of learning about death and dying.
- Educators and persons working with elders must come to terms with the limiting effects of ignoring or denying death on people's learning and relationship-building opportunities and identity options.

Knowledge and subsequent curricular programming will be richer if the sociocultural contexts of learning about death and dying are complemented by the literature in the area from health professions. Finally, the aesthetic of *mono no aware* might be a way for people working within intergenerational programming to frame the experience, thus allowing all involved to be sensitive to the beauty of the juxtaposition of young and old rather than allowing fears of death to adversely interfere with learning and interaction.

Conclusion

This chapter has obvious significance to the field of intergenerational learning, but its focus on the relationship between intended and operational curricula and their corresponding effect on the learning opportunities and positioning of children and elders has implications for all curricula, including literacy curricula. The chapter raises the questions: What is the place of death in life? How do educators respond to this question, and what in turn do they pass on to learners? How do their responses affect their own identities as human beings and educators?

Further, how do the responses colour the lives, including communicational practices and relationships, of elders and young children and
their experiences with aging, death, and dying? Rather than inviting a
single set of right responses to these questions, I ask them as catalysts
for discussions between educators within their own unique contexts, so
they may open up the null curricula and communicate with each other
and their communities about what is literally a life and death issue.

Chapter Seven

The Lessons of Intergenerational Learning Curricula

Because of the strength and meaning of the intergenerational relationships I have had in my life, "the past beats inside me like a second heart" (Banville, 2005, p. 10); its rhythm guides me in my day-to-day and helps me live in a way that would have been otherwise impossible. I carry within me the lessons of my elders, the responsibility of family, community, and mutual care foremost, and I hope that while they were on this earth, just as my son today teaches me about the impetus to communicate, to make meaning and connect, and the myriad ways through which humans might do so, I too was their teacher. It has been a privilege to witness intergenerational learning programs in action. From their aesthetics to the opportunities and products they generate, the programs have stopped me in my tracks and whispered to me to recognize the beauty that is, in the words of educator Gary, "the circle of life."[1]

Studies of intergenerational relationships and learning are today quite broad and focus on familial, communal, and institutional intergenerational situations (e.g., Larkin, 2004). Given, as discussed in Chapter One, contemporary circumstances, particularly in North American society, where many people who are young and old are being cared for outside of the family (e.g., in retirement homes and day cares; e.g., Jarrott & Bruno, 2007; McCain & Mustard, 1999) and that intergenerational opportunities can be sparse in some circumstances (e.g., Kaplan,

---

1 The metaphor of the circle may indeed be in conflict with the notion of ends, though perhaps the ends refer, in Jeanette Winterson's (2012) terms, to *mass* and not *energy*; thus, life may have both ends and be circular.

Henkin, & Kusano, 2002), shared-site intergenerational programs that focus on bringing together skipped generations for learning, communicating, and relationship-building seem urgently needed. *Learning at the Ends of Life* is an attempt to address what it is that participants may do within such programs; it is a description, illustration, and examination of intergenerational curricula at all levels: intended, operational (Eisner, 2005), null (Eisner, 2002), and hidden (Apple, 1971) with a focus on the curricular commonplaces of teacher, learner, subject matter and milieu (Schwab, 1973). Residing within the larger curricular discussion are potential insights into the literacy learning opportunities and practices of participants and their related identity options. Indeed, the specific cases may shed light into the *nested relations* through which individuals, especially those who are at the ends of life, may practise their literacies. These relations, as documented within the book, include those that are particular to the participants in the intergenerational classes, the relations of the participants and their programs, participants and the institutions in which they are positioned (e.g., day care or a retirement home), and the relations between participants and the social Discourses that may be germane to them (e.g., Discourses concerning what is a child or what is an elder). Focusing on the major ideas, the following are some of the key lessons that come from the earlier chapters of this book.

First, learning, communicating, and having a wide array of identity options so that people may see themselves in terms of their own knowledge, strengths, and interests and communicate through these are vital to people *in the here and now*. Education that is focused on a delayed future that positions children and their learning as valuable "capital," and that measures human worth in terms of this capital is dehumanizing. Also, because it negates the Levinasian "face," such education is unethical. Intergenerational curricula, with their emphasis on what learning can foster today for all people regardless of their relationship to capital and their insistence on meaningfulness for all generations (e.g., Jarrott, 2007) at the ends of life is the antidote to this. It is an example for all education.

Second, Rowsell & Pahl (2007) have taught that there is a connection between the social, literacy practices, texts, and identities, and they demonstrate the ways in which identities and the social can themselves be discerned within texts. Given these relations, one might ask how curricula can expand both people's communication and identity options, particularly within an intergenerational setting. The cases suggest that curricula that create opportunities for expansive communication and identity options are those that support participants through all aspects of the communicational trajectory (Kress & Jewitt, 2003), including what to signify and how with consideration for the occasion of the communication. Such curricula emphasize the social aspect of communication and make good on the notion that within each text (or utterance) is the implied other, the implied audience (Bakhtin, 1986). This raises the question of how when text is produced within a generationally diverse context, the text itself might be enriched.

Third, in terms of the materiality of the literacies, the studies that undergird the book relate that child participants seemed to be better able to move from mode to mode and medium to medium and create visually complex texts. Adults seemed more constrained. These findings relate to what has been observed previously in the literature (e.g., Fraser & Gestwicki, 2002). These differences in terms of generations' literacies also applied to the question of what to signify. One might ask how curricula could help children and older adults support each other to keep open semiotic possibilities, support their facility with modes and media, and widen people's identity options, thus perhaps creating new semiotic possibilities for all. What, for instance, might adult participant Mona have been able to create if her milieu had offered her identity (and material) options that were wider than the silence of aging, death, and dying?

Fourth, while there were moments of semiotic and identity restriction such as just described, much of the intergenerational curricula included in this book moved towards new possibilities for young and old. For instance, they demonstrated what it might mean to enact an ethical curricula that respects that alterity is the precondition for personhood (e.g., Robbins, 2001) and brings together its participants *as equals* who are responsible to each other. These curricula resist the segregation, pathologization, and control of the dominant forms of curricula of the school and the medical model that are so often applied to older adults in, for example, nursing homes. Intergenerational curricula bring together what is seldom together and start from a place of working from people's funds of knowledge (Moll, 1992). These types of curricula can foster great relationships, although the forms of these relationships may differ and even be missed by those outside of them. Regardless of the structure of a relationship, curricula that allow one person to be present to another, to recognize the face of that other, may help to engender an ethical relation (e.g., Robbins, 2001), and this is certainly a lesson for inter- and monogenerational teaching and learning circumstances.

Fifth, intergenerational curricula can be *queer* (e.g., Britzman, 1998) in that certainly within their operational or hidden curricula, they destabilize the "tidy stories of happiness, resolution, and certainty" (p. 79) of life. They necessarily raise the questions and perspectives of long and short lives such as *Where does a life come from? What is a life for? Where does a life go?* The question of the suitability of these queries for young children to contemplate brings with it new questions like *What is a child? Who is a child? What aspects of life and knowledge might a child not participate in and who decides?* The response the children in Chapter Six gave around issues of death, dying, and intergenerational relationship is that children are persons with capacities for relationship, desire, and responsibility beyond what many of the "normate" (Thomson, 1997) adults around them might recognize. The queering of curricula might allow children and older adults to be *seen* and *heard* (Hall & Rudkin, 2011) by themselves, each other, and the world at large. Intergenerational curricula can also queer the normate's understandings of old age, death, and dying. When they attend to what the adult participants in the studies were asking of the people around them, curricula must answer the demand of the face "not to die alone" (Levinas & Kearney, 1986, p. 24). Acknowledging the ends of life is a movement towards this. Being a young child and an adult who is close to death who are seen and heard has implications, as evidenced throughout this book, for people's communication and identity options.

Sixth, while there are certain issues that must be addressed at a societal level for optimum learning with and for young children and older adults (e.g., the valuing of childhood, old age, and those who educate and care for them) within a specific teaching and learning situation the following may help to create learning opportunities: respecting people's personhood (e.g., considering what meaning learning holds for the individual and group); establishing a community where people find pleasure and support in each other's company and can develop meaningful relationships; ensuring participants' safety and comfort and remembering the significance of rhythm and routine; providing a purpose for learning tasks and venues for sharing products; allowing for participant decision-making; and focusing on learning that is challenging and meaningful to everyone through differentiated projects.

The lessons above may be worthy of being called secrets, for they might engender the types of teaching and learning opportunities the music teacher at the beginning of this book was looking for. Indeed like secrets, they are not well known; yet for these very reasons I want everyone to hear about them. Thus, just as adult participant Irene in Chapter Six wanted to "go out with the trumpets," I too would like to blast and share widely the lessons of intergenerational learning programs and the people who have lived them. Perhaps instead of sending them out on the trumpet's vibrations, I can let the lessons dance on a song that my Nonna sang to us as children. The lyrics are now unsteady in my mind, but the tune is fresh and alive. Like the analysis of the intergenerational curricula and their participants, my sharing of the lyrics has gaps and holes, unknowns that defy my reach. Still, what is discernible is suggestive of something more, the contours haunting and calling for recognition.

See-saw, see-saw, see we go up and go down ... like an automobile that goes riding and gliding in ... town,
Now it's see-saw, see-saw, see we're not young anymore
We'd give all our ... just to be girls and boys on that old see-saw ...

Appendix I

INTERGENERATIONAL HANDS

INTERGENERATIONAL HANDS*	• Watercolour • Subject – Hands
Overview	This project invites physical interaction between children and elders as they are invited to look for visual details while drawing one another's hands.
Materials	• Pencils (Fat primary ones for better grip) • Watercolours • Paint brushes • Water containers • Sponges for dabbing wet brushes (optional) • White paper (medium-sized) • Several small bouquets of flowers to act as inspiration
Setting the Stage	• Talk about hands – what they look like, what we use them for. If possible, read a book or a poem about hands to introduce today's topic. • Pair each child with an adult. Direct them to close their eyes and feel their partner's hand beside them. Have them take turns to describe how it feels, including skin texture, bumps, jewellery, etc. Point out that these details make their hands their very own.

---

* Adapted from http://www.artmuseums.com/intergenerational.html by Tara-Lynn Scheffel and Rachel Heydon

- Next, hold up Picasso's print *Fleurs et mains* (1958) and ask participants to share what they see in the image. Point out the flowers on the table and ask what details they notice (e.g., colour, texture, shape).
- Share that today they are going to work together to draw and paint their very own pictures of hands holding flowers.

Technical Information
- Invite participants to take turns drawing their partners' hands and add the details they have been talking about.
  ○ First, ask participants to draw each other's hands on a white piece of paper. Remind them to keep an opening between the thumb and forefinger (this is where the stems of the flowers will go). Also have them position their hands so that one is above the other.
  ○ Second, participants may use their pencils to fill in the details for each hand together, talking about what to include and where.
  ○ Third, encourage participants to look at the flowers displayed and use them as a guideline for drawing flowers in the hands they have just completed.
  ○ Finally, provide watercolours and brushes for painting in the pictures.

Closure
- Invite participants to sign their work and collect the texts.
- Showing one at a time, see if the class can tell whose hand is represented in each text. Remind them to look at the details to make their guesses.
- Invite the children to give one of the real flowers to the adults to say thank you for spending time with them.

Textual Links
- Visual Texts: "Generational Hands" by Pablo Picasso
- Picture Books: *My Hands* by Aliki
- Music: "Grandma's Hands" by Bill Wither
- Poetry for all ages: "Her Hands" by Maggie Pittman (http://www.familyfriendpoems.com/family/poetry.asp?poem=1966)

Appendix II

HEARTMAPS

HEARTMAPS*	• Drawing • Subject – What is in my heart
Purpose	Based on Sara Fanelli's *My Map Book* (1995), this project invites participants to visually record those things that hold a special place in their hearts. These special people, places, events, foods, and the like are drawn within a large heart shape and labelled. Participants may then share and compare the special things that are the same and different from those on other heartmaps.
Materials	• 11″ × 17″ drawing paper – 1 per person • Coloured pencils • Fine, permanent markers (e.g., Sharpie) • Variety of maps • *My Map Book*
Setting the Stage	• Put out the maps on the tables and encourage the participants to talk about what they see. • Ask: "What is the purpose of a map?" What kinds of things do they show?" Encourage the participants to discuss other kinds of maps that they have seen or used.

*Lesson adapted by Wendy Crocker and Rachel Heydon from Bainbridge, J. & Heydon, R. (2013). *Constructing Meaning: Teaching the Language Arts K-8* (Toronto: Nelson)

- Tell the participants that today's class is going to be about maps – but a very unique kind of map that leads to the special things that they keep deep down inside.
- Share *My Map Book*. Focus the discussion on the heartmap. List on a visual chart some of the special things that are in your heart.
- Explain that in order to make a heartmap, we must draw the outline of a heart, and then fill it with our special things and carefully label them just as we saw on the road maps, or the maps in the book. Model a *"Think Aloud"* – draw and "think aloud" what you would add and narrate your work as you draw in front of the participants.

Technical Information

- Demonstrate how to make a heart for those who need assistance.
- Encourage participants to begin with the heart, draw and colour the items with pencil crayons and then label with the Sharpie markers.

Closure

- Invite participants to share their favourite thing from their map while it is held by a volunteer for the group to see *or* the child can hold the adult's map while the adult shares his/her favourite part of the map and then exchange.

Textual Links

- Fanelli, Sara (1995). *My map book*
- Interactive map site at http://wikimapia .org/#lat=42.9833&lon=-81.25&z=10&l=0&m=b

Appendix III

HOLIDAY MEAL

HOLIDAY MEAL*	• Watercolour Painting • Subject – Special foods
Overview	Participants share their personal experiences and traditions surrounding a special family meal.
Materials	• Permanent markers (Sharpies) • White paper (heavy) • Watercolour brushes • Sponges • Water tubs • Water colour trays or liquid watercolours
Setting the Stage	• Ask, "What does your family eat for a special holiday meal? Where do they get it?" (Frequently elders will answer, "We grew it" or "Our neighbour raised turkeys.") Ask questions like, "How do potatoes grow?" Ask also, "How is that dish made? Who does the cooking?"
Technical Information	• Explain that today we will pretend that your paper is your placemat. On it you will draw your plate with the marker (life-sized) and all the food on it that you like to eat for your special holiday meal.

*Lesson designed by Bridget Daly and implemented by Tara-Lynn Scheffel and Rachel Heydon

- Remind participants to draw the utensils which they use to eat. Other suggestions (ask the class) can include a napkin, glass, knife, and spoon.
- After the drawing is complete, pass out painting materials and demonstrate painting technique, reminding participants to rinse their brushes in the water and tap lightly onto the sponge before changing colours.

Closure

- At the end of class invite participants to share their dinner paintings and describe the foods they chose.

Textual Links

- Still life artwork with food can be found in the following artists' works:
  - Paul Cezanne (1839–1906): http://www.ibiblio.org/wm/paint/auth/cezanne/sl/
  - Marsden Hartley (1877–1945): http://www.tfaoi.com/aa/2aa/2aa10.htm
  - Nell Blaine (1922–1996): http://www.borghi.org/american/blaine.html
  - Elizabeth Geiger (1967–): http://www.mcjunkingallery.com/Elizabeth_Geiger/index.html

Appendix IV

COMMUNITY STRUCTURES

COMMUNITY STRUCTURES*	• Three-dimensional construction from found materials • Subject – Special places in the community
Overview	• This project is planned to foster awareness of creating visual texts in three dimensions and to foster communication between intergenerational partners in their choices of building design, materials for construction, placement of features, and additional features. In this project participants are invited to collaboratively create special structures using found materials.
Materials	• Variety of found materials (e.g., boxes, tubes, egg crates, foam trays) • Adhesive choices – stapler, tape, glue, Velcro, brads • Scissors – adult and children's sizes • Photos of structures and special places, especially those germane to the local community (e.g., farms, parks) • Plans of buildings
Setting the Stage	• Prior to the class, if possible, take participants for a walk to look at the neighbourhood. Or take pictures of special places, architecture, and struc-

*Lesson designed by Wendy Crocker and Rachel Heydon

tures to display on overhead or a large screen (e.g., via PowerPoint) and use these images to stimulate discussion.

- Lead a discussion about neighbourhoods and communities. What do we find in a neighbourhood? Who is part of our neighbourhood? Invite participants to think about characteristics of their neighbourhoods now or one where they have lived in the past. Can they suggest some important things to have in a community? What has changed in neighbourhoods from the past to today? What has stayed the same? Make a visual list as they give their comments. The list can include plants, animals, specific people, houses, bikes, cars, playground, birds, and businesses.
- Discuss what structures and buildings they would find in their local neighbourhood or community
- Read selected pages of *Iggy Peck, Architect*. Discuss what structures Iggy is creating. Share ideas about the different materials that the character is using for some of his buildings.
- Show the plans of a variety of structures as the plans or ideas that architects have before they build. Give each intergenerational pair or group of participants a piece of paper to draw the plan for their building and label what they will need to build.
- Discuss how the nature of plans and how a structure grows out of the paper like a sculpture – it is 3-D.

Technical Information

- Encourage participants to follow their plans and to talk about what materials they will use to create their building.

Closure

- Share the finished structures with the group and describe the materials that were used in the construction.
- Display the 3-D structures, along with their plans.

Textual Links

- Beaty, Andrea (2007). *Iggy Peck, Architect.*
- Frank Lloyd Wright – "Wright on the Web" at http://www.delmars.com/wright/flw8.htm

- Gothic architecture at http://images.google
  .com/images?hl=en&um=1&q=gothic+
  architecture&sa=N&start=20&ndsp=20
- Byrne Design Architects at http://www
  .byrnedesigninc.com/Portfolio_Residential.php

Appendix V

COLLOGRAPHS

COLLOGRAPHS*	• Printmaking • Subject Matter – Home
Overview	This project invites participants to share and compare where they live; they create an image of home using a printing process that entails making a plate from layered paper.
Materials	• 12″ × 18″ tag board, 1 per person • White glue or glue sticks • Black crayons or markers • Scissors • 4–6 brayers (depends on class size) • 4–6 colours of water-based block printing ink (depends on class size) • Cookie sheets or plastic sheets • Selection of 12″ × 18″ white and coloured construction paper to serve as the background for the prints (preferably with not too rough a surface)
Setting the Stage	• Begin by showing photos of many types of dwellings – English cottage, yurt, mansions, and huts.

*Lesson designed by Bridget Daly and implemented by Tara-Lynn Scheffel and Rachel Heydon

- Invite participants to pair-share, "What does your home look like?" Encourage the adult to remember places they have lived in the past. Invite all participants to take turns describing their homes. Encourage visual descriptions by asking about colour, how many windows, are there stairs, trees, a porch, etc. Point out commonalities ("Vera also lived in a green house!")
- Explain how participants will be invited to make a print of their house or maybe a house they would like to live in. (Most people are familiar with using a rubber stamp to make a print. You can explain printmaking using that example.)
- Using emphasis tell them, "Nothing you *draw* will show up in your print, only what you *cut* will print." You will need to repeat this several times during the session, especially in your demonstration.

Technical Information

- Demonstrate drawing the main/biggest shape of the tagboard (name the shape while drawing it). Cut it out and set it aside. Draw and cut the next biggest shape (roof, porch, second floor) and so on, cutting out windows, doors, stairs – even pets, shingles, and trees.
- Using glue and a Q-tip or a glue stick (always put glue on the back of the smaller piece) stick pieces together.
- To print: show participants the colours of ink and the colours of paper. Invite them to choose a combination that has a lot of difference or contrast. Squeeze about a 1" worm from the tube (about ½ tsp. from a jar) onto the cookie tray.
- Using the brayer, roll the ink out top to bottom and side to side repeatedly until the brayer is evenly covered with ink. About a dozen back and forth strokes should do it. Immediately roll the ink onto the surface of the cut-out house. Pick up more ink from the tray with the brayer and roll onto the house template, repeating the process until it is completely covered. The participant should be encouraged and assisted to do this part quickly, before the ink dries out.

- Immediately flip the house template face down on the paper. Using a brayer rolled with a different ink colour, roll the brayer across the back of the template (to burnish the image) and right on over the edge to create a "halo" around the outside.
- Carefully peel the template off the print and allow both to dry completely.

Closure

- The results of each print are shared.

Textual Links

- Use photos of many types of dwellings cut out from magazines, newspapers, etc.
- Beatty, A. (2007). *Iggy Peck, Architect.* NY: Abrams Books for Young Readers.

Appendix VI

AMATE

AMATE*	• Cut paper • Subject matter – Symmetry
Overview	This project introduces the concept of symmetry, culminating in a cut-paper project of South American origin.
Materials	• Pencils • Precut brown paper bags – around 13″ × 16″ • 18″ × 22″ white paper • Scissors • Glue sticks • Waxed paper • Iron • Newspaper padding
Setting the Stage – Part One	• Begin by asking participants if anyone knows what the word 'symmetry" means. Explain that when you draw a line down the centre of a thing, if one side matches the other side then we say it is symmetrical. Draw an imaginary line down the centre of your face and ask if they think that one side is the same as the other. Reference other objects around the classroom, asking the same question.

*Adapted from Jo Miles Schuman, *Art from Many Hands: Multicultural Art Projects,* by Bridget Daly and implemented by Tara-Lynn Scheffel and Rachel Heydon

○ Note: Not all answers are obvious. A clock's shape may be symmetrical, although (as a child will, no doubt, point out) the numbers are not. Your body (in most cases) is symmetrical, but your hand is not.

• Once participants get the idea, draw a dotted line on the white board and a half circle on one side. Ask what you should draw on the other side of the line to make the shape symmetrical. Repeat the practice with a half-heart shape.

Setting the Stage – Part Two

• Explain that the Otomi, an indigenous tribe in South America, strip bark from the amate tree to make paper. They soak it, pound it with rocks and lay it out in the sun. When it is dry they will sometimes paint pictures on it and sometimes cut out symmetrical designs to decorate their homes. Tell them that the people of the Otomi tribe really use their imaginations to combine pictures of animals, plants, and people in their cut-outs; objects that reflect their life and their community.

• Show some examples of the project. Explain that in this class they will not use tree bark, but they will use something that we find a lot of in our environment: grocery bags. They will cut out a symmetrical design and later make it look like tree bark.

Technical Information

• Invite participants to begin by drawing a dotted line down the middle of the back of their bag. Don't worry if it is not exactly straight. Invite participants to draw their designs on one side of the dotted line. Remind them that they will have the same thing on the other side when they cut it out; it will be symmetrical.

• When their drawing is complete (check each one to make sure it is viable) they are ready to start cutting. Demonstrate folding the paper in half along the dotted line with the drawing on the outside. Tell them that it is very important that they not cut entirely through the dotted line or their picture will be cut in half. They can, however, cut portions of the dotted line out to make it look fancy.

- When they are finished cutting remind partici- pants that you are going to make their paper look like tree bark. Using a precut sample of your own, crumple the design into a tight ball. (Make a spectacle of it so everyone is aware of the process. This should relieve some of the shock when they crumple their own.) Then care- fully open it up and flatten it out on the news- paper padding. Lay the waxed paper sheet on the "good" side (without pencil marks) and iron the design flat, simultaneously melting wax on the wrinkles. Show them how it now looks like amate bark.
- When the paper cut-out is flattened flip it over on some newsprint and cover the back with glue. Rub the glue stick carefully from the centre out over the edges to avoid ripping. Gently slip the newsprint out from underneath and, leav- ing the sticky side up, cover the cut-out with a large white sheet of paper, rubbing the back side firmly to make sure it sticks. Using a large sheet of white paper makes it easy to cover the entire piece, and it can be cut down and centred after- wards.

Closure

- Invite the participants to share their work with one another. If time permits, have them title their artwork and explain why they have chosen that title.

Textual Links

- To learn more about amate paper, take a look at: http://www.home.earthlink.net/~kering/ amate.html

Appendix VII

STYROFOAM PRINTS

STYROFOAM PRINTS*	• Printmaking • Subject Matter – Winter
Overview	This project invites participants to view and represent images of winter through printmaking. Time permitting; the lesson might also encourage discussion about recycled materials.
Materials	• Styrofoam meat or fruit trays (wash thoroughly with hot, soapy water and let dry completely) ◦ Cut the edges off of the trays and cut the trays to get the biggest flat piece possible without an imprint. • Ball-point pens • Scissors • Water-based block ink • Brayers • Thick plastic sheet or cookie try to roll out ink • Paper
Setting the Stage	• Read *Stranger in the Woods* and/or display images of winter as an introduction to what the artists notice about the world during the wintertime.

*Lesson designed by Bridget Daly, implemented by Tara-Lynn Scheffel and Rachel Heydon

• Explain that they will be invited to create their own winter scenes by drawing a picture in a piece of Styrofoam then rolling it with ink to make a print.

Technical Information

• Demonstrate how to press into the Styrofoam with the pen to engrave your drawing. Invite each participant to feel the drawn line. When the drawings are complete, make sure the lines are sufficiently deep so the print will be clear.
• Demonstrate the printmaking technique. To print:
  ○ Place a small amount of ink (the size of a kidney bean) on the plastic sheet.
  ○ Participants may roll the ink flat, varying direction (about 15 times so that the ink is not too thick).
  ○ Once the brayer is evenly covered in a thin layer of ink, roll it onto the Styrofoam plate. (Invite the participants to observe that the ink lies on the surface of the plate but does not fill the lines they etched in ballpoint.)
  ○ Lay a piece of paper on top and rub it firmly all over with your fingers.
  ○ Peel off the print and let dry.

Closure

• Make multiple prints from each plate (you can use different colours of paper and/or ink). Encourage the participants to trade prints.
• If time permits, explain that there are many "throw away" items in our lives that can be reused or recycled to make art. Use the Styrofoam tray as an example. The adults will be able to share many examples of "recycling." For example, in the early 1900s:
  ○ clothing was sewn from flour sacks,
  ○ quilts were made from old clothing, and
  ○ dolls were made of apples or corncobs

Textual Links

• Suggested picture book about winter:
  ○ *Stranger in the Woods* by Carl R. Sams and Jean Stoick.

Appendix VIII

MINIATURES

MINIATURES*	• Coloured pencil drawing • Subject matter – Everyday life
Overview	In this project, participants explore fitting big ideas into a small format. Additionally they may recognize that they enjoy similar home activities to their classmates, young and old.
Materials	• 4″ × 6″ cartridge paper • Felt-tip markers • High-quality coloured pencils
Setting the Stage	• Talk about how small (intimate) the samples are: How small might the brush be to paint them? What kind of arm movement would the artist use to make the brush strokes? Point out the decorated borders. • Persian and Indian miniatures often depict events of everyday life. Sometimes they mix in religious figures or mythic animals. Ask about an activity they do (at home or at school) every day that they would like to draw.
Technical Information	• Begin by drawing a border about an inch in from the edge of the paper.

*Lesson designed by Bridget Daly and textual links by Rachel Heydon and Tara-Lynn Scheffel

- Draw the picture with a felt-tip marker.
- Decorate the border – you can use just shapes or lines or you can think of something that would relate to your picture (e.g., flowers, rain, or clouds around a gardening scene; spoons and forks design around cooking).
- Colour in with pencils, and remind to colour around things – cover the white.

Closure

- Invite participants to share and talk about their miniature. Ask what is it they enjoy about the activity they choose to depict.

Textual Links

- Persian miniatures: http://www.farhangsara .com/miniature_gal.htm
- Slideshow of images: http://www .mihanfoundation.org/gallery8/index.html
- Indian Miniatures: http://www.ubu.com/ aspen/aspen10/indian.html

Appendix IX

ACCORDION BOOKS

ACCORDION BOOKS*	• Coloured pencil • Subject matter – All about me
Overview	This project invites participants to share and illustrate bits of personal information in a 4-page linear format. Participants may then share and compare this information, finding similarities and differences.
Materials	• Mat board (any colour precut to 4¼" × 5¾"; two pieces per participant; this will act as the covers of the book) • Legal-sized white paper (16" × 5½"; this will act as the body of the book) • Black felt-tip pens • Coloured pencils or fine-point coloured markers • Glue sticks • Prompts: on small slips of paper, type or print short statements that the participants can illustrate. Choose 6–8 statements and make as many copies as there are participants in the class. Some examples: This is where I live; Yikes! I'm scared; My favorite pet; This makes me smile; Yum!; This is what I do best; My friend.

*Lesson designed by Bridget Daly and implemented by Rachel Heydon, Tara-Lynn Scheffel, and Wendy Crocker

Setting the Stage

- Think-pair-share: Ask the class, "What's one important thing about you?" After giving participants time, have them tell the person next to them. Then have a few people share with the whole class their responses and what they have heard from others.
- Introduce an accordion book that you've made about yourself. Do not tell the participants it's about you. Tell them it's about someone and they need to guess who.
- Conduct a picture walk through the book.
- Now read the print text.
- Discuss how the words in the book often tell us things about the illustrations and how the illustrations show us what the words say.
- Have the participants guess the author of the book.
- Invite the participants to create their own accordion book. Their book will tell the reader something about the person who made it using pictures and words.

Technical Information

- Explain that the participants will choose phrases typed on little strips of paper and create illustrations to go with them.
- Read each prompt aloud, pausing between to ask for suggestions on possible illustrations. For example, "Yum!" can be illustrated with a favourite food. Let participants share and compare their likes and preferences.
- Read the prompt through again, this time inviting participants to raise hands for the ones they choose. They may choose four, one for each page of their book.
- Distribute the white paper, one sheet to each, and demonstrate the fold. Start by folding the paper in half, end to end. Then turn back one open edge, line up to the fold and crease. Flip the paper over and turn back the other open edge to the fold and crease. Some people will need help with this accordion fold.
- Demonstrate how to use a glue stick, making sure to apply the glue to the backside of the prompt. Next, have participants glue one prompt to each page.

- Hand out the black felt-tip pens and invite participants to draw using only the pens.
- When the drawings are complete, distribute coloured pencils or markers to complete the drawings.
- When the pages are complete, invite the participants to rub glue on the back of the front and back pages and attach a piece of mat board to each for the covers.
- The cover(s) may be decorated now with words or drawings, as time permits.

Closure

- Share books. This may be done as a whole group, in small groups, or in pairs.

Textual Links

- Educators may also include picture books that address the topic "All about me." Some great titles include:
  ○ Martin, B. (1998). *Here are my hands*. New York: Henry Holt and Company.
  ○ Ewald, W. (2002). *The best part of me*. Boston: Little, Brown.

Appendix X

MOBILES ON TWIGS

MOBILES ON TWIGS*	• Collage • Subject matter – "Things we love"
Overview	This project invites participants to use a 3-dimensional format to identify and create images of "things they love."
Materials	• Twigs (small 8"–14" with multiple branches) • Coloured embroidery thread or twine • Construction paper of various colours • Pencils • Scissors • Glue sticks
Setting the Stage	• Begin by showing the group a 3-D item and a 2-D representation of that item (e.g., a real flower and a painting of a flower). • Discuss the comparison. • Explain what a mobile is and show works by Alexander Calder and Karen Rossi. • Pair-share: Ask the class to think about something or someone they love and share it with the person next to them. Then they can take turns telling the class.

*Designed by Bridget Daly implemented by Tara-Lynn Scheffel and Rachel Heydon

Technical Information

- Invite participants to create images of 5 or more things they love by drawing, cutting, and gluing. Demonstrate paper folding such as:
  - How to make an accordion fold in order to create "springs" that will allow paper pieces to stick out and become 3-D.
    Note: Emphasize variation in size and colour of pieces.
- After all pieces are completed use a hole punch at the top of each piece and attach a length of embroidery thread. (Typically these tasks are too difficult for small or arthritic hands – help is needed.)
- Give each participant a twig and help them to tie their pieces to it.

Closure

- Share mobiles, looking for commonalities in subject matter. Also, point out how the pieces can be seen from all sides and how they move.

Textual Links

- Alexander Calder (1898–1976) was an American-born artist and sculptor who invented a type of sculpture called the mobile. For images of his work, please view: http://www.calder.org/ SETS/work/work.html
- Karen Rossi is best known for her metal sculptures and her whimsical mobile creations. An example of her work can be viewed at: http:// karenrossi.com/fineartgallery-mobiles.htm
- Books to read:
  - Rodgers & Hammerstein's *My Favourite Things*, illustrated by Renee Graef.

Appendix XI

CROWNS

CROWNS*	• Medium – Collage • Subject – Kings and queens
Overview	Participants can fantasize about an ideal country where they make the rules, ultimately creating a crown specific to their ideas.
Materials	• Tag board strips 8" × 26" • Coloured markers • Glue sticks • Scissors • Scrap (collage) paper • Optional: foil, feathers, sequins, glitter, sticky dots, other gee-gaws.
Setting the Stage	• Begin by talking about kings and queens. Explain how kings and queens wear crowns and in this class, they will make their own crowns. • In some countries a king or queen gets to make the rules, so we say they "rule" their country. Have them think about how they would rule a country if they were a king or queen. Invite them to "pair-share" their thoughts. What would their country be named? What would be important in their country and what kind of people would live there? What would the weather be like?

*Lesson designed by Bridget Daly

Would cookie trees line the roads? Would there be schools, wars, monsters, cars, beaches?

- Have them think about what kinds of pictures they could make to show people what their country is like. A picture that represents something in a simple way is called a symbol. Some countries use symbols on their flags. Now they can make their own crown decorated with symbols. Tell the participants that the symbols on their crown will let people know what their country is like.

Technical Information

- Demonstrate how to cut out the top edge of the crown. The edge can be jagged, curved, free-form, or any uncomplicated pattern. Many participants will find it easier to draw the line first and then cut it out.
- Show a variety of completed crowns. Once the top edge is cut, hand out materials and let them create. When they are finished, size to fit and staple the two overlapping ends together in several places.

Closure

- Make sure to invite them all to wear their crowns at once. Take a picture!

Textual Links

- Choose some pictures of flags.

Appendix XII

CHALK ON CLOTH

CHALK ON CLOTH*	• Pastel chalk on cloth • Subject – Summer
Purpose	This project invites participants to share and illustrate personal experiences of summer through drawing. Specifically, the adults will be able to reminisce and share about the world they grew up in as the children then compare and contrast the memories shared with their own experiences of the environment today.
Materials	• 12″ × 18″ piece of canvas • Milk (approximately 1 pint per 12 people) • Pastel chalk • Newspaper padding (both to iron on and to use as a work surface for the damp canvas) • Iron set on medium • Scrap paper
Setting the Stage	• Begin by explaining that many artists use fabric instead of paper. Artists of all kinds paint on canvas, a coarsely woven cotton. Faith Ringgold paints as well as sews on canvas to make quilts. (Some of her quilts are used as illustrations in

* Adapted from *Discovering great artists: Hands-on art for children in the styles of the great masters* by M.F. Kohl & K. Solga (1996) by Bridget Daly

children's books, so some of the participants may be familiar with them.)

- Show the class some of Ringgold's work and point out the beautiful, multicoloured borders.
- Explain how Ringgold's quilts tell stories about her life and her feelings. Many of her quilts include pictures of people in her life enjoying a pleasant activity together including summertime activities.
- Invite participants to give their impressions of the environment. For example, adults can talk about where they used to like to go swimming or fishing. Prompt discussion on how we now have days when the beaches are closed due to pollution and there are fewer fish to catch than ever before.
- Explain that for the theme for today's project will be "Summer."

Technical Information
- Thoroughly wet the canvas pieces with milk. (This is easily accomplished in a shallow bowl.) Let the excess milk drip off and help this process by giving the canvas a good squeeze before placing the wet canvas flat on a few sheets of newspaper padding.
- Remind the class of how Ringgold's patterned edges help to frame her picture while you demonstrate the process. Invite them to draw their pictures with the coloured pastels.
- When they have completed the drawing they can take it to the "ironing station."
- With the iron set on medium, cover the canvas with scrap paper or aluminum foil and iron the canvas until it is dry or nearly so. The milk is the secret ingredient that will set the pastels so that they are fixed permanently as long as the canvas is not washed.

Closure
- Finished pieces can be pinned to a bulletin board for sharing and subsequent display.

Textual Links
- Works by Faith Ringgold (e.g., *Tar Beach*)
  - Some of Ringgold's quilts are used as illustrations in children's books and may be familiar to the children. Also, many of her quilts in-

clude pictures of people in her life enjoying a
pleasant activity together, which leads nicely
into discussions of art as storytelling.
- To learn more about Ringgold's work, check out
  her website at: http://www.faithringgold.com/
  ringgold/default.htm

Appendix XIII

PASSPORTS

PASSPORTS*	• Collage • Subject – Myself moving out into the world
Purpose	Everyone needs a passport to enter a different place. As a culmination to our look at special people and special places, participants will team up to take each other's photo, and then each participant will select a background and "dress" their photo to participate in activities in that setting
Materials	• Digital camera and printer • Various backgrounds from travel brochures and magazines • Catalogues, paper for creating clothing • Markers, scissors, and glue
Setting the Stage	• Cover the large table with pages and pages of travel brochures. This will stimulate discussion among the participants and increase anticipation about the class. • The technique of collage will be introduced to the participants with illustrations from fine art books. Discussion about technique, overlapping of different materials, etc. will take place in the whole group.

*Lesson designed by Wendy Crocker

- Think-pair-share between partners about special places that participants like to visit.
- Adults will introduce children and their special places. Children will introduce adults with "This is _____ and he would like to visit _____."
- Discuss that sometimes you need to have a special "ticket" in order to visit places. Show samples of passports and stamps from different countries. Share a sample of today's Passport activity.
- Explain that pairs will be working together to create passports to visit a special place. Today's work has two important parts:
- Part One is the selection of a background location for their collage. Using the pages on the tables, encourage children and adults to discuss and share a variety of potential "locales."
- Part Two occurs while the participants are looking for background pages. Partners will take turns using a digital camera to take photos of each other. These pictures will be used as collage against the background for their "passport."
- While the photos are being printed, participants will create clothing for themselves using magazines, construction paper, and markers using collage technique. Encourage the participants to create an outfit which is in keeping with their selection of location, e.g., a bathing suit, sunglasses, sunhat for a warm locale.
- Finally, the participants will "dress" their photo and mount it onto the travel photo background to finish their "passport."

Technical Information

- Provide instruction and support for taking the photos.
- It is best if the camera is large enough for the adults to hold easily, yet not too bulky for the children.
- Ensure that you can print the photos as the participants are working on the collage clothing. If printed digital photos are not an option, try Polaroid film.

Closure	• All participants have an opportunity to share their passport with the group explaining where they are going and how they are dressed
Textual Links	• Samples of collage from Eric Carle books http://www.ladyfingerssewing.com/prodimages/3877M%20cropped.jpg
	• (video) http://www.eric-carle.com/video_misterseahorse.html

References

"About us." (N.d.). *Journal of Intergenerational Relationships*. Retrieved 14 December 2010 from http://jir.ucsur.pitt.edu/about.php

Aday, R.H., McDuffie, W., & Sims, C.R. (1993). Impact of intergenerational program on black adolescents' attitudes toward the elderly. *Educational Gerontology, 19*, 663–73.

Albers, P. (2001). Literacy in the arts. *Primary Voices K-6, 9*(4), 3–9.

– (2006). Imagining the possibilities in multimodal curriculum design. *English Education, 38*(2), 75–101.

– (2007). *Finding the artist within: Creating and reading visual texts in the English language arts classroom*. Newark, DE: International Reading Association.

– (2008). Theorizing visual representation in children's literature. *Journal of Literacy Research, 40*(2), 163–200.

Albers, P., & Cowan, K. (2006). Literacy on our minds: A student-inspired symposium. *Language Arts, 83*(6), 514–22.

Angersbach, H.L., & Jones-Forster, S. (1999). Intergenerational interactions: A descriptive analysis of elder-child interactions in a campus-based child care center. *Child & Youth Services, 20*(1–2), 117–28.

Apple, M. (1971). The hidden curriculum and the nature of conflict. *Interchange, 2*(4), 27–40.

Ayala, J.S., Hewson, J.A., Bray, D., Jones, G., & Hartley, D. (2007). Intergenerational programs: Perspectives of service providers in one Canadian city. *Journal of Intergenerational Relationships, 5*(2), 45–60.

Bainbridge, J., Heydon, R., & Malicky, G. (2009). *Constructing meaning: Balancing the elementary language arts* (4th ed.). Toronto: Thomson Nelson.

Bakhtin, M.M. (1981). Discourse in the novel. In M. Holquist (Ed.), *The dialogic imagination: Four essays* (Trans. C. Emerson & M. Holquist) (pp. 259–422). Austin: University of Texas Press.

– (1986). The problem of speech genres. In C. Emerson & M. Holquist (Eds.),

Speech genres and other late essays (Trans. V.W. McGee) (pp. 60–102). Austin: University of Texas Press.

Banville, J. (2005). *The sea.* New York: Vintage.

Basman, S., Blackman, B., Botticella, M., Coelho, E., Daly, L.A., Liss, J., et al. (n.d.). *Young and old together: A resource manual for developing intergenerational programs.* Toronto: Ministry of Community and Social Services of Ontario.

Bearne, E. (2009). Multimodality, literacy and texts: Developing a discourse. *Journal of Early Childhood Literacy, 9*(2), 156–87.

Beaty, A. (2007). *Iggy Peck, architect.* New York: Abrams Books for Young Readers.

Beynon, C., Heydon, R., O'Neill, S., Crocker, W., & Loerts, T. (2011). *Mixed voices: Attending to the multiple voices of young children in an intergenerational singing program.* Paper presented at the meeting of the Canadian Society for Studies in Education, Fredericton, NB.

Bobbitt, J.F. (1971). *The curriculum.* New York: Arno Press.

Bourdieu, P. (1990). *The logic of practice* (Trans. R. Nice). Stanford: Stanford University Press.

Britzman, D. (1998). *Lost subjects, contested objects: Toward a psychoanalytic inquiry of learning.* Albany: State University of New York Press.

Brummel, S.W. (1989). Developing an intergenerational program. *Journal of Children in Contemporary Society, 20*(3–4), 119–33.

Buscaglia, L. (1982). *The fall of Freddie the leaf: A story of life for all ages.* Slack.

Butts, D., & Moore, L. (2009). *Generations unite: Mix wisdom with energy.* Aging Services of California. Retrieved 15 December 2010 from http://www.aging.org/i4a/pages/index.cfm?pageid=2182

Carle, E. (1998). *Draw me a star.* New York: Penguin.

Childs, P., & Wimmer, M. (1971). The concept of death in early childhood. *Child Development, 42*(14), 1293–1301.

Christian, L.G. (1997). Children and death. *Young Children, 52*(4), 76–80.

Cole, B.V. (2001). Helping children understand death. *Journal of Child and Adolescent Psychiatric Nursing, 14*(1), 5–7.

Cook, J. (1989). Should young children be shielded from knowledge of death? In W. McDuffie & J. Whiteman (Eds.), *The intergenerational activities program handbook* (3rd ed.) (p. 25). Binghamton, NY: Broome County Development Council.

Cowan, K., & Albers, P. (2006). Semiotic representations: Building complex literacy practices through the arts. *The Reading Teacher, 60*(2), 124–37.

Cox, R., Croxford, A., & Edmonds, D. (2006). *Connecting generations tool kit: Best practices in intergenerational programming.* Toronto: United Generations Ontario.

Cummins, J. (2001). *Negotiating identities: Education for empowerment in a diverse society* (2nd ed.). Los Angeles: California Association for Bilingual Education.

Cummins, J., Baker, C., & Hornberger, N.H. (Eds.). (2001). *An introductory reader to the writings of Jim Cummins*. Clevedon, England: Multilingual Matters.

Cummins, L. (2004). The funeral of Froggy the frog: The child as dramatist, designer, and realist. *Young Children, 59*(4), 87.

David, B. (2010, 29 October). Golden years shinning brighter: Canadian seniors living longer, better. *Calgary Herald*. Retrieved 9 November 2010 from http://www.calgaryherald.com/life/Golden+years+shining+brighter+ Canadian+seniors+living+longer+better/3749265/story.html?cid= megadrop_story

David, T., Raban, B., Ure, C., Goouch, K., Jago, M., & Barriere, I. (2000). *Making sense of early literacy: A practitioner's perspective*. Stoke on Trent: Trentham.

Dillon, J.T. (2009). The questions of curriculum. *Journal of Curriculum Studies, 41*(3), 343–59.

Dodson, C.B. (1993). *Genji, Keats, and "mono no aware."* Paper presented at the annual meeting of the College English Association, Overland Park, KS, 1–4 April.

Doherty, G., Friendly, M., & Beach, J. (2003). *OECD Thematic Review of Early Childhood Education and Care Canadian Background Report*. Ottawa: Her Majesty the Queen in Right of Canada.

Donmoyer, R. (2001). Paradigm talk reconsidered. In V. Richardson (Ed.), *Handbook of Research on Teaching* (pp. 174–97). Washington, DC: American Educational Research Association.

Dupuis-Blanchard, S., Neufeld, A., & Strang, V. (2009). The significance of social engagement in relocated older adults. *Qualitative Health Research 19*(9), 1186–95.

Dyson, A.H., & Genishi, C. (2005). *On the case: Approaches to language and literacy research*. New York: Teachers College Press.

Edwards, C., Gandini, L., & Forman, G. (1998). *The hundred languages of children: The Reggio Emilia approach – advanced reflections* (2nd ed). Greenwich, CT: Ablex.

Egan, K. (1978). What is curriculum? *Curriculum Inquiry, 8*(1), 65–72.

Eisner, E.W. (2002). *The educational imagination: On the design and evaluation of school programs* (3rd ed.). Upper Saddle River, NJ: Prentice Hall.

– (2003a). The arts and the creation of mind. *Language Arts, 80*, 340–4.

– (2003b). Artistry in education. *Scandinavian Journal of Educational Research, 47*, 373–84.

– (2005). *Reimagining schools: The selected works of Elliot Eisner*. London: Routledge Falmer.

Elders Share the Arts. (n.d.). Retrieved 3 November 2009 from http://www
.elderssharethearts.org/

Essa, E.L., & Murray, C.I. (1994). Research in review: Young children's understanding and experience with death. *Young Children, 49*(4), 74–81.

Fanelli, S. (1995). *My map book.* New York: HarperCollins Publishers.

Fei, V.L. (2004). Developing an integrative multi-semiotic model. In K.
O'Halloran (Ed.), *Multimodal discourse analysis: Systemic-functional perspectives* (pp. 220–46). London: Continuum.

Fraser, S., & Gestwicki, C. (2002). *Authentic childhood: Exploring Reggio Emilia in
the classroom.* Albany, NY: Delmar Thomson.

Friedman, B. (1997). The integration of pro-active aging education into exciting educational curricula. In K. Brabazon & R. Disch (Eds.), *Intergenerational
approaches in aging: Implications for education, policy and practice* (pp. 103–10).
Binghamton, NY: Haworth Press.

Gandini, L., Hill, L., Cadwell, L., & Schwall, C. (2005). *In spirit of the studio:
learning from the atelier of Reggio Emilia.* New York: Teachers College Press.

Gee, J.P. (1996). *Social linguistics and literacies: Ideology in discourses* (2nd ed.).
London: Taylor & Francis.

Gillen, J., & Hall, N. (2003). The emergence of early childhood literacy. In N.
Hall, J. Larson & J. Marsh (Eds.), *Handbook of early childhood literacy* (pp.
3–12). London: Sage.

Greenberg, J. (1996). Seeing children through tragedy: My mother died today
– when is she coming back? *Young Children, 51*(6), 76–7.

Greene, M. (1995). *Releasing the imagination.* San Francisco: Jossey-Bass.

– (2001). *Variations on a blue guitar: Lincoln Center Institute lectures on aesthetic
education.* New York: Teachers College Press.

Gregory, E., & Williams, A. (2000). *City literacies: Learning to read across generations and cultures.* London: Routledge.

Gregory, E., Long, S., & Volk, D. (Eds.). (2004). *Many pathways to literacy: Young
children learning with siblings, grandparents, peers, and communities.* New York:
Routledge Falmer.

Griff, M.D., Lambert, D., Fruit, D., & Dellman-Jenkins, M. (1996). *LinkAges:
Planning an intergenerational program for preschool.* Menlo Park, CA: Addison-
Wesley.

Habermas, J. (1972). *Knowledge and human interests* (Trans. J.J. Shapiro). Boston:
Beacon Press.

Hall, E L., & Rudkin, J.K. (2011). *Seen and heard: Young children's voices, young
children's rights.* New York: Teachers College Press.

Halliday, M.A.K. (1978). *Language as social semiotic: The social interpretation of
language and meaning.* London: Edward Arnold.

Handsfield, L. (2006). Being and becoming American: Triangulating habitus, field, and literacy instruction in a multilingual classroom. *Language & Literacy, 8*(3), 1–27. Retrieved 22 January 2009 from http://www.langandlit.ualberta.ca/current.html

Hare, J., & Cunningham, B. (1988). Effects of a child bereavement training program for teachers. *Death Studies, 12*(4), 345–53.

Hare, J., Sugawara, A., & Pratt, C. (1986). The child in grief: Implications for teaching. *Early Childhood Development and Care, 25*(1), 43–56.

Harste, J. (2003). What do we mean by literacy now? *Voices from the Middle, 10*(3), 8–12.

Hawkins, M., & McGuire, F. (1999). Exemplary intergenerational programs. In *Preparing participants for intergenerational interaction: Training for success*. New York: Haworth Press.

Hayes, C.L. (2003). An observational study in developing an intergenerational shared site program: Challenges and insights. *Journal of Intergenerational Relationships, 1*(1), 113–31.

Henkin, N., & Kingson, E. (1999). Advancing an intergenerational agenda for the twenty-first century. *Generations, 22*(4), 99–105.

Heydon, R. (2005). The de-pathologization of childhood, disability and aging in an intergeneration art class: Implications for educators. *Journal of Early Childhood Research, 3*(3), 243–68.

– (2007). Making meaning together: Multimodal literacy learning opportunities in an intergenerational art program. *Journal of Curriculum Studies, 39*(1), 35–62.

– (2008). Communicating with a little help from friends: Intergenerational art class as radical, asset-oriented curriculum. In R. Heydon & L. Iannacci, *Early childhood curricula and the de-pathologizing of childhood* (pp. 100–29). Toronto: University of Toronto Press.

– (2009). We are here for just a brief time: Death, dying, and constructions of children in intergenerational learning programs. In L. Iannacci & P. Whitty (Eds.), *Early childhood curricula: Reconceptualist perspectives* (pp. 217–41). Toronto: Detselig Press.

– (2012a). Intergenerational learning from a curriculum studies perspective: New directions, new possibilities. In N. Howe & L. Prochner (Eds.), *New directions in early childhood education and care in Canada*. Toronto: University of Toronto Press.

– (2012b). Multimodal communication and identity options in an intergenerational art class. *Journal of Early Childhood Research, 10*(1), 51–69.

Heydon, R., & Daly, B. (2008). What should I draw? I'll draw you! Facilitating interaction and learning opportunities in intergenerational programs. *Young Children, 63*(3), 80–5.

Heydon, R., & Hibbert, K. (2010). "Relocating the personal" to engender critically reflective practice in pre-service literacy teachers. *Teaching and Teacher Education, 26,* 796–804.

Heydon, R., & Iannacci, L. (2008). *Early childhood curricula and the de-pathologizing of childhood.* Toronto: University of Toronto Press.

Heydon, R., O'Neill, S., Beynon, C., Crocker, W., & Zheng, Z. (2011). Listening for the voices: A study of the initiating and sustaining factors, prevalence, curricula, and opportunities of intergenerational learning programs. Paper presented at the meeting of the Canadian Society for Studies in Education, Fredericton, NB.

Heydon, R., & Wang, P. (2006). Curricular ethics in early childhood education programming: A challenge to the Ontario kindergarten program. *McGill Journal of Education, 41*(1), 29–46.

Hicks, D. (2002). *Reading lives: Working-class children and literacy learning.* New York: Teachers College Press.

Hirakawa, S. (2005). *Japan's love-hate relationship with the West.* Kent, UK: Global Oriental.

Hodge, R., & Kress, G. (1993). *Language as ideology* (2nd ed.). London; New York: Routledge.

Hopkins, A.R. (2002). Children and grief: The role of the early childhood educator. *Young Children, 57*(1), 40–7.

Iannacci, L. (2005). *Othered among others: A critical narrative of culturally and linguistically diverse (CLD) children's literacy and identity in early childhood education (ECE).* London, ON: University of Western Ontario.

Illinois Intergenerational Initiative. (1997, March). This way, everybody wins: Intergenerational curriculum enrichment. *Education Digest, 62*(7), 22–4.

Intergenerational Programming – Rationale – Why Now? (n.d.). In *Marriage and Family Encyclopedia.* Retrieved 3 September 2009 from http://family .jrank.org/pages/902/Intergenerational-Programming-Rationale-Why-Now.html

Jarrott, S.E. (2007). Programs that affect intergenerational solidarity. *Proceedings of the United Nations Expert Group Meeting "Intergenerational Solidarity: Strengthening Economic and Social Ties."* Retrieved 29 September 2009 from http://www.un.org/esa/socdev/unyin/documents/egm_unhq_oct_07_ jarrott.pdf

Jarrott, S.E., & Bruno, K. (2007). Shared site intergenerational programs: A case study. *Journal of Applied Gerontology, 26*(3), 239–57.

Jarrott, S., Gigliotti, C., & Smock, S. (2006). Programming: Where do we stand? Testing the foundation of a shared site Intergenerational program. *Journal of Intergenerational Relationships, 4*(2), 73–92.

Jenks, C. (2004). Constructing childhood sociologically. In M.J. Kehily (Ed.),

An introduction to childhood studies (pp. 77–95). New York: Open University Press.

Jewitt, C., & Kress, G. (2003). *Multimodal literacy*. New York: Peter Lang.

Kamler, B. (2001). *Relocating the personal: A critical writing pedagogy*. Albany: State University of New York Press.

Kaplan, M., Henkin, N., & Kusano, A. (2002). Preface. In M. Kaplan, N. Henkin, & A. Kusano (Eds.), *Linking lifetimes: A global view of intergenerational exchange* (pp. ix–xvi). Lanham: University Press of America.

Kaplan, M., Duerr, L., Whitesell, W., Merchant, L., Davis, D., & Larkin, E. (2003). *Developing an intergenerational program in your Early Childhood Care and Education Centre. A guidebook for early childhood practitioners*. Pennsylvania State College of Agricultural Sciences. Retrieved 8 November 2010 from www.scribd.com/.../Developing-An-Intergenerational-Program-Early-Childhood-Care-Center

Kastner, J. (Director, Producer, Writer). (2004, 15, 16, & 19 September). *Rage against the darkness: Aging: a Canadian snapshot* [Television broadcast]. Toronto: CBC.

Keene, D. (1988). *The pleasures of Japanese literature*. New York: Columbia University Press.

Kendrick, M. (2004). *Converging worlds: Play, literacy, and culture in early childhood*. Bern: Peter Lang.

Kraut, L. (2009, June/July). *Response 1*. Teaching Young Children, 2(5). Retrieved 15 December 2010 from http://www.naeyc.org/tyc/lounge/past

Kress, G. (1997). *Before writing: Rethinking the paths to literacy*. London; New York: Routledge.

– (2003). *Literacy in the new media age*. London: Routledge.

Kress, G., & Jewitt, C. (2003). Introduction. In C. Jewitt & G. Kress (Eds.), *Multimodal literacy* (pp. 1–18). New York: Peter Lang.

Kress, G., & van Leeuwen, T. (2006). *Reading images: The grammar of visual design*. London: Routledge.

Kuehne, V.S., & Collins, C.L. (1997). Observational research in intergenerational programming: Need and opportunity. In K. Brabazon & R. Disch (Eds.), *Intergenerational approaches in aging: Implications for education, policy and practice* (pp. 183–93). New York: Haworth Press.

Kuehne, V.S., & Kaplan, M.S. (2001). *Evaluation and research on intergenerational shared site facilities and programs: What we know and what we need to learn*. Washington, DC: Generations United.

Laden, N. (1998). *When pigasso met mootisse*. San Francisco: Chronicle Books.

La Porte, A.M. (2000). Oral history as intergenerational dialogue in art education. *Art Education, 53*(4), 39–44.

La Porte, A. (2004a). The educational, social, and psychological implications of intergenerational art education. In A. La Porte (Ed.), *Community connections: Intergenerational links in art education* (pp. 2–13). Reston, VA: National Art Education Association.

– (Ed.). (2004b). *Community connections: Intergenerational links in art education.* Reston, VA: National Art Education Association.

Larkin, E. (2004). Introduction. In E. Larkin, D. Friedlander, S. Newman, & R. Goff (Eds.), *Intergenerational relationships: Conversations on practice and research across cultures* (pp. 1–3). Binghamton, NY: Haworth Press.

Larkin, E., & Newman, S. (1997). Intergenerational studies: A multi-disciplinary field. In K. Brabazon & R. Disch (Eds.), *Intergenerational approaches in aging: Implications for education, policy and practice* (pp. 5–16). Binghamton, NY: Haworth Press.

Lather, P. (1991). *Feminist research in education: Within/against.* Geelong, Vic: Deakin University.

Levinas, E. (1991). *Otherwise than being or beyond essence* (Trans. A. Lingis). Boston: Kluwer Academic Publishers.

Levinas, E., & Kearney, R. (1986). Dialogue with Emmanuel Levinas. In R. Cohen (Ed.), *Face to face with Levinas* (pp. 13–33). Albany: State University of New York Press.

Lewison, M., Flint, A.S., & Van Sluys, K. (2002). Taking on critical literacy: The journey of newcomers and novices. *Language Arts, 79*(5), 382–92.

Linkages Society of Alberta (May, 2008) *"LINK Project: Linking Intergenerational Needs and Knowledge – Train the Trainer." Intergenerational Best Practices Guidelines.* Retrieved 9 November 2010 from: http://www.linkages.ca/pdfs/researchdocs/igp_guidelines.pdf

Luke, A., & Freebody, P. (1999). Further notes on the Four Resources Model. *Reading Online.* Retrieved 16 November 2010, from reading online.org/research/lukefreebody.html

Lyons, C., Newman, S., & Vasudev, J. (1984). The impact of a curriculum on aging on the elementary school students. *Gerontology and Geriatrics Education, 4*(4), 51–63.

MacGregor, C. (2007). Explaining death to your child. *Pediatrics for Parents, 23*(9), 17–20.

Malaguzzi, L. (1998). History, ideas, and basic philosophy: An interview with Lella Gandini. In Edwards, C., Gandini, L., & Forman, G. (Eds.), *The hundred languages of children: The Reggio Emilia approach – advanced reflections* (2nd ed.) (pp. 49–97). London: Ablex.

Marriage & Family Encyclopedia. (n.d.). *Intergenerational programming, rationale, why Now?: Program models, intergenerational interactions, impact on families, international intergenerational programming efforts.* Retrieved 22 May 2012 from http://family.jrank.org/pages/908/Intergenerational-Programming .html

McCain, M., & Mustard, F. (1999). *Reversing the real brain drain: The early years study.* Toronto: Ontario Children's Secretariat.

McDuffie, W. (1989). But what if someone dies? In W. McDuffie & J. Whiteman (Eds.), *The intergenerational activities program handbook* (3rd ed.) (p. 24). Binghamton, NY: Broome County Development Council.

McDuffie, W., & Testani, B. (1989). A history of Broome County Intergenerational Activities Program. In W. McDuffie & J. Whiteman (Eds.), *Intergenerational Activities Program Handbook.* Binghamton, NY: Broome County Child Development Council.

Mellonie, B., with Ingpen, R. (1983). *Lifetimes: The beautiful way to explain death to children.* New York: Bantam.

Minnesota Department of Health. (2005). Demographics of an aging population. Retrieved 15 December 2010 from http://www.health.state.mn.us/ divs/orhpc/pubs/healthyaging/demoage.pdf

Moll, L. (1992). Funds of knowledge for teaching: Using a qualitative approach to connect homes and classrooms. *Theory into Practice, 31*(2), 132–41.

Moseley, P.A. (1976). *Developing a curriculum for death education: How do children learn about death?* Annual meeting of the American Education Research Association, San Francisco, 19–20 April 1976.

New London Group, The. (2000). A pedagogy of multiliteracies: Designing social futures. In B. Cope & M. Kalantzis (Eds.), *Multiliteracies: Literacy learning and the design of social futures* (pp. 9–38). London: Routledge.

Newman, S. (1985). *A curriculum on aging in our schools: Its time has come. Generations Together.* Pittsburgh, PA: University of Pittsburgh.

Northcott, H.C., & Wilson, D.M. (2008). *Dying and death in Canada* (2nd ed.). Peterborough, ON: Broadview Press.

Olaniyan, D.A., & Okemakinde, T. (2008). Human capital theory: Implications for educational development. *European Journal of Scientific Research, 24*(2), 157–62.

Ontario Ministry of Education. (2006). *Kindergarten program (revised).* Toronto: Author.

Pahl, K. (1999). *Transformations: Children's meaning making in a nursery.* Oakhill, England: Trentham Books.

– (2009). Interactions, intersections and improvisations: Studying the multimodal texts and classroom talk of six- to seven-year-olds. *Journal of Early Childhood Literacy, 9*(2), 188–210.

Pahl, K., & Rowsell, J. (2005). *Literacy and education: Understanding the new literacy studies in the classroom*. London: Sage.

Penn State College of Agricultural Sciences (2003). *Developing an intergenerational program in your early childhood care and education center: A guidebook for early childhood practitioners*. University Park: Pennsylvania State University Press.

Pitri, E. (2001). The role of artistic play in problem solving. *Art Education, 54*(3), 46–51.

Purcell-Gates, V. (2001). What we know about readers who struggle. In R. Flippo (Ed.), *Reading researchers in search of common ground* (pp. 118–28). Newark, DE: International Reading Association.

Ringgold, F. (1991). *Tar beach*. New York: Crown.

– (1998). *Dancing at the Louvre: Faith Ringgold's French collection and other story quilts*. San Diego: University of California Press.

Robbins, J. (2001). *Is it righteous to be? Interviews with Emmanuel Levinas*. Stanford: Stanford University Press.

Robson, C., Sumara, D., Luce-Kapler, R., Coll, B., Hogan, R., Hurst, G., Innes, V., Morrissey, C., & Spencer, C. (2010). Writing and reading subjects: Fixing and unfixing identity through close literary practices. *Changing English, 17*(4), 385–98.

Robson, C., Sumara, D., & Luce-Kapler, R. (in press). Performing an archive of resistance: Challenging normative life narratives through literary reading and memoir writing research. *International Journal of Education through the Arts*.

Rogers, W.S. (2004). Promoting better childhoods: Constructions of child concern. In M.J. Kehily (Ed.), *An introduction to childhood studies* (pp. 125–44). New York: Open University Press.

Routman, R. (2000). *Conversations: Strategies for teaching, learning and evaluating*. Portsmouth, NH: Heinemann.

Rowsell, J., & Pahl, K. (2007). Sedimented identities in texts: Instances of practice. *Reading Research Quarterly, 42*(3), 388–404.

Ryerson, M.S. (1977). Death education and counseling for children. *Elementary School Guidance and Counseling, 11*(3), 147–73.

Sandstrom, S. (1999). Dear samba is dead forever. *Young Children, 54*(6), 14–15.

Schwab, J.J. (1973). The practical 3: Translation into curriculum. *School Review, 81*, 501–22.

Schulman, L. (1987). Knowledge and teaching: Foundations of the new reform. *Harvard Educational Review, 57*, 1–22.

Schwalbach, E., & Kiernan, S. (2002). Effects of an intergenerational friendly visit program on the attitudes of fourth graders toward elders. *Educational Gerontology, 28*, 175–87.

Seachrist, D. (June/July, 2009). Response 2. Teaching *Young Children, 2*(5). Retrieved 15 December 2010 from http://www.naeyc.org/tyc/lounge/past

Seefelt, C. (1989). Part III: Impacts. Intergenerational programs – Impact on attitudes. In S. Newman & S. Brummel (Eds.), *Intergenerational programs: Imperatives, strategies, impacts, trends* (pp. 185–194). New York: Howarth Press.

Simon, R. (1992). *Teaching against the grain: Texts for a pedagogy of possibility.* Toronto: OISE Press.

Spiezia, V. (2002). The greying population: A wasted human capital or just a social liability? *International Labour Review, 141*(1&2), 71–113.

Stein, J.G. (2001). *The cult of efficiency.* Toronto: Anansi.

Stein, P. (2008). *Multimodal pedagogies in diverse classrooms: Representation, rights and resources.* London; New York: Routledge.

Teachers.tv. (n.d.). Early years education: Sweden versus the UK. Retrieved 14 December 2010 from http://www.youtube.com/watch?v=cmdHvkcMhZ4

Thew, N. (2000). Race, class and gender. In J. Mills & R. Mills (Eds.), *Childhood studies: A reader in perspectives of childhood* (pp. 131–44). London: Routledge.

Thomson, G.R. (1997). *Extraordinary bodies: Figuring physical disability in American culture and literature.* New York: Columbia University Press.

Thompson, E., & Wilson, L. (2001). The potential of older volunteers in long-term care. *Generations, 25*(1), 58–63.

Turcin, D. (June/July, 2009). What can early childhood educators do when a child dies? *Teaching Young Children, 2*(5). Retrieved 15 December 2010 from http://www.naeyc.org/tyc/lounge/past

Tyler, R.W. (1949). *Basic principles of curriculum and instruction.* Chicago: University of Chicago Press.

VanderVen, K. (1999). Intergenerational theory: The missing element in today's intergenerational programs. In V.S. Kuehne (Ed.), *Intergenerational programs: Understanding what we have created* (pp. 33–47). Binghamton, NY: Haworth Press.

Viorst, J. (1971). *The tenth good thing about Barney.* New York: Simon & Schuster.

Ward, C.R., Kamp, L.L., & Newman, S. (1996). The effects of participation in an intergenerational program on the behavior of residents with dementia. *Activities, Adaptation & Aging, 20*(4), 61–75.

Wertsch, J.V. (1991). *Voices of the mind: A sociocultural approach to mediated action.* Cambridge, MA: Harvard University Press.

Winterson, J. (2012). *Why be happy when you could be normal?* New York: Grove/Atlantic.

Wohlwend, K.E. (2009). Damsels in discourse: Girls consuming and producing identity texts through Disney princess play. *Reading Research Quarterly*, 44(1), 57–83.

Wood, F. B. (2008). Grief: Helping young children cope. *Young Children,* 63(5), 28–31.

Zolten, K., & Long, N. (2006), *How to talk to children about death*. Fayetteville, AK: Center for Effective Parenting, Department of Paediatrics, University of Arkansas.

Index

230   Index